ADVANCED PRAISE

"I am very pleased to recommend Sam Chess' new book, *Unmasking Revelation*. The New Testament book of Revelation is an unopened mystery to the vast majority of Christians, and this book will do just what its title says; it will "unmask it." It will open up its prophetic visions and make clear its message of the future. Sam has performed a vital service to the Christian community in these days of rising moral chaos, and international conflict. The book of Revelation gives the Believer a sure anchor of hope in these last days and Sam Chess's book does indeed "pull back the cover."

GARY COHEN TH.D. – Translator of the book of Revelation for the New King James Version of the Bible, *Author, Seminary professor, Seminary President, Retired Army Colonel, architect of the Jerusalem model at Holyland Experience, Orlando, Florida.*

T0098647

Unmasking Revelation

UNMASKING REVELATION

A Study of Revelation to Reveal Its POSITIVE MESSAGE that Jesus Wins and Satan Loses

SAM CHESS

NEW YORK

LONDON • NASHVILLE • MELBOURNE • VANCOUVER

Unmasking Revelation

A Study of Revelation to Reveal Its Positive Message that Jesus Wins and Satan Loses

Published in New York, New York, by Morgan James Publishing. Morgan James is a trademark of Morgan James, LLC. www.MorganJamesPublishing.com

Unless otherwise indicated, all Scripture quotations are taken from the Holy Bible, New Living Translation, copyright © 1996, 2004, 2007, 2013 by Tyndale House Foundation. Used by permission of Tyndale House Publishers, Inc., Carol Stream, Illinois 60188. All rights reserved.

*There are two comprehensive Scripture indexes at the end of the book, with additional versions used with permission.

ISBN 9781642796001 paperback
ISBN 9781642796018 eBook
Library of Congress Control Number: 2019943540

Cover Design by:
Christopher Kirk
www.GFSstudio.com

Cover Image by:
Christopher Weise

Interior Design by:
Chris Treccani
www.3dogcreative.net

unmaskingrevelation.com
info@unmaskingrevelation.com
Facebook: Sam Chess – Author

Scroll Photo: Heather Brogan
Four Horsemen Picture: Heather Brogan
Timeline Chart: Christopher Weise and Sam Chess
Second Coming Chart: Penny Worley and Sam Chess

Morgan James is a proud partner of Habitat for Humanity Peninsula and Greater Williamsburg. Partners in building since 2006.

Get involved today! Visit
MorganJamesPublishing.com/giving-back

CONTENTS

Prologue   ix

Introduction   xxv

Part I   **The Revelation of Jesus Christ**   **1**
1   Jesus Is "Walking" Among the Churches   5
2   Jesus Is "Re-forming" the Churches   13

Part II   **The Revelation of Jesus Christ**   **23**
3   A Glimpse into the Throne Room of God   27
4   Finding One Worthy to Break the Seals   43
5   The Lamb is Worthy to Open the Scroll!   59

Part III   **The Revelation of Jesus Christ**   **77**
6   Setting the Stage for End Times   81
7   Opening the Scroll and Seven Seals   94
8   The antichrist (and the Rapture) is Coming!   106
9   The Advent of the antichrist   119
10   The Battle of the Ages I   130
11   The Battle of the Ages II   141

12	The Lamb Becomes King of Kings I	150
13	The Lamb Becomes King of Kings II	164
14	The Second Coming of Jesus Christ	176
Part IV	**The Revelation of Jesus Christ**	**189**
15	The Marriage Feast—and Jesus' Return	193
16	The Millennial Reign of Christ	203
17	The New Heaven and New Earth	213
18	Heaven—Our Eternal Home	226
Epilogue		237
Special Acknowledgement		239
Acknowledgements		241
Answers to End-of-Chapter Questions		243
Scripture By Chapter Index		247
Scripture By Book Index		255
About the Author		263

PROLOGUE

Jesus' disciples are shocked! Their world had turned upside-down. For three years they had witnessed leprous stubs grow into fresh new feet, thousands of shekels of food appear out of nothing, and dead people brought back to life! Six months ago the momentum in their already insane new life had taken a startling shift, and now for the last six weeks they were, literally, living every moment of their lives in mouth-hanging shock!

The gears shifted last fall when their long-awaited, miracle-working Messiah had announced that he was going to die! He had slipped it in at the end of a bizarre moment up in Caesarea Philippi standing in front of the pagan "gates of hell" grotto where human beings were daily being sacrificed. "I will build my church," he had shouted. "The very gates of hell will not stand against it! The 'Church,' my Church," he had said, "will bind and loose on earth what has already been bound and loosed in heaven" *(Matthew 16:18–19)*. What in the world could that possibly all mean they wondered?

As if that hadn't been startling enough for fishermen and tax collector brains to absorb, Jesus began to enlarge on the fact that once they got back down to Jerusalem, he was going to suffer terrible things at the hands of the religious leaders, and then be brutally murdered. "I will be killed," Jesus had said, "but on the third day I would rise from the dead" *(Matthew 16:21)*. That last phrase went right over their heads. It didn't sink in at all. They were still so absorbed and confused by the "I will be killed" phrase! Peter tried to challenge Jesus: "No way, Lord," he had said. "That's never going to happen to you!" Jesus gave him one of his deep-into-your-soul stares and said, "Get away from me, satan! You are a dangerous trap to me. You are seeing things purely from a human point of view, not from God's" *(Matthew 16:22–23)*. Everybody else shut their mouths and tried to make sense out of what seemed senseless.

- **Then he died!** Jesus died, just as he had predicted! Hundreds of people watched his pale, bloodless, lifeless body being hauled down from the cross and carefully packed into Joseph of Arimathea's tomb. Lots of people commented on how accurate Jesus' prophecies about himself had been. Nobody dared mention Jesus' final "rising" line in Caesarea Philippi. To even repeat the line would require faith, and their faith was shattered.

- **Then the sun rose Sunday morning!** When the disciples arrived at the tomb, they were greeted by two men, obviously angels, in dazzling robes asking them, "Why are you looking among the dead for someone who is alive? He isn't here! He has risen from the dead! Remember what he told you back in Galilee that the Son of Man will be betrayed into the hands of sinful men? He will be crucified, but he would rise again on the third day" *(Luke 24:5–7)*!

- **And then, there he was, alive!** They saw Jesus with their own eyes, they talked to him, and they touched him. His words reached deep into their hearts! The religious leaders had rushed around injecting "spin" about his body being stolen from an obviously empty tomb over the next five weeks. But everybody knew it was a lie. Every person who lived in and around Jerusalem had some friend or relative who had literally seen, and heard, and touched the resurrected Jesus!

 The Apostle Paul would soon write: "I passed on to you what was most important: Christ died for our sin, He was buried, and he was raised from the dead on the third day, just as the Scriptures said. He was seen by Peter and then by the Twelve. After that, he was seen by more than 500 of his followers at one time, most of whom are still alive" (1 Corinthians 15:3–6).

During Jesus' last post-resurrection forty days on earth, he had hammered several eternal truths into his Follower's minds:

- "I told you I was going to die, paying the sin debt of the whole world, didn't I?"

  "Yes Jesus, yes, you did!"

- "Remember, I told you I was going to rise again after three days. Did I?"

  "Yes, Jesus—we lost sight of that with you being murdered, and all. Besides, what do we know about resurrections—the only three people we ever saw die and come back to life, were raised from the dead by you, Jesus!"

- Jesus replied, "I know how difficult it is for you to get your heads around things that you've never seen happen before. I need to make sure you get this next part right, because I'm challenging you to teach it to thousands, even millions, of my followers: **I AM GOING TO LEAVE YOU—<u>BUT I WILL BE BACK!</u>**

- "If you missed the part about me rising from the dead, I'm sure you missed the part about my eventual 'Second Advent.' There can't be a 'Second Coming' unless I leave you after my 'First Coming'! I realize that doesn't fit your preconceived thoughts any more than my death and resurrection did, so let me reinforce what I tried to tell you just last month."

  John 14:1–3: "Don't let your hearts be troubled. There is more than enough room in my Father's house. If this were not so, would I have told you that I going to prepare a place for you? When everything is ready, I will come and get you so that you will always be with me where I am."

"Do you understand this?"

"No, no, we don't—Jesus!"

Five weeks later, the Followers find themselves on a ledge of rock with some of the same dazzling angels. As they stare in disbelief, Jesus lifts off the planet.

The disciples' mouths fall open even wider. They keep staring until his body disappears into the clouds. The "dazzlers" seem to have yet more to say. It will set the stage for the disciples' lives. *(And it sets the stage for this book!)*

> **Acts 1:10–11: "As they strained to see him rising into heaven, two white-robed men suddenly stood among them. 'Men of Galilee,' they said, 'why are you standing here staring into heaven? Jesus has been taken from you into heaven, but <u>someday he will return from heaven in the same way you saw him go!</u>'"**

One of the men standing near the outside of the circle was a Jerusalem Commissioner named Ethan. *(We'll follow him as a fictional representative of the Early Church throughout this book!)* Ethan had long been friends with Jesus' younger brother James. James and Ethan had together mocked Jesus' actions before his death. Even when he performed impossible miracles, the two men had managed to discredit him. Jesus' humiliating death only reinforced in their minds that they had been right all along!

<u>**And then they saw him alive**</u>! The sneers were wiped off their faces, their mocking tone turned to hushed awe! They hung on to every single word Jesus said for the next forty days. As Ethan and James watched the last wisp of Jesus' frame disappear into the clouds, the angels' words cut into their heart.

Commissioner Ethan's detail-oriented mind became consumed with preserving everything Jesus had ever said. It was he who encouraged anyone who had notes from Jesus' sermons to bring them to his office. It was he who encouraged his associate, the former tax collector Matthew, to follow the "deep burning in his soul" and begin to condense all the notes into one document.

- The last words of the angels had focused their minds back to Jesus' statement before his death: **"There are more than enough rooms in my Father's house!"** *What could that possibly mean,* **"I am going to prepare a place for you?"** *What place, where is it?* **"When everything is ready, I will come and get you, so that you will always be with me where I am"** *(John 14:2–3). Wait a minute, where are you going to take us? The angels said you are coming back, just as we saw you leave. Doesn't that mean* *you are <u>descending</u> here, <u>to earth</u>, from where you just <u>ascended</u>? How long do we have to wait?* **<u>Jesus, why are you leaving at all?</u>**

- The Old Testament info-nerds among them were frantically flipping through the scroll of Zechariah and shoving it into the faces of the rest of the disciples. "Do you realize that the Messiah just lifted from the Mount of Olives, and Zechariah 14 prophesies that the Messiah is one day going to return to the Mount of Olives and split the Mount to the east and the west? He is going to rule from Jerusalem as the King of the whole earth. All the people of the earth are going to come here, to Jerusalem, and worship him" *(Zechariah 14:4, 9).*

Their minds were churning, their discussion got deep. What would it be like to see Jesus return "the way they saw him go," and then for him to set up an eternal rule from Jerusalem? Would they all still be alive to see it?

- Ethan and Matthew rediscovered the two sentences that Jesus said in front of Caiaphas the High Priest that had so convinced him to condemn the Messiah to death. There had to have been very specific words from Jesus' mouth that would get His Eminence Caiaphas enraged enough to condemn The Anointed One to "die for the sins of the whole world. " *(It was almost as if Jesus had set it all up on purpose!?)*

    Mark 14:61–64: "Jesus was silent and made no reply. Then the high priest asked him, '<u>Are you the Messiah</u>, the Son of the Blessed One?' Jesus said, 'I AM. And <u>you will see the Son of Man seated in the place of power at God's right hand and coming on the clouds of heaven</u>.' Then the high priest tore his clothing to show his horror and said, 'Why do we need other witnesses? You have all heard his blasphemy. What is your verdict?'"

Everybody in the First Century knew exactly what Jesus meant when one whole sentence was **"I AM."** They knew exactly what he was referring to when he called himself, **the SON of MAN**. They had been taught, since they were little kids, that phrase was a **declaration of deity**!

> **Daniel 7:9, 13–14: "As I looked, thrones were set in place, and the Ancient of Days took his seat. His clothing was as white as snow. In my vision, there before me was one like <u>a Son of Man</u>, coming with the clouds of heaven. He approached the Ancient of Days and was led into his presence. He was <u>given authority, glory and sovereign power; all nations and peoples of every language worshiped him</u>. His dominion is an everlasting dominion that will not pass away, and <u>his kingdom is one that will never be destroyed</u>."**

Even now, Daniel's "Son of Man," Ethan mused, has gone somewhere to "prepare a place for us," but **he would one day be coming back again** "on the clouds" *(whatever that might mean)*! Daniel's words sure seemed to be being fulfilled in front of their very eyes!

- **Jesus, the Messiah, the Son of Man—the Son of God**, was apparently in the process of being "given all authority, glory and sovereign power— all nations and peoples of every language would one day worship him. His dominion will be an everlasting dominion that will not pass away, and his kingdom is one that will never be destroyed!"

Ethan didn't have a clue how or when all of this "everlasting dominion" stuff would unfold, but the deeper he dug, the more he discovered. He uncovered the words of Jesus' last big sermon before he had gone to the cross. The final words Jesus had said to his disciples, the most important truth he must have wanted right at the forefront of their minds was, seemingly, this mental picture of him coming back to this earth!

> **Matthew 24:30–31: "And they will see <u>the Son of Man coming on the clouds of heaven</u> with power and great glory. And he will send out his angels with the mighty blast of a trumpet, and they <u>will gather his chosen ones from all over the world</u>—from the farthest ends of the earth and heaven."**

Jesus had clearly stated that there was not just one "Advent/ Coming" of God from heaven to earth, but that there was indeed eventually going to be a

Second Advent! Once Ethan got deep into Jesus' last sermon, he found there was so much more to unpack! Jesus had given the sermon in response to his disciples' question: "What are the signs of your return?" Jesus had clearly laid out signs—lots of them! Ethan, and James, and Matthew poured over the statements one by one.

Jesus had declared that Jerusalem was going to be destroyed! If Jerusalem was going to be destroyed, and the Messiah was going to one day return to it, that had to mean the Holy City was going to one day be rebuilt! If the Jewish people were going to all be scattered to the ends of the Earth, that must mean that Jeremiah and Ezekiel were right to prophesy that the Israelites were going to "come back from the four-corners" of the planet and resettle a new Israel! The possibilities were already hammering in their brains. *How, and when, was it all going to happen?*

- Jesus had clearly stated that at least part of the reason he had to leave *(besides the whole preparing-a-place thing)* was so that his Followers could be immersed in the infilling, empowering, transforming "Spirit of Christ—the Holy Spirit" whose presence would indwell all Believers, transforming them from sinfulness to righteousness *(from the inside out)*, **"leading them into all truth"**! And, just exactly as Jesus had promised, his Spirit came crashing into the lives of the brand new Early Church just 10 days after Jesus' ascension!

The pieces were falling into place! The death of Jesus paying humanity's sin debt, followed by Jesus' victorious defeat of death itself by rising from the dead, followed by the outpouring and infilling of the Holy Spirit—it all sure did give the Church their marching orders. They now knew exactly what needed to be done and they had the empowering Holy Spirit inside them to accomplish Jesus' Great Commission. But what they still lacked *(and longed for)* was any sense of what might be coming next.

In Peter's first Spirit-led sermon **after the Morning of Pentecost**, God began to fill in for them the first of many new inspired clues:

Acts 3:18–21: "But God was fulfilling what all the prophets had foretold about the Messiah—that he must suffer these things. Now

repent of your sins and turn to God, so that your sins may be wiped away. Then times of refreshment will come from the presence of the Lord, and <u>he will again send you Jesus, your appointed Messiah</u>! For <u>he must remain in heaven until the time for the final restoration of all things,</u> as God promised long ago through his holy prophets."

Apparently, Jesus was not coming back immediately! There was going to be a time frame that had to pass, a series of events that had to take place, before his Second Return. "**He must remain in heaven until the time for the final restoration of all things.**" *What things? What must happen before God will send Jesus, his appointed Messiah, back to set up his eternal rule?*

One of the driving, daily facts of Early Church life was trying to figure out when this "Coming Back" was going to take place! Led by James, Jesus' kid brother, the Early Church carefully studied the Old Testament prophesies, and *(long before the Gospels were first put into print)* they poured over every memory and every written note about what Jesus himself had told them!

The Early Church, as it formed over the First Century, didn't get inspired Scripture all at once. From the time Jesus first preached until John wrote the Unveiling of Revelation—was a period of about 68 years. The Epistles and the Gospels began to arrive two decades after Jesus' resurrection, one letter at a time.

(Download your free charts at unmaskingrevelation.com)

Ethan and the New Church he was helping to form poured over Zechariah's prophesies looking for clues about the where, the when, and the how of Jesus' return.

Zechariah 14:4, 6–9, 11: "On that day his feet will stand on the Mount of Olives, east of Jerusalem. And the Mount of Olives will split apart, making a wide valley running from east to west. Half the mountain will move toward the north and half toward the south. On that day the sources of light will no longer shine, yet there will be continuous day! On that day life-giving waters will flow out from Jerusalem, half toward the Dead Sea and half toward the Mediterranean and THE LORD WILL BE KING OVER ALL THE EARTH. On that day THERE WILL BE ONE LORD—his name alone will be worshiped. And Jerusalem will be filled, safe at last, never again to be cursed and destroyed."

- It was all so exciting and yet so confusing! They now knew how the Messiah could be killed and still later become **"king over all the earth"**— **with his name alone being worshipped**. Jesus had victoriously defeated satan, death, and the grave, and had risen victoriously alive forever!

But **when would the "second act" start**? Ethan and everyone he could recruit gathered every scrap of notes that anyone had ever taken while Jesus was speaking. The tax collector turned disciple, Matthew, had a gift for organizing information. He meticulously inscribed the words of Jesus' last sermon *(Matthew 24:2, 5–15)*, emphasizing every point, dissecting every word:

- **"Do you see all these buildings? I tell you the truth, they will be completely demolished. Not one stone will be left on top of another!**
- **"Many will come in my name, claiming, 'I am the Messiah.' They will deceive many.**
- **"You will hear of wars and threats of wars, but don't panic, these things must take place, but the end won't follow immediately.**
- **"Nations will be at war, there will be famines and earthquakes in many parts of the world.**
- **"My followers will be arrested, persecuted, and killed.**
- **"Many will turn away, false prophets will rise.**
- **"Sin will be rampant everywhere, the love of many will grow cold.**
- **"The Good News about my Kingdom will be preached throughout the whole world, so that all nations will hear it; and then the end will come!**

- "You will see what Daniel prophesied; the 'sacrilegious object that causes desecration' standing in the Holy Place." *(Put there by the antichrist—as Daniel predicted!)*

The Early Church was riveted by every one of these facts, and so many more, but their attention was always pulled to the "grand finale" of Jesus' last message:

- **Matthew 24:30–31: "And <u>then at last, the sign that the Son of Man is coming will appear</u> in the heavens, and there will be deep mourning among all the peoples of the earth. And <u>they will see the Son of Man coming on the clouds of heaven</u> with power and great glory. And he will send out his angels with the mighty blast of a trumpet, and they will gather his chosen ones from all over the world—from the farthest ends of the earth and heaven."**

Ethan, and his growing group of intense Scripture students, wrote down their logical *(theo-logical)* list of facts. Jesus had started his "Signs List" by prophesying that **"not one stone would be left on another" in Jerusalem**. Nobody was threatening to destroy Jerusalem at the moment. So if that was going to happen before Jesus' return, his "Second Coming" was almost certainly not going to be in the next week or next month.

- Whatever Zechariah's "returning Messiah standing on the split Mount of Olives, with Jerusalem safe never again to be destroyed, and the Messiah Prince finally becoming KING OVER ALL THE EARTH"—whatever all that meant—a whole lot of other things had to happen first!
- At a very minimum, Jerusalem was going to have to be leveled, and the persecution of Believers was going to begin and grow ever more intense.
- Jesus' final "Commission" was going to have to be carried out of "making disciples of all nations and baptizing them in the Name of the Father, Son, and Holy Spirit," of getting the Gospel of Jesus' Kingdom out to the ends of the earth, wherever that was *(Matthew 28:19)*.
- Only after these things, and more, happened according to Jesus own words—**would the "End come"!**

(Less than 40 years after Jesus' death Jerusalem became a pile of ruins and stayed that way for the next 1900 years. The Early Church could never have imagined it would all take that long!)

Right on cue, at least as far as Jesus' prophesies were concerned, persecution began to sweep through the newly forming Church, and it drove Jesus' Followers *(Christians, as they were mockingly called)* away from Jerusalem. Jesus' brother James hung in there, leading the Church in Jerusalem. He was now so sure that his big brother was the long-awaited Messiah that he would gladly give his life defending the "Good News of Jesus, the Christ"! *(He did!)*

Acts 8:1: "A great wave of persecution began that day, sweeping over the church in Jerusalem; and all the believers except the Apostles were scattered through the regions of Judea and Samaria."

One man, named Saul, became a "one-man killing machine." The New Church was terrified of him! He was infuriated that thousands and thousands of people were committing their whole lives to this "counterfeit" Messiah. *(Whatever would God do to deliver them from this manic killer?)*

Church Elder Ethan, Church Leader James, and the New Church leaders had their hands full with more than just interpreting Old Testament prophesies and recording Jesus' words.

- People who had jobs were losing them. People who owned real estate were selling it to help feed thousands of new Believers who couldn't feed themselves. And as "the Church—the Christians" were driven further away from Jerusalem into the pagan Roman Empire, they sure didn't find a more receptive audience, only increased persecution.

- **What was driving these people?** The empowering and infilling Holy Spirit? YES! But when they woke up each morning and were thinking about the day ahead and whether they and their families would find anything to eat that day; whether they or their families would even be alive that night—what made them so eager to forge straight ahead— straight into the teeth of danger and destruction? And then what made thousands and thousands of other people, including many previous idol worshipping pagans, decide they wanted to join the ranks of the despised Christians?

- Because they so believed that **what their Messiah had started he was going to finish!** He hadn't deserted them! He left to prepare for what was coming next—**BUT HE WAS GOING TO RETURN** as they saw him go! They would one day enjoy his presence forever!

The very first Epistles/letters the Early Church ever received advising them of what to do in their persecuted state were 1 and 2 Thessalonians. It's significant that they came from the Christian-murdering, now converted and Spirit-led, Apostle Paul! It's also very significant that **both Epistles deal heavily with Jesus' Return!** The Early Church's thirst for new knowledge was huge! So every time they got a new inspired letter from Paul, or Peter, or John, they would pour over every word, trying to figure out what God had added on any number of topics. At, or near, the top of their list was always: "**What more does this new letter tell us about Jesus' Second Coming?**"

- Every local First Century Body of Believers **knew every single passage of inspired Scripture, that they had received up to that point**, on Jesus' Second Coming! They could recite, down to the youngest child, how they all fit together to paint a clear picture of when their Messiah Savior would come again!
- As the persecution and imprisonments and killings increased, they became more and more desperate to learn **if, how, and when God was going to bring an end to the control of sin and satan on this earth**!

Elder Ethan, Presbyter James, and the ever-widening Church as a whole became increasingly focused, **not about the IF of Jesus' Second Coming—but about the HOW!** Sure enough, that was one of the questions the Apostle Paul dealt with in his very first Epistle:

1 Thessalonians 4:13–18: "**And now, dear brothers and sisters, we want you to know what will happen to the believers who have died so you will not grieve like people who have no hope. For since we believe that Jesus died and was raised to life again, we also believe**

that when Jesus returns, God will bring back with him the believers who have died. We tell you this directly from the Lord: We who are still living when the Lord returns will not meet him ahead of those who have died. For the Lord himself will come down from heaven with a commanding shout, with the voice of the archangel, and with the trumpet call of God. First, the believers who have died will rise from their graves. Then, together with them, we who are still alive and remain on the earth will be caught up in the clouds to meet the Lord in the air. Then we will be with the Lord forever. So encourage each other with these words."

My goodness, the Early Church found that encouraging! When Ethan thought about his martyred Dad, or the fact that he himself was living every day with the possibility of being hauled off to the arena to fight to the death with some unfriendly lions—the picture of Jesus returning with a commanding shout, and every Believer, both alive and dead, rising to meet him in the air was awesome! The new letters, once spread, filled every sermon and every Bible Study in every local church for months! It drove them out into the teeth of danger. The Early Church had no reverse gear, in fact, they only seemed to have a high gear—**straight ahead, because they had their eye fixed on the goal!** <u>**JESUS IS COMING BACK AGAIN!!**</u>

There was never a day when they didn't talk about it. There was never a gathering of Believers when they didn't discuss it. They schooled themselves and their children to be able to recite <u>in order</u> exactly what Jesus said would have to happen before his return!

(Download your free chart at unmaskingrevelation.com)

Jesus gave his last sermon in direct response to his disciples' question: <u>**"What signs will signal your return?"**</u>

- Jesus gave his list of signs and he **then finished with:** **"at last, the sign that the Son of Man is coming will appear in the heavens"** *(Matthew 24:30)*. There is an order here!

- "Just as the gathering of vultures shows there is a carcass nearby, so these signs indicate that the end is near. Now learn a lesson from the fig tree. When its branches bud and its leaves begin to sprout, you know that summer is near. In the same way, when you see all these things, *(What things?)* you can know his return is very near, right at the door. I tell you the truth, this generation (γενεά *genea- the distance between your parents and you*) will not pass from the scene until all these things take place" *(Matthew 24:28, 32–34). What generation, what things?*

Ethan, and Matthew, and every single person in the growing Church found every single verse, as each Epistle and Gospel became available. And with each added revelation, Jesus' Second Coming became more detailed! They were all dissecting each new little piece of a phrase—taking the newly revealed information and turning it around and around until it slid into place in the bigger puzzle picture.

When the First Century Christian persecution by their fellow Jews waned, it was picked up in spades by the Romans.

- Even before Paul's missionary journeys, the Romans began to persecute, almost accidentally, under wimpy Emperor Claudius. He really did just want "everybody to hold hands and sing cum-by-yah." Please, don't anybody "rock the boat"—but the Christians rocked the boat! They wouldn't take part in the pagan rituals; they did unsanctioned things like starting hospitals for the sick and going to live in leper colonies. The Romans were pantheist, they worshipped many gods. The problem with the Christians was that they didn't!
- The next Emperor, Nero, promptly had his mother stabbed to death and his new young wife beheaded. Then on July 12th 64 AD fire *(accidentally?)* broke out, and Mad Nero blamed the Christians who were fed to wild animals and burned as torches along the Appian Way leading into Rome.
- The next Roman Emperor, evil Domitian, is the one who enjoyed watching people fed to wild animals as sport and turned it into constant Roman family entertainment.

Meanwhile the Early Church was stepping out every day right into the teeth of death and danger. If they had the choice between sharing their faith or hiding out to escape detection, they would share their faith! Scores of stories, circulated through the churches, of fellow Christians going around town picking up sick people who had been discarded to die at the edge of the road or picking up unwanted babies/children that were set out by the street. They proclaimed their faith over and over even though they knew it would almost certainly mean arrest and death!

- **Why were they so brave?** Because they knew Jesus was coming back again, and they were going do their part to take the Gospel to the "ends of the earth"! It didn't matter so much if they met Jesus dead or alive—just as long as **THEY GOT TO MEET JESUS WHEN HE CAME BACK!**

When Ethan and James first received copies of Paul's letter to the newly transformed Christians in Corinth, they immediately commissioned the scribing of scores of copies and sent them to every Church district. Excitement began to build as each Church Body read the words:

1 Corinthians 15:51–57: "But let me reveal to you a wonderful secret. We will not all die, but we will all be transformed! It will happen in a moment, in the blink of an eye, when the last trumpet is blown. For when the trumpet sounds, those who have died will be raised to live forever. And we who are living will also be transformed. For our dying bodies must be transformed into bodies that will never die; our mortal bodies must be transformed into immortal bodies. Then, when our dying bodies have been transformed into bodies that will never die, this Scripture will be fulfilled: 'Death is swallowed up in victory. O death, where is your victory? O death, where is your sting?' For sin is the sting that results in death, and the law gives sin its power. But thank God! He gives us victory over sin and death through our Lord Jesus Christ."

- What excited them wasn't so much the news that a trumpet would blow upon Jesus' return that they knew from the Gospel notes and 1 Thessalonians. It wasn't something new that the dead would be raised they knew that from 1 Thessalonians. It wasn't even news about the "living forever" part, although they weren't yet quite sure what that all meant. The "broken body raised to new life as a spiritual body" was new! But it still wasn't the most important thing they read in Paul newly inspired letter.

- **There was a word in the last section that lodged in the forefront of their brains: <u>VICTORY</u>!!** That word echoed and reechoed in their minds. It pointed them toward one huge blank space in their understanding—one central key puzzle piece—they could not possibly have grasped until they got Jesus'/John's final letter of Revelation!

INTRODUCTION

Finally, God was ready to explode into the minds of his Church electrifying truths that would ignite them from a fast-burning-bonfire into a raging firestorm that would sweep across the Roman Empire.

- As the Christians were being persecuted and martyred for their faith in record numbers, the same exact people were shifting into overdrive, spreading the Gospel message with an explosive potency. Within 200 years, Christianity would reach into the farthest corners of the Roman Empire with such transforming power that vast numbers of pagans would turn to not only the Creator God of Heaven, but specifically to **Jesus as the Saving Messiah of the world**.

Ethan often met other Church leaders to discuss the state of the developing Church. They built a timeline matching prophesied End Time predictions with on-the-ground unfolding developments. But just as Church Leadership began to sense that a momentum was beginning to build, they were horrified by the execution of James in Jerusalem! Ethan was stunned, but not demoralized. "God still has Apostles in key places out in this Empire who knew the Messiah personally," he said, "who personally heard Jesus prophesy about his Second Coming, and heard angels declare that 'he would return the same way they saw him go.'"

Then within five years, the Church received news of the brutal killings of both Peter and Paul by Mad Nero. However, now aging Ethan was determined to press on leading the church down the same path defined by Peter and Paul and James.

When General Titus marched in and destroyed Jerusalem in 70 AD, turning the town into a pile of rubble and driving the surviving Jews out into the pagan world around them, Ethan could see that Jesus' prophesies leading to his return were being fulfilled right in front of his eyes.

- He wrote to the Apostle John, the last surviving disciple who was living in Asia overseeing Church plants there. John responded back that with the leadership all dying off, the churches in Asia were starting to slip away from their "first love." If only there were some catalyst, some newly inspired truth from God that would reignite the church into a holy raging fire—but who was going to hear from God and write some new Epistle with all those God has used in the past now dead and gone?

- Ethan wrote back: There is yet one man—one disciple who after Jesus' resurrection ran to the tomb and found it empty and "he believed"! There is yet one disciple left who saw the resurrected Jesus, talked with Him, touched the nail prints in His hands, heard Jesus' last words commissioning him to "go out into the whole world and disciple all people in all nations, teaching all that He Himself had taught."

- There is yet one man left who watched Jesus ascend into Heaven with a promise to one day return back to Earth. He already wrote a Gospel account about the life of Jesus—that was written like no other writing before or since.

- John began to entertain the thought that possibly God might just use an old man to write explosive new truth.

But then—John heard a knock at his door one dark night. Roman soldiers dragged him off to the local jail. Within days he found himself dumped on a prison island offshore from his home town of Ephesus. "So much for Ethan's challenge, so much for the stirrings in his mind. He was going to die on this forbidden piece of rock—."

- Sunday morning arrived, he found himself lost in worship, and lifted in praise to the Messiah he now so deeply loved. He asked for a pen.

("Because he's old what harm can he do," the guard said.) He reached for the pen and dipped it into the inkwell. He has no idea what he is going to write but it was almost as if Someone was guiding his pen. He began to scribble:

- **Revelation 1:1: "This is a *revelation from Jesus Christ,* which God gave Him to show His servants the events that must soon take place."** "*Revelation*" (*apokalupsis*), "an unveiling" or "taking off the cover." John pictured the great curtain of all history—past, present, and future—begin to fall back, and he started to realize that he is going to be able to look inside. This wasn't going to be a revelation from John—this was going to be a Revelation from Jesus!

John found his pen writing that this "Unveiling" holds an amazing promise that is completely unique to anything John has ever heard before:

Revelation 1:3: "God blesses the one who reads the words of this prophecy to the church, and he blesses all who listen to its message and obey what it says, for the time is near."

John had never seen anything like this—no other books in the Old Covenant or the developing New Covenant had a promise like this. It would be the reader's **"blessing"** to read and study this special unveiling of Jesus Christ! "He will reveal things previously hidden"—by peeling back the cover of God's working past, present, and future!

- John knew the process of being used by God to pen inspired truth. It had happened to him four times before—but this seemed different. Jesus was handpicking him and **dictating exact phrases.** "I want you to write down word for word what I tell you to write," the Risen Christ seemed to be saying. John titled the letter: **"the Revelation from Jesus Christ."** Everyone who read it would understand it to be: the *unveiling,* or *the unmasking, or taking off the cover* by Jesus Christ **of events yet to come.**

As the words flow out from John's pen, Jesus separates them into two distinct parts:

Revelation 1:19: "Write down what you have seen:

1) both the things that are <u>NOW</u> happening and (Chapters 1–4a; from John's day to the present.)

2) the things that <u>WILL</u> happen." (Chapters 4b–22; are the unveiling of what is yet to come.)

John then writes and writes and writes until Jesus stops talking! By the time he finished, he knew beyond a shadow of a doubt that God has just used him in an eternal way! He had captured the "key" that the Early Church was waiting for—one that would ignite them into a roaring wall of spiritual flame.

- "Clearly these inspired words have to get off this piece of rock and out to every Christian Church on the planet."
- Amazingly, Emperor Domitian suddenly dies and "the old man" is released to go back home. John packages the scroll as if it is the most valuable possession on the planet. It is!
- When he arrives home, he is consumed with one thing only, to "carefully copy this scroll and get it immediately into the hands of the Asian churches and then out through them to the rest of the world."
- "And I need one more favor," John said. "I need you to appoint your best scribe because I need a copy made and sent to Ethan the Elder for he will know exactly what to do with it!"

As the Church did their first read through of the new letter, they were excited about the "letter directly from Jesus" part. They loved the "blessing when you read it" part, but there was one key piece they were all looking for—Was this the book that was going to answer all their questions about Jesus' expected return? They didn't have to read far:

Revelation 1:7, 8: "<u>Look! He comes with the clouds of heaven. And everyone will see him</u>—even those who pierced him. And all the nations of the world will mourn for him. Yes! Amen! 'I am the Alpha and the Omega—the beginning and the end,' says the Lord God. 'I

am the one who is, who always was, and who is still to come—the Almighty One.'"

As they read and read, and reread through their new letter, it didn't take long for them to understand that there was more to Jesus' "Second Coming" than just the "pre-signs" Jesus had mentioned that **would happen BEFORE his return**— they were now getting their first prophetic look at **what was going to happen AFTER Jesus' return!**

- The final veil was ripped off their minds—**they now knew how it was all going to end** and they were electrified! They now had the final key to the "Gospel" message; they caught something huge that they hadn't caught before.
- **Satan wasn't going to win his battle against God**! Jesus was going to victoriously clean satan's clock, destroy the chokehold of death, and even the curse of sin itself would be purged off this planet *(Revelation 22:3)*! **Jesus would set up an eternal reign and all the redeemed Believers would be reigning with him!**

Nobody in the Early Church let their "Revelation letter" collect dust. Nobody said, "It is just too hard to understand." They were pouring over it every day, making sure they understood it. The message of the letter was intense *(it still is)*: **Jesus victoriously wins—satan miserably loses!**

Ethan and the Early Church did not see the coming traumatic End Times in the book of Revelation as if they were somehow directed at them, the Church, the followers of Jesus. They read that once **"the Scroll" is opened, God makes all-out, no-holds-barred, take-no-prisoners war on *sin and satan*.** That's the part the Church had not yet heard. For all they knew Jesus was going to be returning to a sin-soaked planet. They might be lifted off, but satan would forever be wrecking this planet, and its future inhabitants, their grandchildren.

Once they read through their final letter of Revelation, they realized that the **returning Jesus was going to deal a death blow to "the evil one"!** Inside that scroll with seven seals was **packaged God's final judgment on sin and hell and death!**

Jesus/John "unveiled" that **satan and the antichrist use every single weapon at their disposal to defeat God and HIS MESSIAH, and <u>they completely, and dramatically, lose the war against the Creator of the universe</u>** *(Revelation 6–20)!*

- The excitement in the Churches reached a level never known before! Their worship services could be heard to the edges of town. The first time the Elders publicly read the account of Jesus' actual return, the church came unglued *(Revelation 19)!* "The King of all kings and Lord of all lords returns to this earth with millions of His Saints."
- In spite of all of satan's efforts to stop them, the Saints have been redeemed from their sins and have received their eternal reward! On the other hand, satan, the antichrist, and those who have refused Jesus' salvation are eternally destroyed with a single sentence from Jesus' mouth!
- **JESUS WINS—satan loses!**

The last paragraph in Jesus' final Revelation hammered that theme—It was the final prayer in every church gathering from that day forward:

> **Revelation 22:12–14, 17, 20: "'Look, I am coming soon, bringing my reward with me to repay all people according to their deeds. I am the Alpha and the Omega, the First and the Last, the Beginning and the End.' Blessed are those who wash their robes. They will be permitted to enter through the gates of the city and eat the fruit from the tree of life. The Spirit and the bride say, 'Come.' Let anyone who hears this say, 'Come.' Let anyone who is thirsty**

come. Let anyone who desires drink freely from the water of life. He who is the faithful witness to all these things says, 'Yes, I am coming soon!' Amen! Come, Lord Jesus!"

Sam's Note:

1900 years have since passed. So much of what the First Century Churches were prophetically looking forward to has already unfolded—in what is now history to us.

- **Only 30% of all Biblical prophesies have yet to be fulfilled—and Scripture seems to suggest they will happen in a snowballing rush!**

But as the prophetic End Times, as detailed by Jesus, move ever closer, something has happened in the minds of many modern day Christians. Jesus' Church has gone from pouring over Jesus', Paul's, Peter's, and John's End Time prophesies to, in some 21st century churches, never bringing the subject up at all!

- We have moved from seeing the Revelation letter **as a victorious call to awe and worship** detailing **the victorious win of Jesus and the massive loss of satan**—to a focus on the antichrist and satan as if they were the main characters of the book! They're not!

- Instead of being drawn to the book, many Christians tell me, they read the first 65 books of God's Word then slam their Bible shut when they get to the 66th book! Why?

- How can we regain the Early Church's intensity in looking forward to Jesus' return? How can we make our priority what they so clearly prioritized? **What will happen to our world when we do?**

The Revelation of Jesus Christ

PART I

REVELATION 1–3:
Unveiling What Jesus Is "Up to Now"

It now becomes our task—to ask ourselves not only what this book said to the Early Church, but what does it say to me? We already know, for certain, the same facts that John himself discovered:

- The book of Revelation deals not only with what is coming at the End of Times, but also with what Jesus is doing (*wanting to do*) in His Church today—"**the things that are now happening.**" That must apply just as much to me today as it did Ethan in the First Century.

Once we grasp that truth, we become ready to study the full "Unveiling" of Revelation. And it's also still just as true that: *God blesses the one who reads the words of this prophecy to the church, and He blesses me when I listen to its message and when I <u>obey</u> what it says.*

- Please notice this often-overlooked fact: **The command to "obey" what Revelation says** *can't apply to Chapters 5–22* **because they reveal what is "yet to come"** in our future. We can't obey what hasn't happened yet, right? So, *the things we are to obey must be found in Chapters 1–3. Yes?*

So we must not fail to study the opening chapters and as we dig through them, we each need to ask ourselves: *"Am I walking in a unique, special blessing promised by Jesus because I am obeying the words of Revelation 1:3—What is happening in my life and in my local church right now that matches the words of Jesus' Unveiling?"*

- And one more great point: The chapters of Revelation that reveal **the things that *will* happen (5–18) cover a period of only about seven years. The chapters that reveal what Jesus is doing right now (1–4) cover more than 1,900 years**—and they contain letters that Jesus personally dictated, and then on through the seven churches in Asia, to every Christian on the planet!

? *That "obey" statement on the previous pages is an eye-brow raiser to many Christians. If the "blessing" connected with Revelation comes from reading and <u>obeying</u> its words, which parts should I be obeying, and how should that be affecting my life right now?*

? *The default Christian answer on what Jesus is doing now is that he "has gone to heaven to prepare a place for us," and "he is interceding for the Saints." So, what's this newly-minted "vocation" of Jesus "walking among the lamp-stands" in Revelation 1–3, and how should that be influencing my life?*

? *Whenever we think of meeting Jesus in heaven, our minds automatically picture a long-haired, white-robed, Middle Eastern man in flip flops holding out his nail-scarred hands. When you one day meet Jesus in heaven, what does Revelation 1 say he will look like?*

1

Jesus Is "Walking" Among the Churches

Nearly 2,000 years have passed since Jesus was crucified, resurrected, and ascended to Heaven. **So just what has Jesus been up to?** *(Preparing us a place? Yes!)* But Paul tells us that He is also "sitting at the right hand of the Father making intercession for the Saints" *(Romans 8:34)*. What does that even mean? Obviously, Jesus is not spending his time sitting on a small throne beside the Father's big throne. That has to be an "idiomatic" way of saying that Jesus is occupying "the seat of honor, power, and influence."

- From that "seat," He is "making intercession" for us as our Divine Defense Attorney, pleading our case before the Throne of God and assuring Him *(and us)* that His sacrifice for us—is fully sufficient to cleanse us from all our sins!

That is powerful, and very important! But Revelation 1–3 unveils **even more** of what Jesus is "up to." John describes a brand-new snapshot of how Jesus appeared to him in his "island unveiling:"

Revelation 1:12–17: "When I turned to see who was speaking to me, I saw seven gold lamp-stands. And standing in the middle of the lamp-stands was someone like the Son of Man. [Daniel 7:13] He

5

was wearing a long robe with a gold sash across his chest. His head and his hair were white like wool, as white as snow. And his eyes were like flames of fire. His feet were like polished bronze refined in a furnace, and his voice thundered like mighty ocean waves. He held seven stars in his right hand, and a sharp two-edged sword came from his mouth. And his face was like the sun in all its brilliance. When I saw him, I fell at his feet as if I were dead."

John knew Jesus as well as any human being on Earth, so why would he "fall at His feet as if dead" when seeing Him again? Because Jesus was no longer the Teacher from Nazareth, who walked the roads of Galilee, on his way to becoming our Suffering Savior! Now, He is very clearly the Divine King of the Universe!

Jesus now vs. Jesus then

The change is so mind-numbing that John is shocked! John's leftover view of a bruised, battered, and crucified Savior" shuffling along in a bloodied white robe is clearly *not* what Jesus looks like anymore. He was such a startling figure that when John saw him, in his vision, it was too much to bear and he hit the ground—hard!

- Truth is, if Jesus walked in on any of us at this moment, we would not be standing chatting with him—even if you are an unbeliever—you would be on your face in awe and worship!

    Revelation 1:17–18: "But he [*Jesus, my friend, my cousin, the Messiah, the Savior of the World*], **laid his right hand on me and said, 'Don't be afraid! I am the First and the Last. I am the living one. I died, but look—I am alive forever and ever! And I hold the keys of death and the grave.'"**

John had more of the Middle Eastern oriental mindset than most of us and was better prepared to understand parables and symbolism than modern Westerners—but even he did not understand what he was seeing. So, Jesus explained it to him.

Revelation 1:19–20: "'Write down what you have seen—both the things that are now happening and the things that will happen. This is the meaning of the mystery of the seven stars you saw in my right hand and the seven gold lamp-stands: The seven stars are the messengers [angels- ἄγγελοι] **of the seven churches, and the seven lamp-stands are the seven churches.'"**

The "reality" behind the "symbolic" is supposed to be clear. It shows us exactly what Jesus is doing right now: He is *"moving among the churches"* which, as we will soon see in Revelation Chapters 2 and 3, is His present, all-consuming focus. The period of time between John's vision and the final beginning of the End Times is all about Jesus getting His Church ready for heaven! It was in the First Century—it's still just as true today!

Take a minute to read these opening three chapters from Jesus' perspective. He had lived His human life here on Earth, raised up 12 disciples, poured into them everything He could about who the Father was, and about what it meant to follow Him. Then He died, rose again, and commissioned His disciples to go out and finish what He began! He then ascended back to Heaven. *("Going to prepare a place for us" John 14:3.)*

Fast-forward some 50 years. The young Church, in spite of the persecution, has grown and spread across the known world. All the rest of the New Testament had been written in some form and was being circulated through the Church. Jesus has this one chance to speak directly back into the life of a Church that had been birthed through the efforts of His disciples. That's the context of the "seven letters" in Revelation 2 and 3, and that makes what Jesus has to say in these letters very important.

So why is Jesus "moving among" the Churches?

The "letters" make it clear that Jesus is consumed with how His Church is functioning. Apparently, His whole focus is to "serve" the churches; encouraging right behavior and exposing sinful behavior. He points out where the churches are missing the mark and exhorts them. He compliments those who are headed in the right direction and encourages them to shift up a gear. He warns those who have slipped a gear or two—that they are in spiritual danger. **That is what Jesus is doing right now**! That is where Jesus says He is investing huge amounts of His efforts. *(So, doesn't it make sense that if "Jesus' Church" and our association with it—is not a big priority to us—that is kind of a big deal considering that it is an all-consuming priority to Jesus?!)*

> **The entire New Testament is all about forming people into local "Church" bodies, from Jesus' great "I will build my Church" speech in Caesarea Philippi—right to this very moment!**

That is the entire backdrop of the book of Acts and all the Epistles! And now here, the first three chapters of Jesus' "Unveiling" are about Him "moving among those churches," adjusting their behavior, and making promises for their *(and our)* future.

"But—I'm not a Laodicean!"

Jesus mentions seven Asian churches by name. If we are not careful, we might mistakenly dismiss what He says to these churches as none of our business. "These letters are to seven specific First Century churches. They were written about them, to them, and for them. So, whatever was wrong with the church at Laodicea does not have any significance to my life today because **I'm not a Laodicean!**"

It would be a mistake to imagine that the God of the Universe would choose "seven little stone churches in Asia," all of which deteriorated back to dust long ago, for this Unveiling. Elder Ethan and all the churches in other locations knew full well that those seven churches represented a cross-section of all people, for all of time, and in every nation.

- These churches are *every church*. "Jesus is walking" among every church with exhortations—until that moment in time comes—when He will finally switch gears toward "the things that are to come."
- Jesus handpicked those seven churches as opposed to the churches in any other dots on the map because what was going on in those seven churches was strikingly similar to what goes on in most churches and among most believers.
- When we study them, we find most of our weaknesses, and get to reap all the benefits of Jesus' exhortations.

We are not going to look at every detail that Jesus emphasized to each church because that is not the point of this book. But neither should we be among those who toss out the first three chapters of Jesus' Unmasking to "get on to the good stuff."

- Jesus' words are here in the beginning chapters of the final book of the Bible, the book that wraps up the Scriptures, the final piece of written Revelation this world would ever receive—because His words are designed to tell us exactly what our Risen Lord is even now expecting from us right at this exact square on our calendar.

(1) If we are like the Believers in the church at **Ephesus**, it may mean that we once had a passionate love for and focus on our relationship with Jesus, but the *pressures of life, and the "stuff" of this world, has made us lose our first love*. If that's you—Jesus' advice is to come back into the closeness you once knew.

(2) If we are like the Believers in the church at **Pergamum**, it may be that we are *drowning in "worldliness."* The pull of what this world offers is far more attractive to us than the eternal things God has to offer. Jesus says: "Think about what matters eternally and put distance between yourselves and this world!"

(3) If we are like the Believers in the church at **Smyrna**, we may be true believers but are *being heavily tested and persecuted* in our daily lives. Jesus has compassionate and comforting words.

(4) If we are like the Believers in the church at **Philadelphia**, we deeply love the Risen Jesus and are solid in doctrine—but we *need to take the message of truth out to others.*

(5) If we are like the Believers in the church at **Thyatira**, we might be *seduced by people teaching a watered-down Gospel* that just seems easier to follow. Jesus commands those people to repent.

(6) If we are like the Believers in the church at **Sardis**, "the church of the living dead," we have a reputation for doing good, but we are simply *going through the motions.* Jesus tells us to "Wake up!"

(7) And if we are like the Believers in the church at **Laodicea** and are lukewarm "one-inch-deep" Christians who *talk faith but don't live it out—*Jesus has very strong words for counterfeit Christians!

How much do I know?

1) Which is not one of Jesus' physical characteristics now?
    a) eyes like flames of fire
    b) voice thundering like ocean waves
    c) long dark hair
    d) feet like polished brass
2) Of the three things the Bible says Jesus is doing right now, what would seem to consume most of his time?
    a) preparing a place for us *(John 14:3)*
    b) interceding for us *(Romans 8:34)*
    c) getting his "Church" ready for heaven
3) What is the repeated phrase that shows up at the end of every Revelation 2–3 letter that shows us that these letters are for all churches for all times?
4) In five of the seven letters, Jesus exposes those who are claiming faith but not living it out, going through the motions, living in worldliness, or are lukewarm. How would you say this is being played out in modern churches?

You can check your answers beginning on page 243.

Number of correct answers on this page:

? *Did you ever wonder why, after dying for humanity's sins, after rising from the dead bringing eternal life to all who believe; why in the world has Jesus waited 2000 years to return? What's the point?*

? *What should be our response when somebody says, "I'm a Christian, but I don't go to church anymore—churches are full of hypocrites"?*

2

Jesus Is "Re-forming" the Churches

It important to realize that these two chapters written to "re-form" Jesus' Churches were written just 65 years after Jesus died. Churches formed after Jesus life-changing resurrection—Churches who had the infilling and empowering Holy Spirit available to "lead them into all truth"—those groups of people within six decades were already getting letters of correction from Jesus. Churches, it seems, are filled with imperfect people!

Many of us have complaints about our churches and fellow church people. Some of us have bad memories of things "Christian" people have said or done. All those things were just as true about Elder Ethan's Early Church and were probably even true of churches John himself led before his exile. Here's the point: Whatever negative feelings we might want to express toward our local churches, we need to remember this fact:

The New Testament makes it very clear just how important the idea of the Church is to Jesus, beginning with the power sentence He made to Peter: **"Upon this rock** *(Peter's confession of his deity)* **I will build my Church, and all the powers of hell will not conquer it."** His Church will be given the **"keys to the kingdom of Heaven, and whatever they** *(the Church)* **binds and looses on Earth has already been bound and loosed in Heaven"** *(present passive participle!) Matthew 16:18, 19.*

The church was not some stray thought to Jesus. **Apparently, the whole reason Jesus went back to Heaven, rather than setting up his earthly kingdom right after his resurrection, was to give time for this all important "Church" to be formed!**—God doesn't just love human beings so much he sent his Son to pay their sin penalty. Jesus, God incarnate, loves the (His) Church!

> **Ephesians 5:23, 25, 27: "Christ is the head of the church. He is the Savior of his Body, the church. Christ loved the church. He gave up his life for her. He did this to present her to himself as a glorious church without a spot or wrinkle or any other blemish. Instead, she will be holy and without fault."**

The Magna Carta (the charter) for Jesus' Church!

Jesus' "Magna Carta" for us collective Believers was this: He was going to build His Church, and all the forces of Hell will not be able to prevail against her *(us)*! Jesus has a great passion for assembling a roomful of the most unlikely miscreants and turning them into a roomful of Brothers and Sisters in Christ. That is what He loves to do and is devoting His time to up until the End Time begins!

- If the thought of a few dozen, or a few hundred vastly different people, from vastly different backgrounds, with vastly different ways of thinking all collected together, has a "hellish" sound to us, we need to be brought up short by the knowledge that just such a scenario has a "heavenly" sound to Jesus!

Ephesians 1:22–23: "God has put all things under the authority of Christ and has made him head over all things for the benefit of the church. And the church is his body; it is made full and complete by Christ, who fills all things everywhere with himself."

Ephesians 3:10: "God's purpose in all this was to <u>use the church to display his wisdom</u> in its rich variety to all the unseen rulers and authorities in the heavenly places."

Imagine that! Jesus' plan is to use the transforming life changes that happen in us, around us, and through us to "wow" the angelic realms in Heaven, and to confuse and confound the very forces of evil in the "not-so-heavenly" realm.

It is what God will do through groups of us, banded together in faith, that will push back the plans of satan in this world! Do we see why this all introduces the Book of Revelation? The whole theme of Jesus' Unveiling in four words is: **Jesus wins—satan loses!** Ethan and the late First Century leadership knew instantly that Jesus expected that principle to start in his Church! *That* is why he has been constantly **"walking among the churches"** from the day of Pentecost right up until this present day. It's what He will still be doing tomorrow, and next week, and next year until He returns to "rapture" His "Bride"! **This is Jesus' Plan A for building the Kingdom among those who follow Him. There's no plan B!**

The next time you hear somebody say, "Organized churches are unimportant and filled with sinful hypocrites," remember this: Churches might indeed be full of hypocrites, but Jesus is pouring Himself into reshaping those hypocrites into saints, His body, His Bride!

"Churches are full of hypocrites!" Bite your tongue!

The seven churches Jesus addresses in his Revelation were no doubt formed under Paul's influence. John knew all these churches and had probably preached in them. He, and Jesus' mother Mary, lived there in Asia until she died and John was exiled to Patmos. The Elders of those churches may have been John's friends.

- There is no doubt that these churches had once been "on fire" for Jesus. They were all "results of the resurrection!" There was a time when they were spreading the name of Jesus all across Asia Minor, and their lives and testimonies were the talk of all Asia.
- These seven churches were probably "cutting-edge" spiritual churches in the 50's and 60's AD, but by the 90's AD (*just 40 or so years later*), five of the seven were getting a correction letter from Jesus Himself!
- That knowledge should set us back on our heels. We are so far removed from that place and time that most of us don't even know where a city called Laodicea was, but if we had lived in 95 AD, we would have understood that a "once-on-fire" Laodicean church had cooled to the point where Jesus threatened to "spit them out" of His mouth.

That is undoubtedly why Jesus chose a cross-section of churches that needed a spiritual jolt. What Jesus said to those seven churches in John's letter was supposed to be passed on to other churches, right down to us in the present day, because every single letter ends with this announcement:

> **Revelation 2:7: "Whoever has ears, let them hear what the Spirit says to the churches."**

Before we dive into what is coming next—we need one hard look at the first letter to Ephesus, so we can get a feel for how these letters read. Ephesus was John (and Mary's) hometown but it was one of the most wicked places on the planet, so Jesus' Church had to be extra sharp. It was—and then it wasn't!

> **Revelation 2:1–7: "To the angel** [leader] **of the church in Ephesus write: These are the words of him who holds the seven stars in his right hand and walks among the seven golden lamp stands. I know your deeds, your hard work and your perseverance. I know that you cannot tolerate wicked people, that you have tested those who claim to be apostles but are not, and have found them false. You have persevered and have endured hardships for my name, and have not grown weary. Yet I hold this against you: You have forsaken the love you had at first. Consider how far you have fallen! Repent and**

do the things you did at first. If you do not repent, I will come to you and remove your lampstand from its place. But you have this in your favor: You hate the practices of the Nicolaitans, which I also hate. Whoever has ears, let them hear what the Spirit says to the churches."

The Nicolaitans were people who taught that since Christians are no longer under the Old Testament law, but under grace—it should not matter how they live, or what they do, or how much they sin because they are covered by Jesus' grace. Imagine what John, or James, or Peter, or the Apostle Paul himself would have said to such blatant error. Jesus pulled no punches—"I hate that doctrine," he said! Fortunately, the whole Ephesian church hadn't yet drifted that far. Some of the other churches, though, had already fallen off a cliff.

- Seven times Jesus offers compliments where compliments were deserved; then five times He moves to convict them of a desperately needed course correction. He always finishes with the phrase, now familiar to each of us looking on years later: "Whoever has ears, let them hear what the Spirit says to the churches" *(Revelation 2:7)*.

Why does He say all that? So that we will avoid making the same mistakes! He is telling us that He is here to help us with all the resources of Heaven because we are His number one concern! He is "walking among the churches" ready and willing to infuse all of us with His Spirit and help us overcome any weakness. He wants to make our light so bright that we will push back satan's darkness!

"Don't be a frog in the frying pan!"

Jesus does not want us to make the mistake that five of the seven Asian churches made and, like "a frog in a frying pan," adapt to the gradual heating of the world until at last we are boiling in our own juices and don't even know it.

The good news here is that none of this need have a sad ending. *Seven out of seven times*, after warning "all who have ears to hear" to focus on what the Spirit is saying to the churches, Jesus issues life-giving promises:

(1) **Jesus promises victorious eternal living, eating from the "tree of life"!** *Wow, we haven't seen that since the Garden of Eden!*

> Revelation 2:7: "Whoever has ears let them hear what the Spirit says to the churches. To the one who is victorious, I will give the right to eat from the tree of life, which is in the paradise of God."

(2) **Jesus promises His followers will live even after dying!**

> Revelation 2:11: "Anyone with ears to hear must listen to the Spirit and understand what he is saying to the churches. Whoever is victorious will not be harmed by the second death."

(3) **Jesus promises to be our "Never-ending Supply"!**

> Revelation 2:17: "Whoever has ears let them hear what the Spirit says to the churches. To the one who is victorious, I will give some of the hidden manna. I will also give that person a white stone with a new name written on it."

(4) **Jesus promises us a future "reigning with Him"!**

> Revelation 2:26–29: "To all who are victorious, who obey me to the very end, To them I will give authority over all the nations. They will rule the nations with an iron rod and smash them like clay pots. They will have the same authority I received from my Father, and I will also give them the morning star! Anyone with ears to hear must listen to the Spirit and understand what he is saying to the churches."

(5) **Jesus promises us eternal acceptance by our Good, Heavenly Father!**

> Revelation 3:5: "All who are victorious will be clothed in white. I will never erase their names from the Book of Life, but I will announce before my Father and his angels that they are mine."

(6) **Jesus promises us citizenship in the "New Jerusalem"!**

Revelation 3:12: "All who are victorious will become pillars in the Temple of my God, and they will never have to leave it. And I will write on them the name of my God, and they will be citizens in the city of my God—the New Jerusalem that comes down from heaven from my God. And I will also write on them my new name."

We'll end this chapter with **the 7th promise,** but first let me show you a startling reality:

- The seven churches Jesus addressed in Revelation Chapters 2 and 3 are all gone! That fact would have been completely unbelievable to Elder Ethan or Peter or John. The Church in Ephesus had grown to as many as 50,000 people—20% of the entire population of Ephesus had turned from perverted sinful practices and become vibrant Christians.

- Yet today, more than 1,900 years later, the population of Turkey is 74 million. The percentage of Christians in Turkey is less than 2% (120,000). Try to grasp the huge significance of that. This area in Asia Minor was the centerpiece of civilized life in the First Century. These cities were home to a huge number of Roman citizens. Asia had more Roman cities than all of Italy. This area was second only to the city of Jerusalem as a focal point of the New Testament.

- The Apostle Paul moved back and forth through this area and spent three years in Ephesus. John, and Jesus' mother Mary, spent the later part of their lives there as well as Timothy, Aquila, Priscilla, and others. Twelve of the 27 books in the New Testament are addressed to people living in this area—Galatians, Ephesians, Colossians, 1 and 2 Timothy, 1, 2, and 3 John, 1 and 2 Peter, James, and Revelation. As a result, thousands and thousands of believers trusted in Jesus Christ!

- This was the place where God proved to the world that he could take the vilest of human-sacrificing pagans and turn them into the holiest of saints. It was from this part of the world that Christianity spread north and west to Spain, and to Europe, and to the British Isles *(which became the heritage on which America was eventually founded)*.

- That is why it is so shocking that *98 out of every 100 people living in that part of the world, today, reject Jesus as the divine Savior of the world!*

We have to ask the question: *What happened?* The imagery of Revelation tells us that Jesus is walking among seven golden lamp-stands *(representing all churches)*. That symbol is very significant:

The lamp-stand is not the light;
the lamp-stand is what holds the light!

The light is the Gospel of Jesus' redemption and forgiveness for the sins of the whole world. The "lampstand" holds the light up—so that it can illuminate and saturate the dark world around it. Jesus said:

Revelation 2:5: "Consider how far you have fallen! Repent and do the things you did at first. If you do not repent, I will come to you and remove your lampstand from its place."

It is certain that Jesus is not hiding around some corner watching for our light to grow dim so that He can jump out and rip out our lampstand. That is the opposite of the point! When our lives are on target, in focus, in harmony with the truths of God's Word, we are automatically holding our lampstand high above the crowd around us so that they are being saturated with the light of the Gospel, whether they want to be or not!

---

(7) Now, let's add in the *final promise* of the final letter to the seven churches. It seems like a visible momentum is building. The end of Chapter 3 offers a gripping promise that is also applied, by Jesus, to each of us today:

Revelation 3:20–21: "Look! I stand at the door and knock. If you hear my voice and open the door, I will come in, and we will share

a meal together as friends. Those who are victorious will sit with me on my throne, just as I was victorious and sat with my Father on his throne."

The mental snapshot of Jesus' standing at the door and knocking has spawned a lot of discussion. "Jesus does not knock the door down—but waits for us to open up to Him. There is no knob on the outside—because the door to our hearts must be opened from the inside."

What? We get to sit on Jesus' throne!

Let's chew on this final eternal benefit of opening the door of our heart and giving our Creator full access to every corner of our soul.

Revelation 3:21–22: "To him who overcomes I will grant to sit with Me on My throne, as I also overcame and sat down with My Father on His throne. He who has an ear, let him hear what the Spirit says to the churches."

Jesus promises to *let us sit on His throne!* What could that possibly mean? That is clearly something far more than "receiving the crown of life" or "being clothed in white garments." To understand why God would give such a huge blessing to us, we must get our heads around just how far Jesus is willing to go for all His redeemed saints in this "Church" He is building. This is really what the End Times are all about.

The heroes of the rest of the story are not the antichrist and satan. THEY LOSE!! They end up in the lake of fire! <u>The heroes at the end of the book, at the end of all time, are Jesus and the victorious redeemed Saints!</u>

Amazingly, we won't deserve a drop of what we receive. It will all be a gift from our wonderful Savior! The Early Church figured that out—and SO MUST WE!

How much do I know?

1) Jesus announces that "He is going to build his church" in Matthew 16:18–19. This happens 6+ months before he is crucified. In Matthew 18, Jesus again stresses the "binding and loosing" privileges of Believers. Just before that in Matthew 18:15–17 we find Jesus teaching on "church discipline." The unrepentant are supposed to be taken in front of the whole "church!" Isn't that odd, considering most people say the "church" wasn't "born" until the Day of Pentecost months later! How would you explain that?

2) Ephesians 3:10: "God's purpose in all this was to use the church to display his wisdom in its rich variety to all the unseen rulers and authorities in the heavenly places." In what ways are we/should we "the Church" be living out an example to "unseen authorities" both good and evil?

3) What do you think Jesus meant by allowing us "Overcomers" to sit with him on his throne? If we are going to "reign with Jesus," who are we going to reign over? Won't every human be either in heaven with us, or in hell with satan?

You can check your answers beginning on page 243.

Number of correct answers on this page:

The Revelation of Jesus Christ

PART II

REVELATION 4-5:

Unveiling Heaven and the Throne of God

For the general church attendee in the 21st Century, the part of Revelation that focuses on End Times is not often thought to even really begin until Chapter 6—the startling chapter that describes the opening of the seven seals. Many modern End Time students would struggle to remember anything that's recorded in Chapters 4–5. That would not have been true for the First Century consuming-everything-prophetic Christian! They would have soon figured out that what is happening in Revelation 4–5 is more "eternally significant" than what happens in Chapters 6–18!

- It should matter to us today, that what John recorded as happening in Jesus' Revelation, Chapters 4–5, was already happening in John's day, it is still happening today, and it will still be unfolding a million years from now. *(In contrast, Chapters 6–18 cover fewer than seven years.)*

Consider these statistics: *(Many people are quoting these figures, although I can't find who sat down and did the counting.* I've added in the percentages.) ☺

- The Bible contains 31,124 verses.
  - 8,352 (26.8%) contain prophecy *(they speak of events to come).*
- The Old Testament contains 23,210 verses.
  - 6,641 (28.5%) contain prophecy.
- The New Testament contains 7,914 verses.
  - 1,711 (21.5%) contain prophecy.
- Of the 8,352 prophetic Bible verses:
  - **6,312 (67.8%) have already been fulfilled** exactly as predicted.
  - *2,040 (32.2%) are yet to be fulfilled.*

The Bible was written over a period spanning 2100 BC to 95 AD. We can count as many as 40 different authors, writing from different locations hundreds of miles apart, and it was all written in three very distinct languages.

- Yet every bit of the Bible fits together with perfect unity, and every single thread of prophecy fits together with machine-like precision—**two-thirds of which has already precisely come to pass!**
- Any Biblically informed, deep-thinking Christian should logically draw the conclusion that **the remaining 2,040 verses of Biblical prophecy will unfold exactly as predicted!**

However—before Jesus reveals how all this prophecy is going to unfold, He Himself, as "the Lamb that was slain," must be found "worthy to open the seven seals" beginning in Revelation 6.

- First, Jesus wanted to make sure that all Believers who read this "blessed" letter will have a picture in their minds that is bigger and more impressive than the horrors the Early Church was facing in the First Century. A picture that is even bigger than the horrors he is going to show us unfolding during the End Times. That's exactly what truths persecuted Ethan and his hunted congregation would have honed in on.
- "The antichrist might soon be arriving on the earth and things could get a little dicey as Believers wait for the Risen Jesus to clean satan's clock. But they-can-know-that-they-know-that-they-know that they have hold of the tail-end of the biggest thing in the whole universe!"

So—**Chapters 4 and 5 <u>present a Heavenly "eternal intermission"</u>** that reached way beyond the mind-numbing chaos and turmoil facing the Church in John's day. My, those persecuted people needed to hear this truth—AND SO DO WE!

(?) *Did John's vision happen with him sitting among the angels in the Throne Room of God—or was he only invited to write what he saw as he "looked through a doorway" into heaven?*

(?) *Heaven, as it exists right now, is described in four different passages in the Bible. Many people can describe what a modern "I was there" book says Heaven looks like but have no idea what the Bible actually records. Can you name three characteristics of what we will actually see when we arrive in God's Throne Room?*

(?) *True or False: Many End Time fans want to start their study of Revelation with "the good stuff" in Chapter 6–18. God purposely put a picture of our future in heaven in Chapter 4, so that we would lock that "future hope" in before studying the difficult last seven years!*

3

A Glimpse into the Throne Room of God

Revelation 4 is a direct follow-up to the last words of Revelation 3.

Revelation 3:21: "To him who overcomes I will grant to sit with Me on My throne, as I also overcame and sat down with My Father on His throne."

<u>**Then Chapter 4 starts**</u>*: (The chapter headings were not originally in John's letter, but it's a tool we all need to use to keep on track.)*

> To him
> who
> overcomes

Revelation 4:1–2: "Then as I looked, *I saw a door standing open in heaven,* and the same voice I had heard before spoke to me like a trumpet blast. The voice said, *'Come up here,* and I will show you

what must happen after this.' And instantly I was in the Spirit, and I saw a throne in heaven and someone sitting on it."

There's so much here that we need to understand before we move on to the rest of this chapter, let alone the rest of this book. Imagine the Early Church trying to get their minds around "a doorway open into heaven"!

- Picture, again, John sitting on his rocky prison island. He has been writing furiously as Jesus is dictating. John thoroughly understood the "seven churches part." He could picture the faces of people in each church. He could picture the places where they met. He had prayed over and over again for people with special needs in each church, and for God to lock the door against those who were satan's antagonists. He knew the churches' strengths and had, himself, probably warned them about their spiritual weaknesses. He must have so enjoyed writing back to them about Jesus' promise of a "crown of life" and "a white robe."

Toward the end, however, John finds himself in uncharted territory. Jesus promises that "**those who overcome will sit with Him on His throne.**" I picture John pausing—putting down his pen—and taking a deep breath before picking it up again to resume writing. He, like all of us, must have been wondering, *"What could it all mean?"* The picture of Heaven doesn't come into focus in the Old Testament. The Hebrew Bible, which was John's Bible, has a lot to say about human thrones here on Earth, but says very little about Heavenly thrones. *(David did briefly mention "heavenly thrones" in the Psalms.)*

- Psalm 47:8: "God reigns above the nations, sitting on his holy throne."
- Psalm 99:1: "The Lord is king! Let the nations tremble! He sits on his throne between the cherubim. Let the whole earth quake!"

We today have the whole New Testament and scores of other books written about Heaven *(some more accurate than others)*. The Apostle John did not have all of our information. Jesus had mentioned God "on His throne" on a few occasions and said that He, the Son of Man, would sit on God's throne. We have no indication that He ever explained it or described God's throne to His disciples. There is no record of a Q&A session where one of the disciples asked Jesus, *"What is the throne of God? Is there really a throne or is it just a way of saying God sits in the seat of power in the universe?"*

Seriously, there is actually a Throne Room in Heaven?

Imagine John's amazement when he heard "the thundering voice" a second time and was invited to peer into the "Throne Room of Heaven," the worship center of the universe! John writes that he saw a "door standing open in heaven." John does not say he got to go in and "chat with the angels," but only that he got to "look through the door."

As John stood in the foyer of Heaven, he got to see what God's Throne looks like. That information was to be sent through the seven Asian churches down the line of history to you and me.

The first point that must have occurred to John—the point that must have exploded its way into the minds of Ethan and Friends, and the point that is also supposed to get through to us—is that **Heaven is an actual place!** John was not looking into some hologram of what Heaven might look like if it actually existed. John was looking into the actual Throne Room of Heaven!

- **We are fascinated with Heaven**. Tens of thousands of people read the book and watched the movie *Heaven Is For Real*. I sincerely hope the book and movie turned some people's eyes toward the reality of Heaven.
- But it's a great irony to me, that many people could detail a modern book's description of Heaven with perfect precision—but if we were to ask some of the same people to give us the *actual* description of the Throne Room of Heaven found in the Bible, many would not know what it was or even that such a Biblical description exists. *It does!*

Here it is:

> **Revelation 4:2–8: "I saw a throne in heaven and someone sitting on it. The one sitting on the throne was as brilliant as gemstones— like jasper and carnelian. And the glow of an emerald circled his**

throne like a rainbow. Twenty-four thrones surrounded him, and twenty-four elders sat on them. They were all clothed in white and had gold crowns on their heads. From the throne came flashes of lightning and the rumble of thunder. And in front of the throne were seven torches with burning flames. This is the sevenfold Spirit of God. In front of the throne was a shiny sea of glass, sparkling like crystal. In the center and around the throne were four living beings, each covered with eyes, front and back. The first of these living beings was like a lion; the second was like an ox; the third had a human face; and the fourth was like an eagle in flight. Each of these living beings had six wings, and their wings were covered all over with eyes, inside and out. Day after day and night after night they keep on saying, 'Holy, holy, holy is the Lord God, the Almighty— the one who always was, who is, and who is still to come.'"

If that description leaves you feeling a bit overwhelmed, put aside for a minute any thought of "that doesn't seem real to me," and just go with this truth: **Heaven is an actual place!** John was clearly overwhelmed by what he was seeing too, but he faithfully wrote down what he saw because he suddenly knew without a doubt that not only was Heaven a real place—but that what he was seeing was actually happening at that very moment.

- It's important to make this point: Throughout Revelation John is writing what he sees *from his frame of reference*. It is almost impossible to describe something that your brain has no "frame of reference" to grasp. For instance, John will describe what *to him* look like huge locusts spitting fire and causing death. Today, we would perhaps see those looking something like this:

It's a giant locust spitting death!

We have a much better frame of reference. We understand attack helicopters that hover in mid-air and spray out death with automatic weapons. How in the world would First Century John or James or Ethan, who walked or rode a donkey everywhere, describe a high-tech helicopter? Perhaps that's not what the fire-spitting locusts in Jesus' Unveiling are, but we need to understand the difficulty John and the New Church would have had picturing things that would not be invented for 2,000 years.

We can imagine how overwhelmed "the Revelator" would have been by the sights and sounds that were filling his eyes and ears as he stared through the door. By the way, John was not the only ancient Biblical writer to glance through a doorway into Heaven. And what do you know—they all saw basically the same thing:

> **Daniel 7:9–10: "The Ancient of Days took his seat; His clothing was white as snow, and the hair of His head like pure wool; His throne was fiery flames; its wheels were burning fire. A stream of fire issued and came out from before him; a thousand thousands served Him, and ten thousand times ten thousand stood before Him; the court sat in judgment."**

> **Ezekiel 1:1, 4–6: "Now it came to pass in the thirtieth year, in the fourth *month*, on the fifth *day* of the month, as I *was* among the**

captives by the River Chebar, *that the heavens were opened* and I saw visions of God. Then I looked, and behold, a *whirlwind* was coming out of the north, *a great cloud with raging fire engulfing itself; and brightness was all around it and radiating out of its midst like the color of amber, out of the midst of the fire.* Also from within it *came* the likeness of four living creatures. And this was their appearance: they had the likeness of a man. Each one had four faces, and each one had four wings."

Ezekiel 1:26–27: "And above the firmament over their heads *was the likeness of a throne, in appearance like a sapphire stone;* on the likeness of the throne was a likeness with the appearance of a man high above it. Also from the appearance of His waist and upward I saw, as it were, *the color of amber with the appearance of fire all around within it;* and from the appearance of His waist and downward I saw, as it were, *the appearance of fire with brightness all around."*

In case we get too impressed with our own 21st Century "enlightenment," and our big-brained sophistication—it is still likely that **if any of us, today, had the chance to catch a glimpse into the Throne Room of Heaven,** we would be slobbering all over our shirts and still find that we are at a complete loss of words to describe what we were seeing because—it would be so far beyond even our modern comprehension!

The tiny glimpses into Heaven that some have claimed to experience must be the most fractional sliver of light. If the door of Heaven were actually swung open to us, we would be absolutely overwhelmed with awe and worship!

Revelation 1:17: "When I saw him, I fell at his feet as if I were dead. But he laid his right hand on me and said, 'Don't be afraid! I am the First and the Last.'"

Imagine how John must have reacted when he found himself looking in on the very presence of the Father, the Son, and the Holy Spirit—in the Throne Room of Heaven!

- Even those beings who have been in God's presence for a long, long time have a very predictable response:

> **Revelation 4:9–11: "Whenever the living beings give glory and honor and thanks to the one sitting on the throne [the one who lives forever and ever], the twenty-four elders fall down and worship the one sitting on the throne [the one who lives forever and ever]. And they lay their crowns before the throne and say, 'You are worthy, O Lord our God, to receive glory and honor and power. For you created all things, and they exist because you created what you pleased.'"**

There is a very important point that Jesus is trying to get through to John, and through John on to *(us)* His Church:

- Heaven is an actual place!
- God is, without question, on His Throne!

Every event in this whole universe unfolds before the omniscient *(all-science)* eyes of God, who is *"seated* on the Throne" of the universe. The Creator and Sustainer of all things does not overlook anything in our lives. That is the message of the fourth chapter of Jesus' Unmasking. **That is the camera *lens* through which God wants us *to understand all that happens in our modern daily lives.***

- The Emperor Domitian was the Roman Caesar when John was writing the Revelation of Jesus. Domitian's brother was Titus who ruled the Roman Empire from AD 79–81. He is famous as the Roman general who completely destroyed Jerusalem in AD 70. *God was on His throne while General Titus destroyed Jerusalem! (In fact, Jesus himself had prophesied it.)*
- Domitian persecuted the Church by allowing horrific purges of the churches and the Believers—he exiled the last living disciple to Patmos

where John faithfully recorded Jesus' Unveiling. After Domitian's death in 96 AD, John returned to live his last days in Ephesus, carrying the Revelation of Jesus with him, to be given to the churches, and it was copied over and over until it now sits in your lap. **God was on His throne when the Emperor Domitian exiled John to Patmos!**

- That is the great truth of Revelation 4: *God is on the Throne!* That is true even if you are being persecuted like the early Believers or are suffering at the hands of your enemies like John on Patmos or are struggling just to make it through one day at a time because life is so hard. *God is on the throne!* Beyond the temporary chaos we live in—there is an Eternal Heaven! And in that Heaven sits the One who created every bit of matter and energy in the universe with one simple phrase "Let there be"!

That is the picture God wants to invade our minds before we study the rest of this book. *In Jesus' Revelation we find a "high definition" picture of Heaven! (That's very much on purpose!)*

> **Revelation 4:1–2: "Then as I looked, *I saw a door standing open in heaven.* And instantly I was in the Spirit, and *I saw a throne in heaven and someone sitting on it.* "**

John did not win the Heavenly lottery offering him a personal tour of Heaven's Throne Room because he was such a good disciple and had outlived the others. The target audience for John's vision was not just John, it was the seven churches and, through them, all the Early Churches and US!—we "who have ears to hear"!

- God wanted John, and the Early Churches, *to lift their eyes above the chaos that was their lives and **focus on the eternal future waiting for them**.* He wanted that message to be passed on to us so we would do the same thing! Whatever you are facing in this life that seems all-consuming right now, know this: **What God has coming for your future will be eternally worth it!**

God did not have to insert a picture of Heaven here, but He did! It was not accidental or incidental. He wants to "lift our eyes off our circumstances—and onto our Savior"! He wants us to realize this truth:

Hebrews 13:14–15: "This world is not our permanent home; we are looking forward to a home yet to come. Therefore, let us offer through Jesus a continual sacrifice of praise to God, proclaiming our allegiance to his name."

That is the axis on which Chapter 4 turns: God wanted this picture of Heaven to settle deep into the mind of the First Century Church, and he wants it to settle deep into our minds—before we study and try to "unmask" the End Time events in Revelation 6–18.

A picture of Heaven fixed in our minds!

When 21ˢᵗ Century American Christians look back at the America of the past we see people who embraced God's Word and lived out His truth in their lives. When we compare that mental picture with our present-day, many of us feel deep sadness or even righteous anger. When many of us turn and look forward toward End Time prophesies, it is easy to feel despair or outright fear.

- Imagine if we had lived in one of those First Century churches in Asia Minor—Pergamum or Sardis or Ephesus—when the sinful sexual perversion of society was far more overt than it is today. (*Many would get life sentences in federal prison today for what they did every day then as part of their pagan "worship."*) What if, instead of a Christian church on every corner, there was a pagan temple literally devoted to the worship of Satan?

When the Seven Asian Churches got their copy of the letter from John, *they would have undoubtedly assumed that the End Times being described would happen in their lifetime!* They were suffering severely as they tried to live out their daily Christian lives. Jesus was exhorting them to be "overcomers" right in the middle of the chaos even though they probably thought that before their generation all died, Jesus' Unveiling would be capped off by the appearance of the antichrist and the "end of the age."

- Ethan and his leadership teams would have been fascinated by the picture inside heaven! Just the detailed snapshot from Chapter 1 must have consumed many, many Bible studies. They would have tried to balance this new knowledge of heaven with the now-known fact that Jesus was returning here to this earth. They were going to "rise to meet Jesus in the air"—yet they were going to "rule with him" right here on this planet! *How could that be?*

- Everybody was talking about a "coming rapture," but when exactly did Jesus, Paul, and now John say that "rapture" was going to take place? Would Jesus return BEFORE the anti-christ arrived or AFTER his attempt to become the counterfeit Messiah? They poured over the clues—.

- They were so deeply buried in persecution and suffering that the thought of a "persecuting antichrist" arriving brought little additional fear.

- It's important to note that there were plenty of teachings in the Early Church writings about a "rapture," but none *(as far as I can find)* that would take the Christians away from this world before "Daniel's 70th week" began. *(What in the world is Daniel's 70th week some will ask—keep reading!)*

The hunted Christians all buried their faces in God's Word and leaned hard into the winds of persecution:

> *2 Corinthians 4:8–9, 10, 16–18: "We are pressed on every side by troubles, but we are not crushed! We are perplexed, but not driven to despair! We are hunted down, but never abandoned by God! We get knocked down, but we are not destroyed!*
>
> *"Through suffering, our bodies continue to share in the death of Jesus so that the life of Jesus may also be seen in our bodies.*

"That is why we never give up. Though our bodies are dying, our spirits are being renewed every day. For our present troubles are small and won't last very long. Yet they produce for us a glory that vastly outweighs them and will last forever!

"So we don't look at the troubles we can see now; rather, we fix our gaze on things that cannot be seen. For the things we see now will soon be gone, but the things we cannot see will last forever."

The Apostle Paul

Paul is saying *(and the Church of Jesus would have quoted it all over and over),* **"We do not, we will not, fix our eyes on our hardships here on earth, but <u>we fix our eyes on Jesus</u>! Our future is not just what we might experience here for a few days or weeks—but <u>what we will be experiencing for all the rest of eternity</u>!"**

Our future is—all the rest of eternity!

- You can be sure that one way or another, as a Believer, *your best days are still ahead (not a handful of them but millions/billions of them!)*
- Start believing today with all of your heart that everything in this final book is describing your eternal victorious future!
- Jesus (and we) ultimately, definitively win!—satan crashes and burns! *(literally!)*

When you think of "God on His throne," ditch the image of a long- white-bearded Ancient of Days resting His weary bones in a big chair. No! The point is: God is in control! The inmates are not running the asylum! Even though humanity careens around exercising the sin nature thinking they are going to conquer the world, they are like a gnat trying to get a foothold on Niagara Falls. There is an infinite God, in Heaven, who created the whole universe with the energy of a single sentence, and He is not reeling from the puny efforts of terrorists or nuclear threats from rogue nations or anything that is, or is not, happening in this world!

- Every possible word of John's vision of God's Throne Room is supposed to help lift us to this place of awe:

> **Revelation 4:2–6:** "Immediately I was in the Spirit; and behold, a throne set in heaven, and One sat **on the throne**. And He who sat there was like a jasper and a sardius stone in appearance; and there was a rainbow around the throne, in appearance like an emerald. **Around the throne** were twenty-four thrones, and on the thrones, I saw twenty-four elders sitting *[these 24 elders likely represent every redeemed saint who has crossed into Heaven],* clothed in white robes; and they had crowns of gold on their heads. And **from the throne** proceeded lightning, thunder, and voices. Seven lamps of fire were burning **before the throne**, which are the seven Spirits of God. Before the throne there was a sea of glass, like crystal. And **in the midst of the throne,** and around the throne, were four living creatures full of eyes in front and in back."

What Jesus, through John, is describing here is not *all* of Heaven. Heaven, as a whole, is probably bigger than our entire universe! Once we see the New Heaven and New Earth described at the end of this book, you may conclude (*rightly*) that this earth will one day become part of Heaven itself. Jesus' Revelation says that the "Heavenly City" is going to **come down to this earth, the New Jerusalem** (*1,400 miles cubed, we'll get to that*).

- What Jesus has chosen to show us here is not a snapshot inside of the New Jerusalem (*not yet!*) where our "mansion" is. What we are seeing in this brief glimpse "through the doorway into the Throne Room" is intended to give us purpose and motivation! Read the rest of Chapter 4 unfolding below. If your tendency has been to jump over it to get to Chapter 6, let this truth wash over your soul!

> **Revelation 4:9–11: "Whenever the living beings give glory and honor and thanks to the one sitting on the throne (the one who lives**

forever and ever), the twenty-four elders fall down and worship the one sitting on the throne (the one who lives forever and ever) and they lay their crowns before the throne and say, 'You are worthy, O Lord our God, to receive glory and honor and power. For you created all things, and they exist because you created what you pleased.'"

And then I think we need here, to insert Chapter 5 into our minds *(We'll discuss it in the next chapter)*. Read it through slowly, it's hugely important to what is coming next!

Revelation 5:1–14: "Then I saw a scroll in the right hand of the one who was sitting on the throne. And I saw a strong angel, who shouted with a loud voice: 'Who is worthy to break the seals on this scroll and open it?' Then I began to weep bitterly because no one was found worthy to open the scroll and read it. But one of the twenty-four elders said to me, 'Stop weeping! Look, the Lion of the tribe of Judah, the heir to David's throne, has won the victory. He is worthy to open the scroll and its seven seals.'

Then I saw a Lamb that looked as if it had been *slain*, but it was now standing between the throne and the four living beings and among the twenty-four elders. He stepped forward and took the scroll from the right hand of the one sitting on the throne. And when he took the scroll, the four living beings and the twenty-four elders fell down before the Lamb. And they sang a new song with these words: 'You are worthy to take the scroll and break its seals and open it. For you were *slain* and your blood has ransomed people for God from every tribe and language and people and nation. And you have caused them to become a Kingdom of priests for our God. And they [us] will reign on the earth.'

"Then I looked again, and I heard the voices of thousands and millions of angels around the throne and of the living beings and the elders. And they sang in a mighty chorus: 'Worthy is the Lamb who

was *slain*—to receive power and riches and wisdom and strength and honor and glory and blessing.' And then I heard every creature in heaven and on earth and under the earth and in the sea. They sang: 'Blessing and honor and glory and power belong to the one sitting on the throne and to the Lamb forever and ever.' And the four living beings said, 'Amen!' And the twenty-four elders fell down and worshiped the Lamb."

Over the years I have often read from Chapter 5 to resoundingly punctuate a worship song or a sermon—"Worthy is the Lamb who was *slain*—to receive power and riches and wisdom and strength and honor and glory and blessing—."

- The point that I/we must not miss is that these are real events happening in real time. There is powerful End Time theology here, and we will refer back to it as the "unveiling" unfolds.

- But, **Chapter 5 is absolutely explosive** in what it unveils about what is coming!

How much do I know?

1) True or False: The Early Church knew little about heaven from the Old Testament. They knew Job had said he would "see God" after dying but they had almost no information on where God was or what Heaven would be like.

2) True or False: To the man or woman in the early Church, whose every day was filled with persecution, loss of property, even the loss of life for them and their family, the picture of a waiting heaven must have been like a drink of ice water to a man in the desert.

3) True or False: Paul's advice that "our present troubles are small and won't last very long. Yet they produce for us a glory that vastly outweighs them and will last forever" are as meaningful for us as they were to the people they were written to. So we should also "fix our gaze on things that cannot be seen. For the things we see now will soon be gone, but the things we cannot see will last forever" *(2 Corinthians 4:16–18)*.

You can check your answers beginning on page 243.

Number of correct answers on this page:

True or False: The picture into the Throne Room of God with angels, and the 24 elders, and millions of redeemed people praising and worshiping God is not some symbolic picture, but those events are actually happening right now and have been since the beginning of human time. People that we know, our redeemed relatives could be praising God in that very Throne Room right now as we are reading this chapter.

True or False: Ezekiel 36–39 is a prophetic "tetrad" (a group of four things you cannot split up). The first two chapters (36–37) are about Israel returning to their country. That has already happened! The last two chapters (38–39) are about a coming battle against Israel. There has been no point since Israel's return in 1948 when the details of those last two chapters have been fulfilled. Therefore, that famous battle must still be coming, perhaps the next thing on the prophetic calendar.

Some massive chaotic event ushers in the End Times and convinces the whole world to accept one leader who can bring them out of the mess. Do you think it might be this yet-to-come Ezekiel 38–39 battle?

4

Finding One Worthy to Break the Seals

By the time Ethan and his fellow Believers read through The Unveiling of Jesus Chapters 4 and 5—they knew they had reached a high point in all of Scripture. They were thirsting for information about Jesus' Second Advent, but there wasn't a chance they were going to rush past "the appetizer" to get to "the meat" of the new letter. Unfortunately, many people today—anxious to move ahead to the unfolding of the End Times in Chapters 6–18—hardly even stop to notice that what we find in **Chapter 5 is the pinnacle of world history. That is no over-statement!**

- God put a picture of Heaven *(4)* in this book purposely to encourage the Early Churches whose members were going through "hell on Earth," and for all of us who would follow them with our own soul-smashing life challenges. But for us today to really understand the huge scale of what is happening in these pages, we have to slow down and unpack one of the "biggest" events in all of history.

- Creation was huge; the fall of man was massive; the incarnation of Jesus in human form was central and explosive; the crucifixion single-handedly changed all of human history; the resurrection of Jesus Christ from the dead made possible the final defeat of sin, satan, death, and

43

hell—and provides complete redemption and eternal life for all who believe!

Revelation 5—A Spiritual Mountaintop!

And then there is Revelation 5! If you are wondering if I am seriously putting the events of Revelation 5 in the "significant event" line up with the Creation, the Fall, the Incarnation, the Crucifixion, and the Resurrection, I can assure you that I am!

- What could be so important in this often-overlooked chapter that qualifies it as such a spiritual mountaintop? Let's read again what John saw when he peeked through the door:

> **Revelation 4:8–11: "Day after day and night after night they keep on saying, 'Holy, holy, holy [Kadosh, Kadosh, Kadosh]** (*to the Hebrews repeating a word twice added emphasis—three times was unsurpassable—God is infinite in holiness*) **is the Lord God, the Almighty—the One who always was, who IS, and who IS still to come.' Whenever the living beings give glory and honor and thanks to the one sitting on the throne (the one who lives forever and ever), the twenty-four elders fall down and worship the one sitting on the throne (the one who lives forever and ever). And they lay their crowns before the throne and say, 'You are worthy, O Lord our God, to receive glory and honor and power. For you created all things, and they exist because you created what [who] you pleased.'"**

- God is not "on His throne" to cater to the whims of humans. It is very much the other way around! *We were created for His pleasure. We were created to glorify God! And one day we will be on our faces in that very Throne Room of Heaven shouting from the bottom of our glorified lungs, "You are worthy, O Lord our God, to receive glory and honor and power."*

That is what is happening *right now* in the Throne Room of Heaven! I, personally, believe the 24 elders probably represent all the redeemed Saints from the Old and New Covenants who have already died and are in the presence of their Creator shouting, "*Kadosh, Kadosh, Kadosh,* Holy, Holy, Holy." *(Our redeemed departed loved ones—a mother, a brother, a child—are perhaps there right now, worshiping the Lord God Almighty.)*

- Imagine the 31,103 verses in the Bible as the pieces of a puzzle God has been working on for 6,000+ years. The whole Bible is one box top snapshot. *Revelation 5 is that last little section where the picture begins to make perfect sense! The few remaining pieces start to click together.*
- ***Here in Revelation 5 it is as though everything is poised in history for the big rush to the finish.*** *The original persecuted Church, when they first read John's letter probably cinched up their robes, canceled their life insurance policies, and got their families ready for the antichrist arrival and Jesus' imminent (just about to happen) return.*

But that was more than 1900 years ago! If everything was "poised" in John's day what "un-poised" the big rush to the finish? Actually, as much as Elder Ethan longed for the "end of times" to arrive—the Church had already sorted and categorized prophesies from Jesus' own mouth that proved it wasn't yet time!

- Jesus was the one who said that Jerusalem would be destroyed. It was! Jesus prophesied that the Jews would be scattered to the ends of the earth. They were! Jesus even said that before the end could come *(Revelation 5–19)* the scattered Jews would have to come back to their Promised Land.

> **Luke 21:24: "They will be killed by the sword or sent away as captives to all the nations of the world. And Jerusalem will be trampled down by the Gentiles <u>until the period of the Gentiles comes to an end</u>."**

This wasn't new news to Elder Ethan *(and it shouldn't be to us).* This verse was right smack in the middle of Dr. Luke's account of Jesus' famous last sermon.

Add that to the all-important Ezekiel prophecy of the "dry bones" coming together *(36–37)*, and finally the New Church also poured over this prophecy from Jeremiah:

Jeremiah 31:8–12: "For I will bring them from the north and from the distant corners of the earth. I will not forget the blind and lame, the expectant mothers and women in labor. A great company will return! Tears of joy will stream down their faces, and I will lead them home with great care. Listen to this message from the Lord, you nations of the world; proclaim it in distant coastlands: The Lord, who scattered his people, will gather them and watch over them as a shepherd does his flock. For the Lord has redeemed Israel from those too strong for them. They will come home and sing songs of joy on the heights of Jerusalem. They will be radiant because of the Lord's good gifts."

"The Jews 'came home' after their exile in Persia," Ethan pondered, "but that sure wasn't 'from the distant corners of the earth'! So, when is Jeremiah's ancient prophecy supposed to be fulfilled? According to Jesus' own words it would have to be—after the period of the Gentiles comes to an end!"

Here is the hinge of history on which Revelation 5 rests: The last major element in Bible history that had to be fulfilled, before the story could move on, was the return of the Jewish people to their "Promised Land." This is the prophecy of the "dry bones" of Ezekiel 37, and the "homecoming" in Jeremiah 31. This was like the "sky part" of the puzzle to the Early Church at the end of the First Century.

- Though they studied more deeply than we tend to—they remained clueless about how all the Old Testament prophesies could possibly fit together into a complete picture encompassing everything predicted by Jesus, and John, and Peter, and Paul. It turns out—we now know they couldn't possibly have worked out all the details—"because some of the elusive 'sky pieces' weren't even in the box!"

- *And those missing "sky pieces" seemed to remain missing for the next 1900 years.* Then something dramatically changed—**the clock started ticking again**. *(What?—How?)*

Strange and evil events began to unfold: Hitler's Nazis annihilated six million Jews in the early-to-mid 1940's murdering them in gas chambers hundreds at a time. It was without doubt a plot of satan to try to stop God's prophetic plan. *(One among several!)*

- At the end of the Holocaust—with ½ of the world's Jewish population GONE!—A lot of heartbroken 20th Century Christians were also looking at their Bibles in complete frustration, wondering how in the world God would ever be able to fulfill Jesus' prophetic words, and return Israel to her homeland so the rest of prophecy could be fulfilled.

Had God lost control? Was satan winning?

- Stunningly, just three short years later—after Adolf Hitler swallowed a cyanide capsule and went to meet the Maker he had so defied—a half-million Jews in Israel declared themselves a new and independent nation while the world was left gasping in amazement trying to make sense of what had just happened. *(Jews began to swarm home from the distant corners of the earth!)*

That was 70 years ago, and in the decades since Jews have been pouring back into Israel. They have come from a hundred countries to their new homeland and have fought off much larger armies determined to wipe them out. **And the prophesy clock started again** *(this time)* loudly ticking toward Revelation 5!

- *But watch this:* Ezekiel had prophesied that Israel *would* return home (Read Ezekiel 36, 37). He then prophesied that *a war would erupt* (Read

Ezekiel 38, 39). In this war, Magog (*which historically was probably the southern part of the former USSR*) will come against Israel—joined by Persia (*undoubtedly modern Iran*), Gomer (*modern Turkey*), and several others surrounding countries, to try once again to wipe Israel off the face of the earth. Ezekiel prophesies that God will step in and rain judgment from Heaven to wipe out all the armies deployed against Israel. (*These are not my words—they're God's!*)

Ezekiel 38:3, 5–9: "Gog, I am your enemy! I will turn you around and put hooks in your jaws to lead you out with your whole army—your horses and charioteers in full armor and a great horde armed with shields and swords. Persia, Ethiopia, and Libya will join you, too, with all their weapons. Gomer and all its armies will also join you, along with the armies of Beth-togarmah from the distant north, and many others. Get ready; be prepared! Keep all the armies around you mobilized, and take command of them. A long time from now you will be called into action. In the distant future you will swoop down on the land of Israel, which will be enjoying peace after recovering from war and after its people have returned from many lands to the mountains of Israel. You and all your allies—a vast and awesome army—will roll down on them like a storm and cover the land like a cloud."

- *If anyone gets incensed that I am speaking against another country, race, or religion—please understand: I am simply trying to faithfully report what the Bible prophetically says is someday going to happen.*

Notice: The battle of Ezekiel 38–39 **comes after** "its people have **returned from many lands** (*Ezekiel 36, 37*) to the mountains of Israel!" (*Israel has now returned to its land—but the Ezekiel 38–39 battle hasn't yet happened!—What does that mean?*)

- I, personally, believe that this coming battle—whether it is two years away or 100 years away—will usher the world into the End Times! Perhaps it is no coincidence that all the players in the Ezekiel 38–39 battle against Israel seem at this very time to becoming a "band of best buds."

- Then again, perhaps it is a coincidence, and their new alliances will crash and burn, and they will become enemies again for the next 50 or 100 years.

One thing is certain: At some point in history the pieces will come together and they will not unravel. Whenever that is, **it is at that exact moment in time—that Revelation 5:1 happens**!

- Revelation 4's Throne Room has been going on since before there was a human race. Your departed grandma, spouse, or child is right now enjoying Revelation 4!
- But Revelation 5 has yet to happen. **All of human history since the fall of mankind in the Garden of Eden has been hurtling towards this moment—a moment so important that it is literally the hinge on which all of history hangs!**

> **Revelation 5:1: "Then I saw a scroll in the right hand of the One who was sitting on the throne. There was writing on the inside and the outside of the scroll, and it was sealed with seven seals."**

In ancient times important documents were rolled up, bound with string, sealed with a blob of wax, and inscribed with a special symbol from the signet ring of the important person who authored the document. The penalty for breaking that official seal was death!

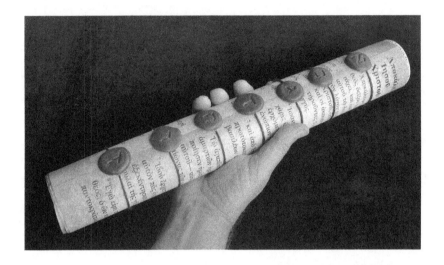

A double seal was used for very important documents, but the wills of Kings and Emperors were **sealed with seven seals**. From God's perspective seven is an often used number *(particularly in Revelation where it shows up more than 50 times)* indicating perfection and completion.

- Ethan and the Early Church caught on instantly that a document "sealed with seven seals" and held in the "right" hand of EL SHADDAI, the Almighty Creator of the universe, would be the hinge on which history turns!

Revelation 5:1–2: "Then I saw a scroll in the right hand of the one who was sitting on the throne. There was writing on the inside and the outside of the scroll, and it was sealed with seven seals. And I saw a strong angel, who shouted with a loud voice: 'Who is worthy to break the seals on this scroll and open it?'"

- Something immensely important is getting ready to happen! And for all we know, right now, the Heavenly Father may be reaching for the scroll with His right hand at this very moment and the strong angel might be expanding his lungs "to shout with a loud voice"!

So, what's in this scroll
that is so incredibly important?

Those well-studied in the book of Revelation might say: "The opening of the first four seals are the 'four horsemen of the apocalypse,' and the fifth seal is the beginning of the Great Tribulation, and the sixth seal is the world coming unglued as the Second Coming of Jesus draws near." All of that is true! But those are actually sub-points to the main point, which is the significance of the scroll in the right hand of the Creator of the universe. For, in the Father's hand, *is the most important document ever in all the universe!"*

- It could only have been written and sealed by the One who had the "power of being" over every molecule in the universe. It is a document that says, *"I am in complete charge, the fullness of time has come, and I intend to set things in order! When I am finished, those who have embraced my redemption will no longer be plagued by sin, or satan, or death, or hell."*
- For thousands of years sin has run rampant through the earth. Satan and his evil angels have done all they could to disrupt the plan of God. Evil has often seemingly won. Sin has saturated every part of human history. Death has taken every human life, but two *(Enoch and Elijah).*

Finally, in Revelation 5–6 God says, "enough is enough," and drops the hatchet to destroy sin's reign and satan's rebellion!

- This is what ripped the veil off the minds of Ethan and Friends. **They now knew how it was all going to end** and they were absolutely ALL IN! (We saw this *before in the introduction—but this is now the WHY!*)
- **Satan wasn't going to win his battle against God**! Jesus was going to victoriously defeat satan—he would destroy the chokehold of death, and even the curse of sin itself *(Revelation 22:3)* would be purged off this planet! **Jesus would set up an eternal reign, and all the redeemed Believers would be reigning with him.**

The First Century Church wasn't pouring over their new letter fascinated by the "third bowl" judgment, or the sound of the fifth trumpet. They really didn't give-a-hoot about the role of the antichrist or the false prophet. Both of them were going to get crushed by the "right hand" of Almighty God!

- It's true that Jesus does detail in the Unveiling that: The (1) opening of the seven seals does lead to (2) the blowing of the seven trumpets, and the blowing of the final trumpet leads to (3) the pouring out of the seven bowls of God's wrath on what is left of this sin-wracked planet.

- **I do not believe, for a moment, that we Believers will be on this planet when the "bowl judgments of God's wrath" are poured out—** *(we'll look at that),* but whatever does comes in those last few gut-stirring months of humanity's timeline, it ends with the Second Coming of Jesus Christ to this earth!

- Jesus, with a word from His mouth, will demolish the power of sin and satan forever and will set up His reign here on Earth where we Believers will be "reigning with Him."

But we're jumping way, way ahead, we need to slow down. We need to unpack this amazing Chapter 5:

> **Revelation 5:2–3: "And I saw a strong angel, who shouted with a loud voice: 'Who is worthy to break the seals on this scroll and open it?'** *But no one in heaven or on earth or under the earth was able to open the scroll and read it."*

A search takes place across the entire universe for anyone who could qualify to open the scroll.

This universe-wide ceremony is a really big deal!

> **Revelation 5:4: "Then I began to weep bitterly because no one was found worthy to open the scroll and read it."**

John was starting to grasp the huge significance of what he was witnessing. "Whatever is in that scroll, **it is God's finalizing all that has gone before**

including enforcing all of what Jesus provided by His death on the cross and His victorious resurrection!"

If only John had actually been *in* the Throne Room he might have, at this point, had his hand up in the air saying: "Oh, oh, oh, I know! I know someone who is worthy! 1) I know the person had to be a human in order to defeat the power of sin over all humanity, and 2) I get the fact that all humanity is locked under the curse of the fall and overwhelmed by the power of sin and satan, but 3) I know a human who was also divine. 4) He faced off with satan as incarnate God-man, and He won the battle. 5) He took all of humanity's sins to a cross and died *their* death to pay *their* sin penalty, and 6) then he defeated death itself by rising from the dead, dealing a fatal blow to satan's power to drop humanity into a godless Hell."

- John must have grasped the fact that what **he was watching was the culmination of everything that history had been moving toward since the fall of Adam and Eve**. He knew instinctively that this scroll had to get opened to finish God's great plan, and that it could only be opened by the Worthiest of the Worthy. If the punishment for breaking the seals on a human scroll was death, imagine the total destruction that would come to an unworthy person who opened the scroll written and seven-times sealed by the Creator of the universe!

> **Revelation 5:5–8: "But one of the twenty-four elders said to me, 'Stop weeping! Look, the Lion of the tribe of Judah, the heir to David's throne, has won the victory. He is worthy to open the scroll and its seven seals.'** *[Jesus, of course, had been presented as a Lion and an heir to King David's throne. Those are fulfillments of prophecy.]* **Then I saw a Lamb that looked as if it had been *slain*, but it was now standing between the throne and the four living beings and among the twenty-four elders. He had seven horns** *[all powerful]* **and seven eyes** *[omniscient, all-wise],* **which represent the sevenfold** *[complete]* **Spirit of God that is sent out into every part of the earth. He stepped forward and took the scroll from the right hand of the one sitting on the throne. And when he took the scroll, the four living beings**

> and the twenty-four elders fell down before the Lamb. Each one had
> a harp, and they held gold bowls filled with incense, which are the
> prayers of God's people."

Clearly this is a huge event in the history of Heaven, one so significant it drops the *four living beings* and the *24 elders* onto their faces. *(Interestingly—they pull out the stored-up prayers of God's people and hold them before the Father and the Lamb.)* This is all such a big deal that it stimulates the singing of a "brand new song" in Heaven.

> **Revelation 5:9–10: "And they sang a new song with these words:
> 'You are worthy to take the scroll and break its seals and open it.
> For you were *slain* and your blood *has ransomed people for God
> from every tribe and language and people and nation. And you have
> caused them to become a Kingdom of priests for our God. And they
> will reign on the earth.'"**

Stay focused, keep trusting—God is on His Throne!

This is one of the reasons why we should not get overly disturbed by the events that begin with the opening of the seven seals in the book of Revelation.

- It will certainly unleash very disruptive events on earth, but the **same event to those in Heaven is so positive that it unleashes a whole new wave of worship and praise!** *Why?*
- The focus of the praise is that the **handoff and opening of the seven seals "clinches the ransoming of people for God from every tribe and language and people and nation!"**
- It now finally opens the path for those "ransomed people" to become "a Kingdom of Priests for our God. And they will reign on the earth." *(What can that possibly mean?)*

And this is not, by any means, the end of what this huge event in Heaven produces. Notice, this is not a single random spurt of heavenly praise. *It is in direct response to the Lamb of God's opening up the scroll with seven seals* which then, finally, sets off the events of Revelation 6–22.

> **Revelation 5:11–14: "Then I looked again, and I heard the voices of thousands and millions of angels around the throne and of the living beings and the elders. And they sang in a mighty chorus: 'Worthy is the Lamb who was slaughtered—to receive power and riches and wisdom and strength and honor and glory and blessing.' And then I heard every creature in heaven and on earth and under the earth and in the sea. They sang: 'Blessing and honor and glory and power belong to the one sitting on the throne and to the Lamb forever and ever.' And the four living beings said, 'Amen!' And the twenty-four elders fell down and worshiped the Lamb."**

So, the "Heir to David's eternal throne," takes the seven-sealed scroll and, surrounded by the singing voices of worship of Heaven, ***launches the final war on satan and sin and hell and death!***

Each seal describes the next judgments prescribed by God's hatred of sin, and His holy wrath at the all-out "blackness" of the willfully unredeemed human heart.

Jesus' words through John to the churches then, and now, promise God's complete and sovereign control over every event of human history.

No matter how powerful evil may seem, no matter how dark the times may become—Jesus Christ is going to return to right all wrongs and set up His everlasting rule!

How much do I know?

1) Jesus prophesied in Luke 21 that the Jews would be killed or sent away as captives to all the nations of the world. That seems to have been fulfilled in 70 AD. He also prophesied that the Gentiles would trample Jerusalem until the time of the Gentiles comes to an end. Did that "time" come to an end on May 14, 1948, when Israel returned and declared herself a nation?

2) The Ezekiel 36–37 return of the Jews, "from the corners of the earth," seems to have been measurably happening over the last seven decades. Notice the Ezekiel 38–39 battle is prophesied to happen AFTER that event. Has there been any time in history when a massive army from the stated countries have surrounded Jerusalem and been driven back by fire from heaven to their mother countries? _____ Has there been any such event witnessed by "all the people of the world" after which all nations will know that God is God—or is that event yet to come?

3) If the final events that the opening of the seven-sealed scroll set in motion are not directed at us Believers, who are they directed at?

You can check your answers beginning on page 243.

Number of correct answers on this page:

The period of time between popping off the first seal on the scroll and Jesus' victorious Second Coming is often referred to as Daniel's 70th Week. Do we have any idea how long that period of time will be?

The Greek phrase "kai eidon" (then I saw, next I saw) shows up twenty-four consecutive times between Revelation 6:1 and Revelation 20:11. What should that tell us about the flow of prophesies in this book?

Who is the one who removes the seven seals off the scroll?

Do you already know what the contents in the Scroll with Seven Seals is going to be?

5

The Lamb is Worthy to Open the Scroll!

The book of Revelation is about Jesus Christ! The entire New Testament is about Jesus! The whole Bible was written to point us to Jesus! If we picture the Bible as an ever-narrowing funnel of inspired truth through which 6,000+ years of human history flows—from the wide mouth, to the narrow stem, to the tiny tip, Revelation 5 is where the stem begins and Revelation 19–22 is the tip, the end-point, when the final flow of human history comes to an end!

The main theme of the New Testament—is often stated to be "salvation by grace through faith" in Jesus' atoning sin payment on our behalf. That's true! That truth, along with "Jesus' victorious resurrection," were the two truths most preached about for the first 300 years of the Church's history. I've come to understand in writing this book that the closest "runner-up" topic in the whole New Testament that is most often discussed in inspired Scripture is: **"The Second Coming of Jesus."**

I personally searched through the entire New Testament, verse by verse, to make sure I get these figures right. I pulled out every reference, categorized them, and was stunned with the results. Not only are there hundreds of verses relating to End Times in both the Old and the New Testaments. There are:

- 260 direct references to Jesus' Second Coming in 7,957 New Testament verses—in 21 of the 27 NT books.

- One out of every 30.6 verses in the NT is directly teaching us about Jesus' Second Coming!
- 342 verses are connected with them in context—one out of every 23.3 verses the NT teaches Jesus' Second Coming!

Oddly, when I did an internet search, I found sites like:
- "4 key verses on the Second Coming."
- "21 verses about Jesus' Second Coming."

I found myself screaming at the screen: "What about all the rest of the verses?" Fortunately, Elder Ethan and Friends had bad internet reception—so they dug and dug through ever increasing pages of inspired Scripture until they had excavated every single reference!

- *I challenge us all, to do Ethan's kind of research on this critical subject. If you don't like doing the digging—write me! I'll send the verses to you, listed and categorized! You'll be stunned at just how much God gave us on the subject of End Times—and how much one can learn from a single compressive read-through.*

The Bible does, without doubt, teach, over and over, that Jesus is going to return to this earth, and at some point, we Believers are going to join Him "in Heaven" for all eternity. For many Christians, not only can we not put those two facts together, but the reality itself is foggy. It always seems like it's an event that is somewhere "out there," not some-thing that has any relevance to this week, this year, or even perhaps our lifetime.

- That was absolutely not true, in the post-resurrection new Church. And it wasn't just our First Century friends that were consumed with the subject of Jesus' Second Advent. Believers throughout the 2nd and 3rd Centuries were just as intensely focused. As wave after wave of persecution ripped through the Empire, the Jesus Followers lived with one consuming thought—Jesus was coming again to "take them to the place He had prepared for them." The big difference in Centuries 2–3 is that they were fortified with the words of the "Unveiling" detailing, for them, exactly how it was all going to end. No wonder they quickly spread the Good News to the very ends of the civilized world!

Revelation is the missing piece of the puzzle!

The Unveiling was designed to cap off all of inspired Scripture! It is supposed to be the missing key that *makes all of human history make sense.* As the first five words of Revelation state, the Unmasking is "intended to lock our attention directly on Jesus"!

Revelation 1:1: "The revelation from Jesus Christ." Note this: No longer is He in the role of our Suffering Savior who came to Earth to pay humanity's sin penalty. That's past—over—done—2,000 years ago! That part of history is finished—Jesus said so on the cross! Now, in this "Revelation" we are watching Him complete the picture of the whole redemption plan. **"Our Redemption"** is not complete until Jesus rescues us from the "sin curse" on this earth, breaks the vice-grip of satan's hold over humanity, defeats satan once and for all, smashes through the rebellion of those who have willingly rejected Him, and elevates those who have followed Him to a place of "rulership" in the universe!

- Many may mock and say that all sounds like a fantasy. The book of Revelation warns us that a large chunk of humanity will still believe that all this **theology *(theos-logos; God logic/reason)*** is a fairy tale—right to the bitter end.

- Humans did not write this final chapter of human history—Jesus did! Whether we agree with it or not makes not one whit of difference! "The King of all Kings and the Lord of all Lords" has already decided these matters!

- The "Revelation of Jesus" is not being offered as one alternative for the end of human history. We do not get to vote on how the final chapter ends. That was already decided by the very One who created all that is—before the first humans sucked the breath of God into their lungs.

As we studied in Revelation 1, *(like John, and James, and Peter, and Ethan before us)* we get a completely new picture of our Messiah in the first chapter of the last book.

> **Revelation 1:13–16: "standing among them [the seven lampstands] was one who looked like Jesus, the Son of Man, wearing a long robe circled with a golden band across His chest. His hair was white as snow, and His eyes penetrated like flames of fire. His feet gleamed like burnished bronze, and His voice thundered like waves crashing. He held seven stars in His right hand and a sharp, double-bladed sword in His mouth, and His face shone like the power of the sun in unclouded brilliance."**

- So, imagine this: Now Israel has returned to their country. Now the End Times clock is again ticking loudly in our ears.
- Now we can almost weekly hear some of the "end time battle" players threatening Israel's destruction.
- Can't you just almost envision the now "glorified" Jesus, his "eyes like flames of fire," his "voice like crashing waves," moving slowly toward the Throne room of Heaven where the Heavenly Father is holding the seven-sealed scroll? **Revelation 5:1: "Then I saw a scroll in the right hand of the One who was sitting on the throne."**

The "Ancient of Days" holds the closing chapter of time as we know it in His right hand. Once the seals are opened, ***the final stopwatch is set for the Second Coming of Jesus!*** When the Father hands off the scroll to the ONE who will open it, when the first seal pops off the scroll, what follows is not some vague or unknown series of events. Everything is clearly recorded in Jesus' Revelation.

- Not only is this not an unknown set of events but it is not an unknown period of time. **From the time the first seal pops loose—to the return of Jesus Christ—is seven years!** This is the long expected "70th week" in Daniel's prophesy.

- When the remaining one-third of the Bible prophesies yet to be fulfilled (2,040) begin to unfold, they will unfold with a rush. *And we learn that the final run to the finish line starts with the opening of the first seal!*

The universe-wide search for One who is worthy to open this most important of all scrolls ends with the Lion of the Tribe of Judah, the One who was slain for the sins of all mankind, for He is found to be the only One "worthy" to become the Judge of the earth! That is what we are supposed to see here. **The same One who gave His human life to bear all our sins in His own body, and then rose to victoriously smash through the "death curse" of sin—is the same One who will soon crush satan and cleanse this whole world from the effects of sin and its curse!**

When the scroll is handed to Jesus, the living beings and the 24 elders fall down in worship. Then millions of angels also worship singing a "new song" about people from every tribe and tongue and nation getting ready to reign with Jesus. And then, finally, every creature in the whole universe shouts out in praise to God.

- **Jesus takes the scroll and reaches for the first seal!** *(Are we grabbing this reality?)*
- The second Jesus touches the first seal, the egg-timer starts to tick, and we are fairly sure we know what will be happening 12 months later!
- We know almost exactly what will be happening 42 months later!
- And we absolutely know what will be going on 84 months later— because it is all right here in the Bible.

Revelation 6:1–2: "As I watched, the Lamb broke the first of the seven seals on the scroll. Then I heard one of the four living beings say with a voice like thunder, 'Come!' I looked up and saw a white horse standing there. Its rider carried a bow, and a crown was placed on His head. He rode out to win many battles and gain the victory."

This is the point in the story when most people begin to shrug, and maybe even shudder, thinking *it just sounds too strange.* I am convinced that the Believers in the Early Church did not find this nearly as weird as we do. They tended to be more symbolic in everyday life than we are. They told parables to get a point across. They used metaphors to refer to one thing, as an example of another, rather than going straight to the point. That is the difference between the ancient eastern mindset and my modern western mindset. It will help if we remember that this letter was not designed to be weird, but instead to present us with a step-by-step unfolding of what is coming in our direction like a freight train.

"Kai Eidon"—Then I saw, or next I saw!

- In this step-by-step account, John uses the phrase, "then I saw" over and over. This is a translation of the Greek phrase **"kai eidon" ("next I saw")**. Jesus inspires John to use this phrase all the way through the book of Revelation, *showing us that **this is a chronological progression!***
- **Some variation of *"Kai Eidon"* shows up 24 successive times:** 6:1, 2, 5, 8, 12; 7:2; 8:2, 13; 9:1; 10:1; 13:1, 11; 14:1, 6, 14; 15:1; 16:13; 17:3; 19:11, 17, 19; 20:1, 4, 11.

The unfolding of End Time events is not as complicated as we often make it out to be! We must consistently focus on the "kai eidon" chronological storyline.

- After the a) sixth seal is opened, the b) seventh seal becomes the blowing of the seven trumpets, and the c) seventh trumpet becomes the pouring out of the seven bowls. After bowl seven is poured out, Jesus returns! It really was designed by Jesus to be just that clear-cut! [IMO]
- *In My Opinion [IMO], I will use this throughout the rest of the book. Many godly, brilliant people have arrived at different conclusions. (But—please read on!)*

So, let's take a look at the seals Jesus opens, and then the trumpet judgments and the bowl judgments—to see if we can pinpoint where we Believers will be when all this unfolds.

"The Four Horsemen of the Apocalypse"

Seals 1, 2, 3, and 4 are what we commonly call:
The Four Horsemen of the Apocalypse.

Though we might want to focus on what color the horse is or who is riding it, the truth **is there is only one rider who matters** because the last three just point to events that will eventually be taking place in the shadow of the first horseman. The first horse and its rider are notably important:

Revelation 6:2: "I looked up and saw a white horse standing there. Its rider carried a bow, and a crown was placed on his head. He rode out to win many battles and gain the victory."

This is the first significant event that starts *(after the Ezekiel 38–39 battle)* as the seven-year clock begins to tick, and this player is there for all seven years. Clearly this person is a world leader, a conqueror. It is significant that he has a bow, but he carries no arrows. He does not conquer the world militarily—yet gains enormous power on earth. He gets a "crown" and amasses influence. *Who is this rider on the white horse?*

- It's not Jesus! Jesus rides in on a "white horse" at the end of the seven years. Could this be *satan's counterfeit messiah, the anti-Jesus, the antichrist? Yes!! Yes, it is!*

- Where does he come from? How could he gain so much world power? *(Other Scripture passages provide more information about him. We'll look at them.)* For now, it is enough to point out that a false "messiah" will rise up during chaotic times, convince a seemingly broken world that he can save their planet, and make a covenant of peace with all of them. In fact, there <u>will</u> be a period of pseudo-peace across the world for a while *(perhaps 24 months into the final seven-year period).* Many will hail this man as a God-like leader and celebrate that the fractured world has decided to COEXIST.

We even know, from Scripture, that this "anti-Jesus'" reign lasts for three-and-one-half of the seven years—at which point he turns into a raging devil exposing who he truly was all along. *(By the end of the seven years, all the armies in the world are gathered outside of Jerusalem where the antichrist has set up his rule.)*

- We should wonder how in the world one person could come to such power on this fractured planet. The Early Church had an easier time with this than we do. They were used to "one world rulers." We fight that now with every fiber of our beings. 21st Century humans are all so different and have such diverse values and allegiances that it is hard to imagine a time in which the Americans, and the Chinese, and the Europeans, and the Russians—and Muslims, and Hindus, and Buddhists, and Jews—all would rally behind one person and say, "We are willing to follow you."
- **Might the catalyst be the battle prophesied in Ezekiel 38 and 39** which is [IMO] the next prophetic event on the calendar? This is a very important approaching event! It is so critical to lock it into our minds because the beginning of "Daniel's 70th Week" rests on this event.

"Daniel's 70th Week"

I promise that we will unfold those defining Scriptures when we get to Chapter 7. But for now—let's continue to unpack more of this "battle" passage we started back in Chapter 3, and try to move our storyline—one step forward at a time:

Ezekiel 39:1–4, 6–8: "Son of man, prophesy against Gog. I will turn you around and drive you toward the mountains of Israel, bringing you from the distant north. I will knock the bow from your left hand and the arrows from your right hand, and I will leave you helpless. You and your army and your allies will all die on the mountains. And I will rain down fire on Magog and on all your allies who live safely on the coasts. Then they will know that I am the Lord. In this way, I will make known My holy name among My people of Israel. And the nations, too, will know that I am the Lord, the Holy One of Israel. That day of judgment will come, says the Sovereign Lord. Everything will happen just as I have declared it."

We've already noticed that the referenced nations seem to be aligning—Russia, for instance, has reportedly helped Iran build nuclear reactors, and even now has military bases in Syria. Is it possible that this prophesied battle could happen in our lifetime? What if it were to happen in the next 10 years? What if Israel were to decide to try to wipe out all of Iran's nuclear reactors? And what if Russia, who seems to have no clear allegiance to Israel, then increasingly tightens its coalition with the other countries and resolves to teach Israel a lesson once and for all? They will not win—because according to Ezekiel 39, God will respond with a massive display of power raining down fire from Heaven clear back to the mother-countries, leaving quite a mess, and quite an impression, on the rest of the world *(Please read all of Ezekiel 38–39)*!

Two results here are very, very important! One is very positive, and one is quite negative! First, the Ezekiel 39 text itself gives us a critical clue about one of the positive spiritual side-effects of this great battle.

Ezekiel 39:7: "In this way, <u>I will make known My holy name among my people of Israel.</u> *<u>And the nations, too (non-Jews), will know that I am the LORD.</u>*"

That is an enormously important sentence in understanding the End Times—*I am absolutely sure that one result of the End Times beginning, will be a mighty, sweeping revival on this planet—a huge spiritual harvest!* This will affect the Jews and every other nation in the world.

- People all over the planet will watch the Divine conclusion of the Ezekiel 38–39 battle on their cell phones and other mobile devices, and **the nations will know that God is God!**

A mighty, sweeping revival on this earth—
a huge spiritual harvest!

At that point, who will God have standing there saying to the world, *"Let me lead you to this God you have suddenly discovered"?* Some Bible teachers would have us believe that none of this matters because God is going to lift all Christians off the earth in a glorious "Rapture" **before** the first traumatic End Time events take place. *(We'll look very closely at those Scriptures.)*

- Let me just share my heart: I do believe Scripture teaches a Rapture of Believers from this planet. **But do I really believe that God would want to take me out of here just before the greatest spiritual harvest in the history of the world?** *(Why? Is that logical, let alone theo-logical?)*
- Do I believe that God would shape me, and millions of other people, as disciple-making leaders for 20-40-60 years—and then not want us to be here when millions, perhaps billions, of people say, **"Well, what do you know? There is a God in Heaven! So, who is He, how do I get to know Him—who can teach me?"** *(Much more on this later!)*

The second repercussion of this Ezekiel 39 finale is worldwide economic turmoil because many of the OPEC nations will have been involved in this massive Middle East fiasco. What if, in the middle of all of this chaos, one superman rises up with the answer to save the planet, and the whole world gathers around his leadership, and so begins a period of relative peace for the next two years?

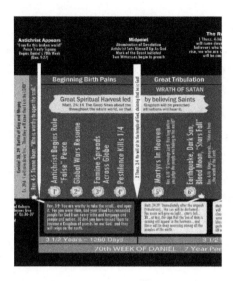

Once again: If the above were the result of the Ezekiel 38–39 battle—during that time—*the world will be a great mission field.* Gone will be all the arrogance that comes from having too much wealth and the shock will long remain of watching Almighty God answer with "fire from Heaven." What if the Bible teaches that Believers are still here? What if, instead of daily diving for the world's financial or political news, or staring mindlessly at useless sitcom reruns, our minds could be consumed with the spiritual harvest across the world and how you, that day, might be able to lead another dozen people into Jesus' Kingdom! *(Please pull the chart you downloaded at unmaskingrevelation.com—and refer to the gold "harvest banner" across the two left red sections.)*

Can you imagine what it would be like for you and your children to be *living in the most exciting spiritual time the world has ever known?* What if every day you were living with an intense spiritual focus that we experience only sporadically now?

- What if you had so prepared your children that they were able, in two or three years, to lead 200–300 people into right relationship with the One who was presently opening the seals to bring sin and satan to an end?

And what if all of that—is why the living beings, the 24 elders, the millions of angels in Heaven, and every creature on Earth gets so excited when Jesus begins to open the seals *(Revelation 5)?*

- I've heard so many people react with—"No, that can't be true—because that's not the way I want it to be." *(And that's not the way I heard my uncle's sister's Pastor preach it when I was a kid!)* I appeal to us all—God is the most logical being on the planet! Everything he does has eternal purpose. He's not focused on "gittin us outta here" so we don't have to suffer anything difficult. He's focused on "saving the whole world from their sins," just like Jesus said!

- Can you imagine a 21st Century Believer sitting down with Early Church Ethan and trying to convince him that God's ultimate passion was to keep his children from any and all suffering? Ethan would have choked on his goat cheese! The idea of one person trying to control the whole world—and when Christians won't bow the knee—persecuting and killing them—was as common to Ethan as the sun rising.

What I am trying to imagine is the team of Early Church Info-Nerds wrestling their attention away from their carefully compiled list of Scriptures on Jesus' Second Advent—and trying for the first time to comprehend the massive nature of what this new Unveiling was laying out for them. This was no longer just about waiting for Jesus to split the Eastern sky! This was about the all-out Cosmic **war of all time between good and evil!** This was about the crashing "end of time" on this earth and the beginning of "eternity."

It would have been easy for them to imagine the anti-Messiah rising to power in their lifetime, a mighty sweeping revival on earth, which already seemed to have begun and then Jesus returning. Can't you just hear their deep discussions as they tried to wrestle these new truths up against the yet unfulfilled—Ezekiel battle, fall of Jerusalem, and the scattering and return of the Jews to their homeland—all prophesies right from Jesus' mouth! The info-nerds pulled out a brand-new papyrus "post-it note" and begin to compile these jarring new details:

- During the first three-and-a-half years *(1,260 days to be exact)*, the time of peace will wear thin and wars will begin to break out all over the planet again. *(Seal/horsemen 2)* And then famine sets in across the world. *(Seal/horsemen 3)* And then "pestilence" takes out one-quarter of the world's population. *(Seal/horsemen 4) That's three more of the "horsemen."* We might say, "Well, that doesn't sound good." It's obviously not, but several Scriptures seem to suggest that God may "protect" His people while they continue the spiritual harvest!

- The *fifth seal* clearly takes us into the "second half" of Daniel's 70th week—the Great Tribulation. The *sixth seal* is "unusual signs" in the heavens that something momentous is about to happen. *(Do you see all this on the chart?)*

There is "sudden silence" in Heaven, then all hell breaks loose—literally!

- Then comes the very important *Chapter 7* in the Unmasking at the end of which there is a very sudden and odd ***"silence in heaven."*** When the silence ends, all hell breaks loose on the earth with the *seven trumpets* followed by the *seven bowl* judgments. Scripture repeatedly calls this "God's wrath" on sin and satan!

But let me stress this—*(and I'm completely sure Ethan and Co. would have reached the same conclusions)*—Believers are not going to be anywhere near this planet when the "trumpet" and "bowl" judgments are poured out on sin and satan! If this all seems too mysterious, hang in there—we'll unpack it all! We will return several times over to the "info-nerds" summary of information until we have, hopefully, peeled back the skin.

- What are the unusual signs in the heavens all about, and why would a place filled with praise to God for thousands of years suddenly go SILENT?

- We'll come to all of that, but the question already filling everybody's mind is: **"When in the world are we Christians going to get off this sin-drenched planet?"**

The seventh chapter of Jesus' Unveiling is often passed over, but is [IMO] one of the most important chapters in the book. Let's just do a quick first read and see if it doesn't sound to you like some huge event is taking place:

Revelation 7:1–4: "Then I saw four angels standing at the four corners of the earth, holding back the four winds so they did not blow on the earth or the sea, or even on any tree. And I saw another angel coming up from the east, carrying the seal of the living God. And he shouted to those four angels, who had been given power to harm land and sea, 'Wait! Don't harm the land or the sea or the trees until we have placed the seal of God on the foreheads of his servants.' And I heard how many were marked with the seal of God—144,000 were sealed from all the tribes of Israel." (Jews!)

7:9–10: "After this *[kai eidon—next on the timeline]* I saw a vast crowd, too great to count, from every nation and tribe and people and language, standing in front of the throne and before the Lamb. They were clothed in white robes and held palm branches in their hands. And they were shouting with a great roar, 'Salvation comes from our God who sits on the throne and from the Lamb!'"

What just happened there?

After the sealing of the 144,000 Jews on earth, a too-vast-to-count crowd shows up in heaven from all over the world. **Who are all these people?** They are all "wearing white robes" *(Jesus' often stated symbol for "redeemed Saints")*.

7:13–14: "Then one of the twenty-four elders asked me, 'Who are these who are clothed in white? Where did they come from?' And I said to him, 'Sir, you are the one who knows.' Then he said to me, 'These are the ones who died in [ἐρχόμενοι—came out of] the great tribulation. They have washed their robes in the blood of the Lamb and made them white.'"

Again, with the "washed in the blood of the Lamb." These are clearly Believers, lots and lots of them, arriving in heaven all at the same time. *Who are they?*

Who in the world is this vast—too great to count crowd from every nation who suddenly appear in the Throne Room?

Some of our modern versions *(including the NLT above)* have thrown us a curve ball by translating the word ἐρχόμενοι as **died in** (the Tribulation). The word ἐρχόμενοι actually means **came out of** (the Tribulation). *These are often said to be martyrs,* millions or billions of them, "a vast crowd, too great to count, from every nation and tribe and people and language," all of whom apparently arrive in heaven all at once before the antichrist has even begun his most intense persecutions. *(How could that be?)*

- I'm pausing here because Jesus' Revelation is designed to be perfectly logical. Note this: If the "rapture" happens BEFORE the Tribulation, and "the graves are opened," then all previous martyrs would by this time be in heaven! That would have to mean that a vast crowd of *newly redeemed martyrs "too great to count"*—would all have to have been saved, and killed, in the first three relatively peaceful years of the antichrist's reign *(which seems unlikely)*. On the other hand, if it is not martyrs— *who is this vast uncountable crowd who suddenly show up in heaven?*

  7:15–17: "That is why they stand in front of God's throne and serve him day and night in his Temple. And he who sits on the throne will give them shelter. They will never again be hungry or thirsty; they will never be scorched by the heat of the sun. For the Lamb on the throne will be their Shepherd. He will lead them to springs of life-giving water. And God will wipe every tear from their eyes."

- I am purposely "salting our oats," trying to make us thirsty. Could it be that this vast crowd showing up in heaven in white robes in Chapter 7 are—"Those who **came out of** the tribulation," those for whom "the Lamb will be their Shepherd and wipe every tear from their eyes?"

Could it be that Chapter 7 is, in fact, describing the "Rapture" of the Saints?

"But Chess, if that were true, we living Believers would have to *(gasp)* live through part of the last seven miserable years!" *Yes, yes we would!*

Sam's Observations:

- Believers in the Early Church would have thought us misguided for even imagining that serving the risen Messiah would not involve eventual persecution. After all, Jesus himself prophesied that reality would be true!

- Believers, now, who live in countries where they are suffering persecution and fully believe they might be called on to suffer even more before they get to Heaven, have an intensity in their walk with God. They have a carefulness about their lifestyle. *Why?*

- A commonly taught Western Christian view that God loves us so much that He is never going to let us suffer anything, but is always going to pour positive gifts on us has [IMO], at the very least, opened the door to overwhelming spiritual shallowness. **Imagine how the Apostle John would have reacted to such a teaching?**

- Many modern Christians apply the next logical step to their End Time viewpoint believing that as we approach End Times, God is going to take us all to Heaven before any possible uncomfortable negative events can occur. *Why? Why would he do that?*

- If a spiritual leader teaches people that there is nothing ahead but smooth sailing and creates in them a false sense of security—but it turns out he/she is wrong, imagine the consequences! If those people find themselves entering the prophesied End Times, they will be subject to spiritual chaos, bewilderment, and shock. What if instead—those people were taught that they would likely be entering the most spiritually exhilarating time of their lives where they would all get to be part of a mega-revival?

- I implore you to dig deep, for you and your family's sake, so you will be ready for whatever comes. *(If I am wrong about what I'm suggesting Revelation 7 is saying about the Rapture, please feel free to nudge me when we get to heaven and remind me how misguided I was.)*☺

How much do I know?

1) When Jesus breaks open the first scroll, a very specific event takes place. A white horse appears with a rider carrying a bow. A crown is placed on his head and "he goes out to win many battles." Who is the rider on the white horse?

2) When Jesus opens the first seal, what happens?

    a) The First Horseman of the Apocalypse appears

    b) The antichrist shows up on earth

    c) The clock of End Times starts ticking

    d) A world leader "saves" the planet from chaos

    e) All of the above

3) If the antichrist appears after the end of the Ezekiel 38–39 battle, will all the people in the world by that time be doubting the existence of the One True God *(Ezekiel 39:7)*?

4) Why is it such a big deal whether the word ἐρχόμενοι in Revelation 7:13–14 means died in (the Tribulation) as the NLT translates it, or it means "came out of" (the Tribulation) as several other versions translate it? This is what is said of that vast crowd from every nation who appear in heaven all at the same time in Chapter 7! *(We'll have to look deeper at this, won't we?)*

You can check your answers beginning on page 243.

Number of correct answers on this page:

The Revelation
of Jesus Christ

PART III

Have you ever heard the phrase "Jesus is coming like a thief in the night?" If we read the whole passage, we soon discover that it says Jesus is coming like a "thief in the night" only to those who don't believe in him. What does 1 Thessalonians 5 mean when it says to us Believers: "You aren't in the dark about these things" or "You won't be surprised when the Day of the Lord comes"?

REVELATION 6-18:
Unveiling End Times

From Chapter 6 on, the Unveiling of Revelation is largely about preparing for the victorious Second Coming of Jesus Christ *(and the destruction of sin and satan that follows)*. The Bible provides us with all kinds of clues so that we can know, with some degree of accuracy, when Jesus' Second Coming will take place. Believers, far from sticking our heads in the spiritual sand and adopting an "ignorance is bliss" attitude, are supposed to be *"knowledgeable"* about these things so we can "be a bright light in the dark world" to everyone else.

Read with me this key passage:

> **1 Thessalonians 5:1–6: "Now concerning how and when all this will happen, dear brothers and sisters, we don't really need to write you. For <u>you know quite well that the day of the Lord's return will come unexpectedly, like a thief in the night</u>. When people are saying, 'Everything is peaceful and secure,' then disaster will fall on them as suddenly as a pregnant woman's labor pains begin. And there will be no escape. But <u>you aren't in the dark about these things</u>, dear brothers and sisters, and <u>you won't be surprised when the Day of the Lord comes</u>. For you are all children of the light. So be on your guard, not asleep like the others. Stay alert and be clearheaded."**

Please look at this familiar passage again carefully: Jesus coming like **"a thief in the night"** is prophetically being said—**about unbelievers!** *The Believers are not in the dark,* they are not supposed to be surprised when the Day of the Lord's Wrath arrives.

If you haven't done so, please download your free charts at unmaskingrevelation.com

1 Thessalonians 5 said we "wouldn't be surprised" when the Day of the Lord arrives. Can you name anything other than the return of Israel to their home-land that would alert us that the End Times are drawing close?

The seven years of "End Times" are considered Daniel's 70ᵗʰ Week. Can you name a period of 483 years in world history that would qualify as the first 69 of the 70 weeks?

Can you think of any reason why, when Jesus pops the seventh seal from the seven-sealed scroll, that there is ½ hour of complete silence in heaven? All the millions of praising redeemed, and all the millions of praising angels who have been making a lot of noise for thousands of years suddenly fall silent. Why?

6

Setting the Stage for End Times

If you are wondering how you can be more knowledgeable about the timing of Jesus' Second Coming, let me share a few clues that may surprise you. Besides the obvious Battle of Magog *(Ezekiel 38–39)* that we discussed earlier, and the rise of a one-world leader whom Revelation calls "the antichrist" *(these are big markers that most of us are [now] familiar with)*, there are some smaller markers that can, to some degree, help us know when Jesus will return.

- **The return of the dispersed Jews to Israel as a nation:** This occurred on May 14, 1948, when Chairman David Ben-Gurion declared the establishing of a new Jewish state called Israel.

- **The increasing speed of world travel and the explosion of available knowledge:** 600 years before the birth of Jesus Daniel was startled by a vision. If we are not watching closely, we might miss these clues:

    Daniel 12:4: "But you, Daniel, shut up the words and seal the book, until the time of the end. Many shall run to and fro, *(rush here and there)* **and knowledge shall increase."**

    Daniel, in a time when it took weeks to travel 500 miles, sees humans racing across the planet. And in a time when only the privileged could read, he sees an explosion of every possible kind of knowledge available to vast numbers of people. Not quite 118 years ago, the Wright brothers took the first flight that spanned 852 feet for a period of 59 seconds. Today, any of us could be halfway around the world by tomorrow morning. Forty years ago, I owned a desktop PC which was fairly rare. Today, we can all get information on every conceivable subject on the cell phone in our pockets within seconds.

- **Instant worldwide video news:** Revelation 11 says that all the world will see the dead bodies of two prophets; 50 years ago any possibility that the "whole world" could witness any event in real time was still science fiction. Not any more!
- **G.P.S. technology:** Revelation 13 speaks of a "mark of the beast" that will be able to keep track of every person's activity. Today, people and pets alike are being micro-chipped willingly and are able to be tracked on most devices! Now, countries like China are conducting almost every aspect of life—based purely on computerized "facial recognition!"

    1 Thessalonians 5:4: **"<u>But you aren't in the dark about these things</u>, dear brothers and sisters, and you won't be surprised when the Day of the Lord comes."**

It should be clear by now that God did not inspire this Book with the intention of having us all scratching our heads in confusion. So, let's get clearheaded! To that end, let's lay out a timeline—with the help of our handy "Timeline chart." This is not just a codifying of the events of Revelation, but a chronology that reaches back into the Old Testament and ties much of prophetic Scripture together.

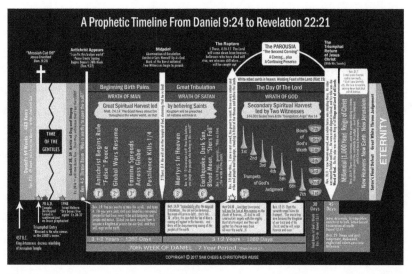

The first part is very important because, even though it doesn't use up much room on the chart, it covers 2,500 years of history and fulfills two-thirds of all biblical prophecy.

*"OK, already! I see it on the chart.
What is Daniel's 70th Week!"*

We have referred several times to **Daniel's 70th week**. What is this strange phrase all about?

The prophet Daniel prophesied that from the time "the King issued the order to rebuild Jerusalem" until the coming of the Anointed One *(the Messiah, or Christ)* there would be a period of 483 years.

> **Daniel 9:24–25: "A period of seventy sets of seven** [49 years] **has been decreed for your people and your holy city to finish their rebellion, to put an end to their sin, to atone for their guilt, to bring in everlasting righteousness, to confirm the prophetic vision, and to anoint the Most Holy Place. Now listen and understand! Seven sets of seven plus sixty-two sets of seven** [434 years] **will pass <u>from the time the command is given to rebuild Jerusalem until a ruler—the Anointed One—comes</u>. Jerusalem will be rebuilt with streets and strong defenses, despite the perilous times."**

(49 + 434 = 483 years. *That is 69 of Daniel's 70 weeks/years.)*

From the time Persian king Artaxerxes issued the decree *in 445 BC* until the time Jesus rode into Jerusalem on a donkey *(as the palm-waving crowd shouted, "Hosanna! Blessed is he who comes in the name of the Lord!")* **was 483** *(lunar)* **years.**

- It shouldn't shock us that thousands of people gathered around a guy on a donkey and quoted the Hillel Psalms reserved for the coming Messiah. *Somebody had been watching their calendar!*
- Within minutes "the entire city was in an uproar." Why? *They were expecting something to happen!* But Daniel had also prophesied, that in spite of the adoration, the Messiah would be rejected—**"the Anointed One would be cut off."**

Daniel 9:26: "After this period of sixty-two sets of seven, the Anointed One will be killed, appearing to have accomplished nothing."

Jesus Himself stopped and cried on the way into Jerusalem and predicted that they were, in fact, going to reject Him. He declared that Jerusalem would be leveled to the ground, and the Jews dispersed. A handful of days later Jesus was crucified, and 40 years later Jerusalem was destroyed!

1) **Notice that 69 of Daniel's 70 weeks have been accounted for.**
2) **A pause of 1900+ years has passed; still no 70ᵗʰ week!**
3) **Daniel's 70ᵗʰ week is still yet to come!**
4) **What's God waiting for?**

For one thing, as we've already noted: The Jews were scattered around the world. Ezekiel prophesied that before the End could come *(who knew it would be 1900+ years)*, the Jews would have to return to their promised homeland from all over the world. *(Is this getting familiar?)*

Ezekiel 36:17, 19, 22–24: "Son of man, when the people of Israel were living in their own land, they defiled it by the evil way they lived. I scattered them to many lands to punish them for the evil

way they had lived. Therefore, give the people of Israel this message from the Sovereign Lord: I am bringing you back, but not because you deserve it. I am doing it to protect my holy name—I will show how holy my great name is—the name on which you brought shame among the nations. And when I reveal my holiness through you before their very eyes, says the Sovereign Lord, then the nations will know that I am the Lord. *For I will gather you up from all the nations and bring you home again to your land."*

Thank God! On May 14, 1948, the nation of Israel was reborn. Now finally, the "time of the Gentiles" is released to wind to an end opening the door for the last unfulfilled week of Daniel's 70-week prophecy to begin. That "one week" (about ¾" of our chart) is the chunk of time that all of biblical history has been, and is still, moving us toward.

Does the Bible say when Daniel's 70th Week is going to arrive and how long it will last?

- Daniel is so specific in his prophecy that he tells us how long the 70th Week will be ***to the day***. In Chapter 12:7–12 he says that the first 3½ years *(time, times and ½ time; **1,260 days**)* will lead up to the antichrist's "abomination of desolation" *(where he declares himself god and demands that the whole world worship him)*.
- Then exactly 1,260 (+30) days later Jesus will return. Daniel even tosses in a mysterious, but exact, 45-day period at the end after which the 1,000-year millennial reign of Jesus on this earth will begin. *(You will find more about this in the next chapter.)*

So, if we are still breathing Earth's air when all of this goes down, where can we Christians expect to be during the first 1,260 days of Daniel's 70th Week?

- Even more importantly, where will we be during the second 1,290 days, the first half which the Bible calls "the Great Tribulation," and the last half which is called "the Day of the Lord's Wrath" *(when the judgments of God destroy every-thing sinful on the planet and wipes out the influence of satan and the antichrist)?*

- Where will we be when Jesus returns in His long-expected Second Coming? And where will we be during the Millennial *(1,000-year)* reign of Jesus on this earth?

Where will I be when this final chapter of human history unfolds?

Let's put together, in **one place**, the same things that Ethan, Matthew and the info-nerds would have been carefully listing, and then see if we can move those points on into a real "theo-logical" understanding of Jesus' Second Coming. How many of these chronological points can you now click off in your own mind? *(Can you locate these 10 points on your chart?)*

(1) We are living right now in the Revelation 1–3 time frame. During which the risen Jesus is *"walking among the seven lampstands"*—His Church— forging sinners into saints, creating what He calls "overcomers."

(2) Chapter 4 lets us look through a *doorway into Heaven* and see where we are all going to victoriously arrive when this earthly saga is over.

(3) Ezekiel 36–37 promises *a worldwide return of the Jews* to Israel setting the stage for the events in Revelation 5–22. *(Since 1948, eight million—more than ½ of all Jews on the planet—have returned to their homeland!)*

(4) Ezekiel 38–39 then *prophesies a coming battle* of the surrounding countries against Jerusalem, at which time God will step in and rain destroying fire down from Heaven on the attackers "as the world watches."

(5) Ezekiel 39:7 says, "In this way, I will make known My holy name among My people of Israel. And **the nations, too** *[non-Jews]*, **will know that I am the LORD [Yᴀʜᴡᴇʜ!]."** The **whole world will then be ripe for the harvest** which is also described in Jesus' prophecy:

> Matthew 24:14: "And this gospel of the kingdom will be proclaimed throughout the whole world as a testimony to all nations, and then the end will come."

The Gospel—proclaimed—throughout— the whole world!

Has that happened yet? If not, when will it happen? I believe *(and thankfully many others do too)* that if we are still alive when all this unfolds, we Believers will remain here into the first part of Daniel's 70ᵗʰ Week—and be a part of seeing Matthew 24:14 fulfilled!

- *In spite of being taught a "pre-tribulation rapture" view as a child, again in Bible College, and again in Seminary; I found myself wrestling with overwhelming Scriptural evidence that suggested we Believers will not be raptured until the events described in Revelation 6 and 7!*

- *For those of us who have unbelieving family and friends, his words would actually be good news—because if we Believers are here when "God answers with fire from heaven," many of our lost loved ones will undoubtedly become very open to the truth of Jesus as the Savior. ("They will know that I am the LORD!")*

(6) In Revelation 5, **God holds the scroll** of time's completion, and Jesus alone is found worthy to open it, which moves all the creatures in heaven and earth to explode in worship.

(7) In Revelation 6, **Jesus begins to pop open the seals and the End Time egg-timer begins to tick**. The first seal is the antichrist, one who rises up to save a chaotic world and brings in three-and-a-half years of false peace. *Remember John's phrase "now I saw"* (kai eidon) *shows us that (almost) all that follows is a chronological progression.*

(8) Seal 6 in Chapter 6 are **"cosmic disturbances"** announcing that God is getting ready to do something big. (*We'll take a closer look.*)

It appears that Seals 1–6 take us past the midpoint of the seven years. So, if I were to teach that the rapture happens in Revelation 7—I would not be advocating a "mid-Tribulation Rapture," but simply suggesting that **whenever Revelation 7 shows up, that is when we go up**!

(9) In **Revelation 7**, God holds back angels who are ready to harm the earth, puts a protective seal on 144,000 Jews, and [IMO] right then, right there, **raptures the church** in advance of His wrath being poured out. *(Lets' briefly bring back Revelation 7 and add even more additional important information to what we already started in Chapter 5.)*

> **Revelation 7:9–10, 13–15: "After this *[kai eidon]* I saw a vast crowd, too great to count, from every nation and tribe and people and language, standing in front of the throne and before the Lamb. They were clothed in white robes and held palm branches in their hands. And they were shouting with a great roar, 'Salvation comes from our God who sits on the throne and from the Lamb!' Then one of the twenty-four elders asked me, 'Who are these who are clothed in white? Where did they come from?' And I said to him, 'Sir, you are the one who knows.'**

> "Then he said to me, 'These are the ones who died in [came out] [ἐρχόμενοι -coming out of, newly arrived] of the Great Tribulation. They have washed their robes in the blood of the Lamb and made them white. That is why they stand in front of God's throne and serve Him day and night in His Temple.'"

- I looked at every reference in the NLT where they translated the word ἐρχόμενοι. 255 times they translated the word "**to come, coming, came**" *(which is the root meaning of the word)*. One time in Revelation 7:14 they translated it "**died in**." *Why would they do that?*
- It's the same word used in Revelation 22 when Jesus says: "I am coming soon." It's the same word used when Jesus says: "Let anyone who is thirsty come." It is the same as the phrase at the end of the book: "Come, Lord Jesus!" Where in the world did the word "die" come from?

By Revelation 7:9, the redeemed Saints are now in heaven!

All those who have "washed their robes in the blood of the Lamb" are now with Jesus and will continue to be there with Jesus throughout the balance of the seven years—all during the period that Scripture calls: **"The Day of the Lord, the Day of Wrath."**

SILENCE

The next thing we notice is shocking—it is supposed to be. We go from a vast crowd too great to count shouting with a great roar to **SILENCE!**

(10) There was **silence in Heaven!** Picture this: The Lamb, Jesus, pops off the seventh seal. As the last seal falls away, the scroll begins to open allowing its

actual contents to become visible. ***Everybody falls silent.*** The four beings, the 24 Elders, billions of angels, and the vast redeemed throng too great to count: *Silent!*

- Inside the scroll *is God's pent-up wrath on satan and sin.* What comes next is what the Bible refers to as *"the Day of the Lord."* There are many prophesies in Scripture, going back in the Old Testament, to this final day of God's wrath being poured out on satan and sin.

- The prophet Zephaniah even prophesies: "**Stand in silence in the presence of the Sovereign LORD, for the awesome Day of the LORD'S Judgment is near. The LORD has prepared His people for a great slaughter and has chosen their executioners**" *(Zephaniah 1:7).*

This is without question going to be the outpoured "wrath of God," which will finally cleanse the effects of sin and the curse from the earth. However, ***God's wrath will NOT fall on His redeemed children. THEY ARE GONE—in heaven with Jesus!***

> 1 Thessalonians 1:10: "**and to wait for his Son from heaven, whom he raised from the dead—Jesus, who <u>rescues us from the coming wrath</u>.**"

> 1 Thessalonians 5:9–10: "**For <u>God did not appoint us to suffer wrath</u> but to receive salvation through our Lord Jesus Christ. He died for us so that, whether we are awake or asleep, we may live together with Him.**"

So, if we are not going to be on Earth suffering the poured-out wrath of God on satan and sin, where will we be? What will we be doing?

- Let's briefly jump forward to enlarge the picture: It seems that by Chapter 19 of Revelation the residents of heaven *(us)* are observing the successful destruction of satan on Earth and are once again expressing ourselves:

> Revelation 19:1–9: "**After this I heard what sounded like the roar of a great multitude in heaven shouting: "Hallelujah! Salvation and glory and power belong to our God, for true and just are his**

judgments. And again they shouted: 'Hallelujah.' The twenty-four elders and the four living creatures fell down and worshiped God, who was seated on the throne. And they cried: 'Amen, Hallelujah.' Then I heard what sounded like a great multitude, like the roar of rushing waters and like loud peals of thunder, shouting: 'Hallelujah! For our Lord God Almighty reigns. Let us rejoice and be glad and give Him glory! <u>For the wedding of the Lamb has come</u> [new event!], <u>and His bride</u> [Church] <u>has made herself ready</u>. Fine linen, bright and clean, was given her to wear.' (Fine linen stands for the righteous acts of God's holy people.) Then the angel said to me, 'Write this: <u>Blessed are those who are invited to the Wedding Supper of the Lamb!</u>' and he added, 'These are the true words of God.'"

The "raptured" Believers are clearly in heaven with Jesus shouting, "Hallelujah!" Yes? We'll unfold this "Supper of the Lamb" in the pages to come, but it seems that once the Heavenly Feast is finished, immediately after comes Jesus' long-awaited Second Coming—and we are part of it!

      Revelation 19:11–16: "I saw heaven standing open and there before me was a white horse, whose rider is called Faithful and True. With justice he judges and wages war. His eyes are like blazing fire, and on his head are many crowns. He has a name written on him that no one knows but he himself. He is dressed in a robe dipped in blood, and his name is the Word of God. The armies of heaven *[US!]* were following Him, riding on white horses and dressed in fine linen, white and clean. On His robe and on His thigh He has this name written: KING OF KINGS AND LORD OF LORDS."

But—we are getting way, way ahead of ourselves (again), but I do want us to be able to plant each part of the unfolding picture inside of the chronological storyline. *It's a bit like putting together a puzzle, and stopping occasionally to look at the box top to get a feel for what the finished puzzle will look like!* Let's hit the rewind button, go back and unfold Chapter 6.

How much do I know?

1) The first 69 weeks of Daniel's prophecy lasted from the time King Artaxerxes degreed the rebuilding of Jerusalem's walls until?

2) You caught, I trust, that the word ἐρχόμενοι is used 255 times in the NT and is always translated: to come, coming, came. One time in Revelation 7:14 it is translated "died in." Why would the translators do that?

3) True or False: The sudden silence in heaven does not happen because everybody has grown seriously tired of praising God 24 hours a day. As the final seal falls away and the scroll totally opens, the full wrath of God against sin and satan is exposed and everybody in the Throne Room knows exactly what is coming next.

4) Matthew 24:14 says the "Gospel of the Kingdom will be proclaimed throughout the whole world as a testimony to all nations, and _then the end will come_." For a variety of reasons, the Gospel has not yet ever been "proclaimed throughout the whole world" _(as Jesus commanded in his Great Commission)_. What are the circumstances where this prophecy will finally be fulfilled?

You can check your answers beginning on page 243.

Number of correct answers on this page:

Which is more "real" in your life right now? The raise you are expecting at work next week, the 78.75 year (U.S. average) lifespan you will spend on this earth, or the billions and billions of years you will spend in eternity "reigning" with Jesus Christ? Which one consumes almost all our thoughts?

1 Thessalonians 1:10 says that we Believers are going to be "saved, by Jesus, from the coming wrath." 1 Thessalonians 5:9 says that we Believers are "not appointed to suffer wrath." If we could determine when the "wrath of God" falls on sin and satan—we would know when Christians will definitely be off this planet! Do you know exactly when the book of Revelation says the "wrath of God" is going to come onto this earth?

Satan has been, since the beginning, constantly trying to stop God's eternal plan. He started with Adam and Eve in the Garden. He tried to take out Jesus several times, including Herod killing all the male toddlers in Bethlehem and murdering Jesus on a cross—only to have Jesus victoriously rise from the dead! Is the antichrist satan's attempt to raise up a false messiah, a counterfeit Christ, a replacement savior?

7

Opening the Scroll and Seven Seals

Can't you just picture Elder Ethan doing the same thing we are doing— every once in a while sneaking a look forward at the whole box-top view of Revelation? Then he would force his attention back to search word by word— undoubtedly burying himself for days on *(our)* Chapter 6—where God the Father, in the Throne Room of Heaven, holds the "most important document in the universe" *(a scroll with seven seals)* in His right hand. A universe-wide search ends with the only One in the whole universe worthy to open the seven seals— the slain Lamb, the Son of God who gave His life for the salvation of humanity. Jesus' finger hovers over the first seal—

- Let's move slowly here, because if we are not careful this will begin to sound "Bible story-ish." By that I mean that our minds tend to separate Abraham and Moses and David and Paul from "real life" where "real life" is about work, and issues at home, and kids, and bills. The risk is that we will do the same thing with Jesus' opening the seven seals.

- Our task here is to unfold the truth— *the prophetic reality* that is happening outside our three-dimensional line of sight is not only real, but it is *more real than what we did Thursday at work or what we had Wednesday for lunch.*

- An overwhelming percentage of what consumes us in this life will have no meaning in the life to come—the man who sideswiped our car in the

Walmart parking lot, the job promotion for which we work 80-hour weeks, the petty dispute with the neighbor over the fence, or the stock market's effect on our retirement account.

- The challenge here is to wrestle our shallow human minds *right now* from "which woman at the grocery store stole our parking spot" to: "I wonder if right now, Jesus is getting ready to take the scroll from the Father, assume His final role as King of all Kings—and is getting ready to pop the first seal, change the whole world as we know it, and drop into gear His final judgment against sin and satan in this world?"

That's the point of Revelation 6–19! It presents the "reality" of Jesus as the final Judge—who **destroys the power of satan, destroys his antichrist, raptures His saints,** cleanses the whole world of sin, and returns to set up a 1,000-year reign. So, if it ever begins to sound "storybook-ish," step back and, by faith, grasp the fact that this prophetic reality is what Almighty God is guiding this universe toward!

- If you are a believer in the Bible, *this is your reality!* If you are a follower of Jesus Christ, this is where belief in the crucified and risen Jesus leads you!

- One day, perhaps soon, Jesus will open the first seal and the prophesied events of Revelation, Matthew 24, the book of Daniel, Zechariah, etc. will unfold. That "one day soon" part is what we wrestle with. Most of us have no problem believing the prophecy of Revelation—as long as it is not something we are going to deal with. But let's ask ourselves this: *What if it is?*

What if Jesus pops the first seal sometime in the next 5, 10, or 15 years? Many *(perhaps most)* Bible students and scholars do agree that the first seal is the appearance on the world stage of this "anti-christ"—anti-messiah, the one who will show up with a solution for world peace and economic healing.

And many agree that after a whole series of progressing events unfold during the last half of the seven years, with the seals off **the scroll—God's judgment on sin and satan unleashes in the final and horrendous "Day of the Lord's Wrath."**

- God gave us "inspired assurances" that we **Believers are not going to be the direct recipients of the final wrath of God** on sin and satan. Let's again review our two previous passages—then add a third great promise to them:

  1 Thessalonians 1:10: "**and to wait for his Son from heaven, whom he raised from the dead**—*Jesus, who rescues us from the coming wrath.*" *(Hell? Or hell on earth?)*

  1 Thessalonians 5:9–10: "*For* **God did not appoint us to suffer wrath** *but to receive salvation through our Lord Jesus Christ. He died for us so that, whether we are awake [alive] or asleep [dead], we may live together with Him.*"

  Revelation 3:10: "**Because you have obeyed my command to persevere,** _I will protect you from the great time of testing that will come upon the whole world to test those who belong to this world._"

But an assurance that God will save Believers from his poured-out wrath—is not the same as an assurance that we will not be here when the antichrist arrives!
- If we are on this earth to fulfill Jesus' Great Commission and the full-blown grand fulfillment of the Great Commission is going to happen in the first half of the final seven years—**why would I as a Jesus-following Believer want to be anywhere else?**
- I'm going to be in heaven for all of eternity. Shouldn't I be willing to stay here for as long as God needs me to finish the task he commissioned me to do? ☺

So right on cue:

Satan's false-messiah, the anti-christ, appears!

Revelation 6:2 makes the **antichrist** *(I don't use a capital letter with satan or the antichrist; they don't deserve it!)* sound like just another international leader out to save the planet. We already noticed, however, that after three-and-a-half years this dude is going to make Stalin look like a Sunday School boy *(Revelation 13)*.

- If Daniel's 70th week is say 20 years away, it could be that the antichrist is, at this moment, playing marbles with his friends on a dusty street in the Middle East. Or perhaps he is in Europe at some exclusive prep-school that trains future world leaders.

We must realize that what we are, perhaps, about to see unfold is something that is not even remotely being played out on a human level. Adolf Hitler, Joseph Stalin, Mao Zedong, and Saddam Hussein were despicable human beings who callously murdered and tortured others—thousands, in some cases, millions of others. These men had what the Apostle Paul called "a spirit of antichrist." They were horrible, sinful people who orchestrated human horrors as far from the grace of Jesus Christ as one can get. They operated in an "antichrist" mentality, **but the one who is coming is not operating "in the spirit of antichrist"—He is the antichrist! He is satan's messiah, the evil one's attempted replacement of Jesus!** You see, in spite of several major setbacks, satan still believes he will beat God!

- During Jesus' first coming, Herod's attempt to kill all the baby boys in Bethlehem was not just some psychotic king's jealousy, but was actually a legitimate attempt by satan to take out the coming Redeemer of the world! We tend to think eternally small, and our "reality" tends to be a rather tiny bubble. God tries to get us to see that there is a whole lot more going on in the universe than the events on our cul-de-sac!
- When the Jewish leaders and the Romans brought Jesus to die on a cross at Golgotha, that idea was not hatched in some stone building inside Jerusalem—but rather was spawned in the pit of hell! Killing Jesus was not the High Priest's idea. It was, once again, another attempt by satan to stop the redemption of humanity!

- And when **Jesus said, "It is finished," satan thought he had won**! I have celebrated (*in sermons*), more than once, satan's rather embarrassing stupidity in thinking he had beat Jesus by killing Him, when in reality he had played right into Jesus' hands! A trumped-up charge was the very tool God used to allow Jesus' shed blood to pay the sin penalty for all of humanity!

- **On Resurrection Sunday, we celebrate the horror satan must have felt when Jesus ripped away the gates of death and hell and rose victorious from the grave, slamming open the doorway to complete forgiveness and eternal life to all *who believe!***

But if we then picture "the evil one" slinking off into a corner somewhere licking his wounds, giving up, and slithering off into eternal oblivion, we are not reading our Bibles correctly. The Epistles tell us that satan is still fighting tooth and cloven hoof against every Believer "seeking whom he may devour." And the book of Revelation makes it clear that he is going to be clawing his way to the very end still believing to the last tick of the timer that he can, somehow, take out God's Messiah!

The devil is a counterfeiter!

- **The antichrist is satan's substitute for the real Christ!** He even dies and is miraculously healed *(Revelation 13:3)*. The number six is the number of "man without God" in the Bible, and perhaps 666 indicates a trinity between satan, the antichrist, and the false prophet to finally destroy humanity. *Make no mistake: The antichrist is not some "boy next door gone bad"!*

- When the final *"Battle of Armageddon"* comes amid Jesus' return, we find the antichrist with all the final devil-filled armies left on this earth turning every drop of satan's accumulated power toward the returning Christ *(along with all of us saints and all the mighty angels who will be returning with Him)*. The antichrist, the false Jesus, will marshal every last drop of satanic power on the planet one last time against the real Christ—somehow still believing that he can conquer Him.

- But instead, **the incarnate Son of Almighty God, the King of Kings and Lord of Lords, defeats satan, the antichrist, the false prophet, and every other sin-filled person on the earth with nothing more than the power of His WORD!**

That is all still to come—but for now, it is important that we 21st Century Believers step back a few yards and see a bigger picture than what we think we see on the nightly news. The evil one is, right now, deeply involved (*unsuccessfully*) in trying to thwart God's eternal plan. For instance:

- Israel is all over the news in our day—fending off an attack here or responding to a rogue nation's vow to destroy the Jewish state and wipe all Jews from the earth. The governments of the world issue their predictable response—urging Israel to remain calm.
- **Since 2001, more than 15,200 rockets and mortars, an average of 3 attacks every single day, have landed in Israel** (*IDF—Israel Defense Forces Blog*).
- Many people look in the direction of Israel and say, "What's the big deal? People in that region have been duking it out for centuries. Let them go at it so long as it isn't hurting us in our part of the world. Unless the problems affect the flow of oil to the West and the price of gas skyrockets, what goes on, on the other side of the world, means nothing to me."

Who cares? What's the big deal?

Well, to be honest, un-believers evaluating the world can have that view, but for Believers that view is totally misguided. We must understand that **according to the Bible, Israel** (*regardless of whatever they have or have not done right*) **is the geographical center-point of the world!** (*No one is more aware of that—than satan!*)

- For Americans, like me, who like to think the world revolves around the United States of America, we need to remember this: From a Bible history, and Bible prophecy standpoint, our country does not even get honorable mention! God, for whatever reason, decided to take Abraham from Ur of the Chaldees *(modern-day Iraq)* and lead him to the "Promised Land" in Israel.

  Genesis 12:1–3: "The Lord had said to Abram, 'Leave your native country, your relatives, and your father's family, and go to the land that I will show you. I will make you into a great nation. I will bless you and make you famous, and you will be a blessing to others. *I will bless those who bless you and curse those who treat you with contempt.* All the families on earth will be blessed through you.'"

God was saying in effect, "I will send my promised Messiah—God incarnate—to the earth to redeem the souls of mankind. I will not send Him to Moscow or London or New York City. He will be born just five miles south of the capital city on this little spit of land that I have carved out."

- All the prophecies of the Old and New Testaments will unfold around *"Jeru-shalom"—"the city of peace."* And yet Jerusalem, God's chosen city, the geographical centerpiece of the earth, has seen more bloodshed that any other city on the face of the earth!
- "Jerusalem has been attacked 52 times, captured and recaptured 44 times! It's been besieged with intent to destroy 23 times, and completely destroyed twice" *(Wikipedia),* but make no mistake:
- The Almighty God of Heaven saw to it *(using Nehemiah and Ezra)* that this city was there for His Son, the Messiah, to die in—and He made sure that when He flung back the stone from the mouth of the tomb, it was right there in that city!
- The forces of satan have opposed the forces of righteousness all over the world, but never more often nor more viciously than right there in God's city. There in that region satan tried to take out the world's Redeemer once, twice, and will ultimately try a third time! It is no accident that

satan's antichrist will one day install himself right there in that town demanding that the entire world worships him.

The real Christ, the true Messiah will one day descend from Heaven and land on the Mount of Olives on the east side of town *(Zechariah 14:4, 9)*. From there He will destroy the antichrist, the false prophet, and all the satanic armies of the world. And there in Jerusalem the victorious Jesus Christ will set up His millennial reign! **"And the *LORD will be King over all the earth.* On that day there will be one LORD, His name alone will be worshiped."** It does not matter what great politician or world leader comes against God's chosen city or His chosen people, they will ultimately fail and be erased from the face of the earth. Not because God's chosen people are so strong or even because they are so faithful, **but simply because they are God's chosen people!**

So, when you hear about Hamas lobbing rockets into Israel or breathing hellish threats against all Jews everywhere, know that this is more than just a little skirmish on the other side of the world. It is all part of a much bigger cosmic battle!

>**Genesis 12:1–3: "The LORD had said to Abram, 'I will make you into a great nation. I will bless you and make you famous—***I will bless those who bless you and curse those who treat you with contempt.'"***

The Unites States has traditionally been a *(best)* friend to Israel, and whether or not the United States continues to be a friend of Israel is extremely important, *not to the future of Israel but to the future of the United States!*

- Think about this: Why is there such vicious animosity toward this little spit of land and the growing number of people living on it? Because Hitler killed half of the entire Jewish population 70 years ago, *the total population of Jews in the world today is less than 15 million, which is less than 50% of the population of the state of California! Israel itself is only 263 x 70 miles—a tiny sliver of land!*

- Israel would fit inside my own state of Florida almost eight times and is surrounded by people, some of whom, want the Jews—all of them— dead. Yet when their neighbors begin lobbing rockets over their cities—

the world tells them to "stay calm." Imagine how calm we Floridians would have been if in 1962 Cuba had started lobbing rockets at us!

I may not be the sharpest knife in the drawer, but—

There are a lot of things I am not sure of in life, but this is not one of them. *Whoever comes against Israel will be soundly defeated because they are not fighting a handful of surrounded, lonely Jews BUT THE VERY GOD OF HEAVEN!*

- Israel has already done their exile, *(Daniel, Nehemiah, Ezra)* and the Jews are now back in their God-given Promised Land.
- The "Time of the Gentiles" is winding down. Revelation 1–3 records events that are all happening simultaneously during the Time of the Gentiles as Israel is returning and the Jews are repopulating their Promised Homeland. They daily continue to return to the land of "Zion," which means that the nations around them are/will be lining up for the second part of Ezekiel's Prophesies *(Chapters 38–39).*
- It sure does seem to me—that the next thing on Israel's prophetic timeline and therefore on the Christian prophetic timeline is the second half of the Ezekiel "Tetrad."

Ezekiel 39:1, 3–4, 6: "'Son of man, prophesy against Gog. I will knock the bow from your left hand and the arrows from your right hand, and I will leave you helpless. You and your army and your allies will all die on the mountains. And I will rain down fire on Magog and on all your allies.'"

How much do I know?

1) True or False: The devil is a counterfeiter, and the anti-Christ is satan's substitute for the real Christ.
   Which aspects of his life seem to be an attempted reproduction of the "Real Christ?"

2) Satan has been, since the beginning, constantly trying to stop God's eternal plan. Besides the obvious murder of Jesus on a cross, can you name three other times in history when satan was obviously trying to bring God's eternal plan to a halt?

3) Is God's promise to Abraham in Genesis 12:1–3 still in effect? ("I will bless those who bless you and curse those who treat you with contempt.") a) The Ezekiel Battle centering around Jerusalem, b) the antichrist setting up his short reign in Jerusalem, c) God's protection of 144,000 redeemed evangelizing Jews around Jerusalem...are they all evidence that God still has a plan for the Jews and the Holy City?

You can check your answers beginning on page 243.

Number of correct answers on this page:

Sam's midpoint note:

You are about halfway through the book! When you get to Chapters 13–18, you are going to get very excited about the "there will be no more delay," and "the King of Kings has now begun to reign" parts. I've read this book many times and I still get misty eyed over the Wedding Feast of the Lamb, our return with Jesus to set up his (our) earthly reign, the arrival of the New Jerusalem here on earth where the "mansion Jesus went to prepare for you" is.

But in the next four chapters you are going to need to put on your "swimmies" and paddle out into the deep end. There are so many moving parts, with the antichrist constantly showing up, and the Rapture taking place, and the antichrist beginning his wrath against humanity, and God's judgments beginning to fall on the earth, and God wiping out the false religious systems on earth once and for all.

It would be a good idea for the next 60 pages or so to put aside all distractions, locate your chart, read through the text of Revelation itself, and thoroughly study this fast-moving section of the coming End Times. This is where so much confusion lies—and it doesn't need to be so!

In 2 Thessalonians 2:1–4 there is a super-important verse that defines critical events that must happen: before "the coming of our Lord Jesus Christ and how we will be gathered to meet Him." Do you know what those "must-happen" events are?

When trying to figure out exactly when the saints will be lifted (raptured) off this planet, we first have to determine when the "wrath of God" is going to be poured out. On that point, does this seem like an accurate, logical (theo-logical) statement: "God's wrath will never be directed through the antichrist; it is going to be directed at the antichrist!"

Yes or No: It is very significant that Chapter 6 ends with massive earthquakes, the mother of all solar eclipses and blood moons, the sky rolling back like a scroll while everybody is hiding in caves screaming: "the wrath of God has come onto the earth." Is it significant that immediately following, in Chapter 7, a vast crowd of white-robed people from every nation arrive in heaven?

8

The antichrist (and the Rapture) is Coming!

We should not forget that Jesus' Second Coming is so important that one out of every 30.6 verses in the New Testament directly mentions it. It is the engine driving much of the history of the New Church. Jesus, and the "dazzling angels," told His disciples that He was going to leave Earth for a while before coming back in His Second Glorious Return. He would "come again," as the King of Kings and Lord of Lords, to purge this earth of everything sinful.

But understanding Jesus' Second Coming is not complete without linking it to the defeat of the anti-messiah, the anti-christ. It's God's great eternal plan vs. the evil plan of satan—and guess who's going to win!

(1) As we've noted: in satan's final drama to wrestle control of the hearts of God's beloved children, he pulls out all the stops and sends his "false counter-answer" to Jesus, the True Messiah, to this earth.

(2) He is satan's "**antichristos**"—against or in-place-of the Anointed One. *(So, why Chess do you keep harping about satan's messiah? I thought he didn't eternally matter!)*

- That's ultimately true—but it is going to be very important to understand that in those final three-and-a-half years, *the world, particularly the Jews, are going to have to make a choice either to embrace Jesus as Messiah or to embrace satan's messiah!*

(3) The anti-messiah will wage all out war on humanity though it's really aimed at God. **(The Great Tribulation!)**

(4) Again: God will answer from Heaven with the **"Day of the Lord's Wrath**." *(God's wrath on satan—not on us!)*

(5) Finally: Jesus Himself will "return" to destroy satan, sin, the antichrist, and the false prophet, and all sinfulness will be cleansed from the earth.

(JESUS VICTORIOUSLY WINS—SATAN MISERABLY LOSES!)

First Century Ethan would have said, "The antichrist can't wreak much more havoc than the Roman Empire already has on my family and friends. I'd be so happy if Jesus would just let him arrive during my lifetime so I could see him and satan, once and for all, get their clocks cleaned by the King of all Kings and Lord of all Lords!

2000 years later 21st Century Alfred might say, "Why do I care when the antichrist arrives, I'm going to be raptured out of here before he shows up! I firmly believe Jesus will 'lift-off' the Saints before satan's anti-messiah ever appears on this earth." *(That view has been the majority view for the last 100+ years.)*

- I can show you almost certainly why Elder Ethan would have rejected that view, and it would, indeed, have been based on his intense study of what the inspired Word says. Sooner or later, like him, every modern Bible student has to deal with this 2 Thessalonians 2 passage from the Apostles Paul's pen:

> **2 Thessalonians 2:1–4: "Now, dear brothers and sisters,** *let us clarify some things about 1)* <u>*the coming of our Lord Jesus Christ*</u> *and 2)* <u>*how we will be gathered to meet Him*</u>. **Don't be so easily shaken or**

alarmed by those who say that the day of the Lord has already begun. Don't be fooled by what they say. *For <u>that day will not come until</u> 1) there is a great rebellion [apostasia] against God <u>and</u> 2) <u>the man of lawlessness is revealed, the one who brings destruction.</u>* He will oppose and will exalt himself over everything that is called God or is worshiped, so that *he sets himself up in God's temple, proclaiming himself to be God.*" *(I added the above numbering for our study.)*

- Did you notice the two parts—and what Paul says has to happen—**1) great falling away + 2) man of sin revealed!**

Before the "coming of our Lord" and us being "gathered up to meet him— "apostasy" *(even from those claiming to follow Christ)* and satan's God-rejecting "lawlessness" will become the accepted "normal." I do believe that *the **distinction between righteousness and sinfulness is going to get ever starker***. Even in our day, the sinful actions of unbelievers are often passed off as "moral," and those who do not tolerate or celebrate sinfulness are said to be the "immoral" people in society. By the time the midpoint of the Tribulation comes and the "man of lawlessness" sets himself up as satan's messiah—people are going to have to choose either to follow Jesus or to completely fall in line behind satan's antichrist.

So, when does the Day of God's Wrath finally crush satan's "lawlessness"?

- Most "Tribulation viewpoints" believe that the Saints—Believers, the Church, the Body of Christ—will be "lifted off" this planet before "God's Wrath" is poured out on sin and satan! Since that seems to be exactly what the Apostle Paul wrote, many believe the "timing of the Rapture" to be JUST BEFORE "the Day of God's Wrath" begins. **<u>Our "tribulation" viewpoints tend to hinge on WHEN EXACTLY we believe that "Day of God's Wrath on satan" actually starts!</u>**

Allow me to present a logical (*theo-logical*) case for when the Day of the Lord's Wrath, against sin and satan, the antichrist, the false prophet, and everyone who has willfully chosen to follow them, begins and when we Christians will be "raptured" off this planet.

(1) The first part of the last seven years is a time of false peace—*not a time of God's wrath!*

(2) The war, famine, and "pestilence" of Seals 2–4 do not come from God but are the result of sinful human aggression against other humans.

(3) The horrifying entrance of the antichrist's exposure as "satan incarnate" against the world is *not God's wrath*. That is satan's wrath against humanity. **God's wrath would never be directed _through_ the antichrist; it is going to be directed _at_ the antichrist!!**

(4) When we get to Seal 5, martyrs *(of all time),* including those who have recently run afoul of the antichrist, "shout to the Lord and say, *'O Sovereign Lord, Holy and True, how long before you judge the people who belong to this world and avenge our blood for what they have done to us?'"* (Revelation 6:10) *Note that God's judgment has not yet started!*

And then we come to Seal 6: *(Please refer to your chart)*

Revelation 6:12–14: "I watched as the Lamb broke the <u>sixth seal</u>, and there was a great earthquake. The sun became as dark as black cloth, and the moon became as red as blood. Then the stars of the sky fell to the earth like green figs falling from a tree shaken by a strong wind. The sky was rolled up like a scroll, and all of the mountains and islands were moved from their places."

• Did you detect a noticeable shift that just took place in the Unmasking of Jesus' Revelation? We **JUST WENT FROM WHAT HUMANS ARE DOING TO HUMANS TO WHAT NO HUMAN COULD**

POSSIBLY DO—mountains and islands moving in massive global earthquakes, a blood moon and solar eclipse simultaneously, stars falling, and "the sky rolling up like a scroll."

No human beings could pull off such things! We are at the point where God steps in and says *(by His actions)*, **"I am done messing around with sinful humanity. From now on I am going to take charge of the planet**, and everything you see, hear, and feel from now on will be something you have absolutely no power over. Satan himself will be left gasping and reeling by what I am going to send to the Earth."

- Though we don't know what satan's thoughts will be at that point, we do know exactly what the "power-players" on the earth will be thinking because the Bible tells us:

  Revelation 6:15–17: "Then everyone—the kings of the earth, the rulers, the generals, the wealthy, the powerful, and every slave and free person—all hid themselves in the caves and among the rocks of the mountains. And they cried to the mountains and the rocks, 'Fall on us and hide us *from the face of the one who sits on the throne and from the wrath of the Lamb. For the great day of their (God's) wrath has come*, and who is able to survive?'"

*The most powerful people on Earth are cowering in caves saying, "**the wrath of God has come!**"* That is impressive—an inspired message from God's Word, **a divine clue!** All of a sudden, the planet erupts in preparation for the Rapture of the Saints and the outpoured wrath of God on sin and satan! We need to see these last three verses in Chapter 6, and all of Chapter 7, as a package *(You will discover this exact same sequence of signs → Rapture in Matthew 24:29–31; Mark 13:24–27; and Luke 21:25–28! Please read those sections! They are lined up for you on the 2nd free chart you downloaded!)*

- There are **global earthquakes**, as though every tectonic plate is shifting, a massive solar eclipse, the mother of all blood moons, and then the weird event of the "*sky rolling back like a scroll*" (remember, John had no *frame of reference to describe what he was seeing),* and then *stars falling like figs* from a tree.

"The great day of God's wrath has come!"

• We are never told that these cataclysmic events wreak havoc on human life as the things that come in the "trumpet and bowl judgments" will *(none of it is of human origin).* This stuff terrifies people, but *it seems to be far more about alerting the earth to what is coming, or as the people in the caves are saying:* **"the great day of God's wrath has come."**

If you are still on earth at this point, don't run to your cave/under-ground bunker. You are going to be just fine—finer than fine. I can tell *you (at least in the certainty of my own mind)* exactly what is coming next. We are poised at the end of the sixth seal. Then *the opening of the seventh seal begins, the blowing of the trumpets of God's judgments begin against sin, satan, and the antichrist.*

But there is that **distinct pause** in Scripture that we are absolutely *not supposed to miss:*

6:12–14: Earthquakes, dark sun, blood moon, weird sky, falling stars, sky rolled up. *(Matthew 24, Mark 13, Luke 21)*

6:15–17: World leaders are in caves screaming: "*The Day of God's wrath has come.*"

7:1: Four angels stand at the "corners" of Earth.

7:2: An angel arrives with the Seal of the Living God.

7:3: He yells, "Don't harm the earth just yet!"

7:4: He seals the 144,000 Jews *(who will stay until Jesus comes).*

You better pay attention to what is coming!

Perhaps the darkened sun and the blood moon are God's way of saying: "*You better pay attention to what is coming!*" The stars falling and the weird sky are celestial happenings unfolding in the upper atmosphere. Let's pick up the story line again so we can see more of what that means:

7:1: Four angels at the corners of earth.

7:2: Angel arrives with Seal of the Living God.

7:3: Yells, "*Don't harm the earth just yet!*"

7:4: Seals the 144,000 Jews.

7:9–10: "*after this [you know what that means!] I saw a vast crowd, too great to count, from every nation and tribe and people and language, standing in front of the throne and before the Lamb. They were clothed in white robes and held palm branches in their hands. And they were shouting with a great roar, 'Salvation comes from our God who sits on the throne and from the Lamb!'*"

In my view, we are seeing *(John was seeing)* the **freshly raptured Church!** How else can we explain this critical passage?

(1) What if the earthquakes all over the world are not the destructive kind that come later, but are instead the earth and sea opening up to eject the redeemed saints?

(2) What if the "stars falling like figs" is the massive movement of angels and people through the atmosphere?

(3) We know all this happens amid an eclipse of the sun, and yet there are clearly visuals going on above the earth. If there is no light from the sun, the light must be generated by the "Light-Giver" Himself?

(4) Based on the above Scriptures—I have had to draw the conclusion that the "beginning" of the Second Coming, the rising of the redeemed dead and the "Rapture" of the living Saints, *will be visible to those left on Earth who will be hiding in caves in utter terror!*

(5) We know for sure that at the moment all these weird events are happening on Earth, John suddenly sees in Heaven, *a vast crowd, too great to count, from every nation and tribe and people and language, standing in front of the throne and before the Lamb. They are clothed in white robes and hold palm branches in their hands.*

    (a) These cannot be people who were raptured four or five years earlier: **Revelation 7:14: "Then he said to me, 'These are the ones who came out of the Great Tribulation. They have washed their robes in the blood of the Lamb and made them white.'"**

    (b) Nor are they martyrs. Martyrs die and are put in graves, and the graves are not opened until just before the Rapture, so what would a vast crowd of them suddenly be doing in Heaven in Revelation 7:14, unless the Rapture has just happened?

    1 Thessalonians 4:16–17: "For the Lord himself will come down from heaven with a commanding shout, with the voice of the archangel, and with the trumpet call of God. First, the believers who have died will rise from their graves. Then, together with them, we who are still alive and remain on the earth will be caught up in the clouds to meet the Lord in the air. Then we will be with the Lord forever."

But—why would you wait, God?

"Why, why God would you hold off rapturing "believing saints" until the first half and well into part of the second half of the seven-year Tribulation period? Because—*(please don't get tired of reading this...it is so important!)* **there is going to be a vast spiritual harvest of people coming to Christ during those years.** Remember, the words at the end of the Ezekiel 38–39 battle that leads us into the End Times. **Ezekiel 39:7: "And the nations, too, will know that I am the LORD."**

- In Matthew 24, just after Jesus announced that Jerusalem had rejected Him as Messiah and would be destroyed, and just *before* the Last Supper begins, He *broke out into His last sermon* all of which is prophetic. Matthew 24 lines up exactly with Revelation 6–19. *(Please refer to the 2ⁿᵈ chart.)*

- Right in the middle of it, Jesus says something fascinating: **Matthew 24:14: "And the Good News about the Kingdom will be preached throughout the whole world, so that all nations will hear it; *and then the end will come.*"**

- This is not some stray verse! This is Jesus unfolding, to His disciples, what the final seven years of the world will be like. And right in the middle of it He says, "Oh, by the way, during this last seven years of time as we know it, **the Good News about the Kingdom will be preached throughout the WHOLE world so that ALL nations will hear it and THEN the end will come!"**

The end of what? What constitutes "the end" of what Jesus is prophesying is a little space in time that Jesus often referred to as *"the end of the age."* He had already used this phrase several times in that very sermon. So, when is the end of the age?

End of the Age → *Rapture* →

Day of the Lord's Wrath →

Jesus' Second Coming!

Matthew 28:18–20: "Jesus came and told His disciples, 'I have been given all authority in heaven and on earth. Therefore, go and make disciples of all the nations, baptizing them in the name of the Father and the Son and the Holy Spirit. Teach these new disciples to obey all the commands I have given you. *And be sure of this: I am with you always, even to the end of the age.*'"

It seems, doesn't it, that *Jesus is promising His continued presence to His Church who will be making disciples right up to "the end of the age."* If the "end of the age" is just before the rapture and the rapture is, in fact, described in Revelation 7 as being just before the beginning of God's wrath being poured out, then *Jesus' Church will be actively making disciples until the very end of Revelation 6!*

Believers will be experiencing my continued presence right up to the "end of the age"!

If you are, in fact, still here when the Ezekiel battle ends in triumph for the God of Heaven, you will rejoice even though you now know exactly what is going to come next. A massive worldwide revival will be sweeping the world, and you will be leading others to Jesus all day, every day. It will be the most exciting time of your life as you rejoice that your children and grandchildren get to live out something that others have only dreamed of. You are not going to be waking up each morning wondering what to do to fill your boring day!

But you will also be intensely aware of what is happening when a charismatic leader rises on the global stage and convinces the whole world that he is the answer to all their hopes for peace. When he and the nations of this world *(including perhaps my own US government)* sign a global peace treaty and move toward a one-world government, a one-world currency, you will not be taken in. Instead, you and your fellow Bible-believing Christians will be the ones who open up your Bibles and show people how prophecy is being fulfilled in front of their very eyes!

You will warn people that the period of peace is false and will be short-lived. When people start to lose faith in their new peace treaty and wars begin to break out, you will be proven right. You will warn people that global famine is on the way, and again events will prove you right. You will warn them that a global outbreak of disease is going to take out one-fourth of the world's population. You may even serve on a vast medical team, and all the while, you will be pointing people to Jesus!

You will warn them that the antichrist is going to turn first on the Jews and then on the whole world! You will tell your Jewish friends that the nice new temple the world leader has allowed to be built on the Temple Mount in Jerusalem is going to be desecrated, and that the celebrated world leader is going to turn into a monster, set himself up as god, and demand everybody worship him. When it comes to pass, they will see that you are right and seek the truth.

Now when the antichrist does turn, things will get very dicey, but you will take heart, knowing that you are just a few months away from being taken up by Jesus to be with Him in Heaven.

Then at last—you will become part of that rejoicing crowd in Revelation 7. In Revelation 14, the focus is on the 144,000 Jews, but right in the middle of it all a vast throng is heard singing from the Throne Room of Heaven. **That will be you!** The Believers singing in the Throne Room at that time are the same vast crowd of Saints found in the first part of Revelation 19. They are the Bride of Christ who is invited to the Marriage Supper of the Lamb in the middle of Chapter 19. They are the Saints who mount up with Jesus and return with the King of Kings and Lords of Lords at the end of Chapter 19!

Through it all, you will know that you are in your Heavenly Father's hands, and that you can/will do exactly what you were born on this planet to do!

Are you ready for all of that?

How much do I know?

1) True or False: It is impossible to overstress the importance of these verses. 2 Thessalonians 2:1–4: "Now, dear brothers and sisters, let us clarify some things about 1) the coming of our Lord Jesus Christ and 2) how we will be gathered to meet Him. Paul says before that event can happen there must first be a great rebellion [apostasia]. What is the second event that has to happen before: 1) the coming of our Lord Jesus Christ and 2) how we will be gathered to meet Him?

2) Chapter 6 ends with this: "Then everyone—the kings of the earth, the rulers, the generals, the wealthy, the powerful, and every slave and free person—all hid themselves in the caves and among the rocks of the mountains. And they cried to the mountains and the rocks, 'Fall on us and hide us from the face of the one who sits on the throne and from the wrath of the Lamb. <u>For the great day of their (God's) wrath has come.</u>'"
Is this the announcement of the outpoured wrath of God?

3) If the above is not the cosmic upheaval caused by God opening graves and lifting millions of Believers off the planet all at once, then what is it?

You can check your answers beginning on page 243.

Number of correct answers on this page:

True or False: The prophet Daniel tells us with amazing accuracy exactly when the Messiah would arrive. He even predicts that the Anointed One will die, seeming to have accomplished nothing. Isaiah 53 prophesies this One would be pierced for our transgressions, crushed for our iniquities, that his life would be made "an offering for sin." What is really stunning is that the Jews didn't expect him to show up exactly when he did, and that they didn't seem to expect him to be their suffering, dying Savior.

True or False: Jesus said in Matthew 24:36: "no one knows the day or the hour when these things will happen, not even the angels in heaven or the Son himself. Only the Father knows." However, much like in the prophecy above, the Son, the angels, and all Believers are not left completely in the dark because inspired prophets have already given us dozens of clues.

True or False: Daniel's 70th Week begins when the "Time of the Gentiles" ends.

9

The Advent of the antichrist

Many Believers today find the end-time events prophesied in the Unveiling of Revelation disturbing. As we have already noted, that was not the case for the people who originally received John's book. Ethan's friends and family were already being executed for their faith and many more were regularly being thrown in prison. *(That was the reason John was on Patmos.)* Some undoubtedly expected that Jesus' additional unfulfilled prophesies *(Jerusalem's fall; the scattering and return of the Jews)* would quickly unfold—making the arrival of the antichrist and the beginning of the Great Tribulation right around the corner, but they were not afraid! Instead, they were straining with excitement because they knew it meant that Jesus would soon be returning to take them home to Heaven!

    1 Thessalonians 4:15–18: "We tell you this directly from the Lord: We who are still living when the Lord returns will not meet Him ahead of those who have died. *(The Thessalonians were so looking for Jesus' return that when some of them died, they were concerned that the dead would miss the Rapture.)* **For the Lord Himself will come down from heaven with a commanding shout, with the voice of the archangel, and with the trumpet call of God. First, the believers who have died will rise from their graves. Then, together with them, we who are still alive and remain on the earth will be caught up in the**

clouds to meet the Lord in the air. Then we will be with the Lord forever. So encourage each other with these words."

There is nothing disturbing or scary about that!

And that is your future too! In a follow-up letter to the same group of Believers in Thessalonica, Paul added this promise that we already started looking at in 2 Thessalonians:

2 Thessalonians 2:1–5: "Now, dear brothers and sisters, let us <u>clarify some things about the coming of our Lord Jesus Christ and how we will be gathered to meet Him.</u> Don't be so easily shaken or alarmed by those who say that the <u>day of the Lord</u> has already begun. Don't believe them, even if they claim to have had a spiritual vision, revelation, or a letter supposedly from us. Don't be fooled by what they say. <u>For that day will not come until there is a great rebellion against God and the man of lawlessness is revealed</u>—the one who brings destruction. He will exalt himself and defy everything that people call god and every object of worship. He will even sit in the temple of God, claiming that he himself is God. Don't you remember that I told you about all this when I was with you?"

- This puts the "gathering up to meet Jesus, those who are still alive and remain caught up to meet the Lord in the air" event, ***BEFORE*** <u>the</u> <u>Day of the Lord's Wrath</u>! As we saw earlier in these same two "first-to-arrive" Epistles, Paul promises the Thessalonians that Believers will be exempted from God's wrath on satan, the antichrist, and the *purposely rebellious (1 Thessalonians 1:10, 2 Thessalonians 1:9–10).*
- But, **the Day of the Lord's Wrath has to come *AFTER* the antichrist** <u>arrives on the scene</u>, even after the antichrist is exposed as an evil monster, blaspheming the God of Heaven, setting himself up as the god of the earth, demanding worship, and wreaking havoc on all who refuse to worship him, particularly Christians and Jews! We know this

happens halfway through the final seven years because the Bible says so in no uncertain terms.

That all exactly fits what Daniel's prophesied about Jesus' First Advent *(600 years before it happened)*, and the antichrist's first advent *(2600+ years before it happens)*. It's all here, in Daniel 9–12:

> **Daniel 9:25–26: "Now listen and understand! Seven sets of seven plus sixty-two sets of seven [483 years] will pass from the time the command is given to rebuild Jerusalem until a ruler, the Anointed One comes. After this period of sixty-two sets of seven, *the Anointed One will be killed, appearing to have accomplished nothing,* and a ruler will arise whose armies will destroy the city and the Temple."**

Was the Anointed One killed? *(Yes, 483 years later.)* Did a ruler destroy Jerusalem? *(Yes, Roman General Titus—70 AD.)* Did Jesus prophesy that the Jews would then be scattered across the world? Yes! Does the Bible say that they would one day return? Yes. Does the Bible prophetically link the return of the Jews to their Promised Land to the completion of God's prophetic timeline? Yes, it does!

So, assume with me, if you will, that Israel's return as a nation triggered the beginning of the next phase of prophecy:

Sixty-Nine Weeks → Jesus Arrival → Death → Resurrection →
Fall of Jerusalem → Time of the Gentiles→
Return of the Jews → Ezekiel's Battle →
Beginning of Daniel's 70th week! → ??

Let's move on to the next verse of Daniel's prophecy:

> **Daniel 9:27: "The ruler will make a treaty with the people *[of Israel]* for a period of one set of seven, but *after half this time, he will put an end to the sacrifices and offerings. And as a climax to all his terrible deeds, he will set up a sacrilegious object that causes desecration,* until the fate decreed for this defiler is finally poured out on him."**

That's the anti-messiah's advent—it is not happy news, so Daniel continues to prophetically probe for answers:

> **Daniel 12:7–8, 11–12:** *"It will go on for a time, times, and half a time. [3½ years] When the shattering of the holy people has finally come to an end, all these things will have happened. I heard what he said, but I did not understand what he meant. So I asked, 'How will all this finally end, my lord?'*
>
> *"From the time the daily sacrifice is stopped and the sacrilegious object that causes desecration is set up to be worshiped, there will be 1,290 days. [3½ years] And blessed are those who wait and remain until the end of the 1,335 days!"*

- If you are one who believes that prophesy is a confused, hodge-podge mess of stray ideas with no rhyme or reason, you might want to reset your theology right about now.
- We are not sure exactly when the Time of the Gentiles will come to an end, but it will! When it does—the antichrist will appear on this planet right on time!

Follow the "kai eidons"!

If we just let the **"kai eidons"** *(next I saw)* in Chapters 6–18 unfold as a chronological storyline, particularly as they relate to the actions of the antichrist and what is going on in the world around him, it all begins to make sense.

- Remember the critical starting line has to be Israel's returning to and populating the Promised Land. Once they are *there (as they now are)*, something will happen that will lead to such a disruption in world events that will cause the entire world to say, "We need someone who can save us."
- Clearly Israel is not the kind to squeal to an outsider to "come and rescue them." They may be only 8 million people in a world of 7 billion, and they may be crammed onto a stretch of land one-eighth the size of

Florida, but they are as independent as humans get. (That's why so many prophecy students puzzle over the world-saving "beast from the sea." *Revelation 13:1—a non-Jew?*)

- **Why would the Jewish people sign a peace treaty with any Gentile, and then give him such access to their country that 3½ years later he is desecrating the temple he gave them permission to rebuild,** and proclaiming that he is their god, not Yahweh! He demands they worship him and only him, which sends the bulk of them running for the wilderness *(Chapter 12)* while he takes over their country in an attempt to rule the world!
- Something must happen that is serious enough to stop the world in its tracks and make all people *(and governments)* rethink the path forward.
- And that something is [IMO] this prophesied, yet unfulfilled, battle of Ezekiel 38–39. *You are probably tired of hearing about this battle, but to unpack the story, let's examine some parts of this account that we have not yet discussed.*

Adding more pieces to the puzzle!

As previously noted: Magog *(probably Russia)* joins with Persia *(definitely Iran),* Gomer *(almost certainly parts of Turkey),* and other surrounding countries to eliminate Israel once and for all. *(These were actual people-groups in ancient times; we now try to figure out what countries occupy that same geography.)* "Magog" is going to form a multi-nation union that will invade Israel. In the last few years, the Russians have made clear movement toward just such an alliance, strengthening economic trade agreements and signing long-term military contracts. Current Russian President Vladimir Putin has already tried to work out a peace treaty. For their part, Iran has repeatedly stated its desire to wipe Israel off the map.

Although we do not know when the players the Bible specifies will move to fulfill the prophecy of Ezekiel 38–39, *it is certain that at some point they will! And that is where the story of the "rush-to-the-end" truly begins.* Let's take a closer look at some parts of the story that we did not yet dig out:

> Ezekiel 38:18–20: "But this is what the Sovereign LORD says: When Gog invades the land of Israel, My fury will boil over! In My jealousy and blazing anger, I promise a *mighty shaking in the land of Israel* on that day. All living things—the fish in the sea, the birds of the sky, the animals of the field, the small animals that scurry along the ground, and *all the people on earth*—will quake in terror at My presence. Mountains will be thrown down; cliffs will crumble; walls will fall to the earth."

This seems to be the mother of all Middle Eastern earthquakes. It is so "divinely" terrorizing that "all the people on earth will quake at God's presence."

> Ezekiel 38:21–23: "I will summon the sword against you [Gog] on all the hills of Israel, says the Sovereign LORD. *Your men will turn their swords against each other.* I will punish you and your armies with disease and bloodshed. I will send torrential rain, hailstones, fire, and burning sulfur! In this way, I will show My greatness and holiness, and I will make Myself known to all the nations of the world. *Then they will know that I am the LORD!*"

Ezekiel 39:12 prophesies that it will take Israel seven months to bury all the bodies. We have already looked at verse 21–22 from the angle that the world is becoming ripe for a vast spiritual harvest, but let's look at it from a different angle.

- What if this is, in fact, the event that throws the world into such chaos that world banks will crumble, governments will tumble, and oil will become like gold? Right out of the pit of Hell comes satan's incarnate solution to finally taking control of God's beloved children. We're not under any illusions—the Bible calls this one "the son of Hell" specifically empowered by satan *(2 Thessalonians 2:9)*. He comes from "the abyss."

- I want to point out this contrast because it is very important. God shows his power more strongly than at any other time in all of history. People who know nothing of the God of Heaven, who have seen nothing of the real supernatural hand of God, have now seen something that has left them "shocked and awed."

- At this exact moment in history when God is supernaturally showing His great power, the son of satan, his counterfeit messiah, the "*antichristos*" steps onto the world stage as the newly-minted leader of the world.

The war between good and evil that has been raging on Earth since the Garden of Eden has reached the boiling point!

Picture the contrast: On one side, a great spiritual awakening reaching *(according to Jesus' own words)* "every nation, language, people, and tribe."

On the other side, at the same time, a *mass of pure evil in the world led by satan himself and his false messiah is growing like a deadly cancer.* The light of God is shining brighter, to greater numbers than the world has ever known, and the Spirit of God is sweeping thousands, even millions, into the Kingdom of God. As that scene is unfolding, God's arch-enemy is gearing up to snuff out the light with pure darkness because he has reached a point of utter desperation.

- It's got to be bad déjà *vu* for the evil one whose last great campaign to thwart God's plan of redemption is just as certainly going to be foiled by God—just like it was when satan brought Jesus to death on a cross *only to watch in horror as Jesus rose from the dead!*
- The same kind of thing happened during Adolf Hitler's hellish efforts to wipe out every Jew on Earth. Satan tried so hard to make a lie out of end-time prophecy—but only succeeded in advancing the plot as the Jews returned from the ends of the earth to their Promised Land in Israel.
- Satan's grand attempt to wipe out Israel again in the Ezekiel war will be met with the supernatural power of God, and the whole world will awake to the possibility of One True God! For just as satan succeeds in planting his anti-messiah into world leadership, a huge wave of spiritual conversions will sweep across the earth reaching into places where

people had never before heard the name of Jesus, and millions, perhaps even billions, will be saved!

Try to imagine the tension that builds between the two sides: pure righteousness versus pure evil!

We Americans are distressed as we witness, in our own country, the advancing of evil that threatens to snuff out our Christian roots and values.

- In England, once the heartbeat of great revivals and mission outreach, only 4–5% of the population attends church on Sunday.
- In Iraq we've watched a Christian holocaust unfolding. According to the Christian advocacy group, *Open Doors*, there were 1.5 million Christians in Iraq in 2003. Today that number has dwindled to less than 200,000.

Imagine what it will be like when the tension we are witnessing today is all amped up *in a world where pure light is running against pure darkness*. We begin to get a sense of what the first three-and-a-half years of Daniel's 70th week will be like. How exhilarating this time will be for Believers who will feel absolutely alive consumed with eternal purpose. No one will be worrying about whether he has the latest model car or the biggest house!

- *There will be zero room for half-committed Christians;* because on one side of life will be Jesus Christ—and on the other side will be the antichrist! No one will be able to "**be a part-time Christian against a full-time devil!**"

And the choice will get starker and starker:

> **1 John 4:3: "But if someone claims to be a prophet and does not acknowledge the truth about Jesus, that person is not from God. Such a person has** *the spirit of the Antichrist, which you heard is coming into the world and indeed is already here.*"

As we get closer and closer to the End of Time, the stark differences between the two sides are going to become more and more clear. **All the muddiness** about what is "of Christ" and what is "of antichrist" will become increasingly "pure light versus pure darkness." When we get to the midpoint of Daniel's 70th week, the antichrist drops all pretenses, sets himself up as god, and demands the Jews and the whole rest of the world worship him. The same 2 Thessalonians 2 that we were looking at about the antichrist at the beginning of this chapter (vv. 6–7) then tells us: *"the One who is holding him back steps aside,"* and then all hell breaks loose as we enter the second half of Daniel's 70th Week.

Revelation 13:5–8: "Then the beast was allowed to speak great blasphemies against God. And he was given authority to do whatever he wanted for forty-two months. And he spoke terrible words of blasphemy against God, slandering his name and his dwelling—that is, those who dwell in heaven. And the beast was allowed to wage war against God's holy people and to conquer them. And he was given authority to rule over every tribe and people and language and nation. And all the people who belong to this world worshiped the beast. They are the ones whose names were not written in the Book of Life that belongs to the Lamb who was slain before the world was made."

The antichrist comes out with his "Mark of the Beast" in the second half of Daniel's 70th week. I've heard people express concern that a Christian might accidentally take "the mark of the beast." I don't think that is even remotely possible.

Could I accidentally accept the "mark of the beast"?

- By the time the "mark" shows up, what is "of Christ" will be so vivid and what is "of antichrist" will be so blasphemously anti-God that to follow the antichrist will be to turn from God, and purposely walk into the arms of satan and his messiah.
- Sadly, many will do just that!

How much do I know?

1) Why <u>would</u> the Jewish people sign a peace treaty with any Gentile, and then give him such access to their country that 3½ years later he is desecrating the temple he gave them permission to rebuild, and proclaiming that he is god, not Yahweh?

2) Picture the contrast: On one side, a great spiritual awakening, on the other side, at the same time, a mass of pure evil in the world. In what ways are we seeing the beginnings of this in the world today in what the Apostle Paul calls "the spirit of antichrist"?

3) **1 John 1:7: "If we are living in the light, as God is in the light, then we have fellowship with each other** [God and us]**, and the blood of Jesus, his Son, cleanses us from all sin."** How can we Believers today assure that our lives are moving into ever increasing light, not slipping into darkness?

4) **Revelation 13:16–17: "He required everyone—small and great, rich and poor, free and slave—to be given a mark on the right hand or on the forehead. And no one could buy or sell anything without that mark."** What do you think the "mark of the beast" might be and why would the antichrist followers be so ready to accept it?

You can check your answers beginning on page 243.

Number of correct answers on this page:

True or False: The Book of Revelation isn't the story of the antichrist; it is the story of Jesus who cleans the false messiah's clock! The real Christ utterly defeats the antichrist! Jesus is the conquering hero of the book! Satan is not all powerful—God is!

*True or False: When we read the book of Revelation, we are supposed to see the final, all-out, once-and-for-all, conflict that ends with God's finally prevailing and wiping out sin and satan! When the Early Church received the book of Revelation, it ignited them to spread the Gospel all over the civilized world in the next 200 years. It was like a shot of adrenaline straight into their spiritual hearts because finally, for the first time, they had a clear-cut, inspired, Biblical assurance that satan was finally going to be defeated and eternally destroyed. Sin would be conquered, and righteousness would prevail. **God wins and satan loses!***

10

The Battle of the Ages I

I know we've spent some time defining the role of the antichrist—because that's what Revelation does—but I have no desire to make the antichrist seem more important than he is. He only exerts limited influence on this planet for seven years **compared to God's infinite influence** over the whole universe for eternity past and eternity yet to come.

And the whole point of an End Times study and the whole point of the book of Revelation is *not to glorify the power of the antichrist. Rather, it is to show us that **the Real Christ utterly defeats the antichrist!*** The power of the antichrist is built on the *limited power* of satan, which is a spider web of lies, deception, fraud, inaccuracies, false promises, warped thinking, etc.

Satan is not all powerful—God is!

Satan does not have all knowledge—God does! Remember, one of the overarching points that Ethan and the Early Church picked up in their first read-through of their new Unveiling letter was to show them that **satan, and the antichrist, use every single weapon at their disposal to defeat God and HIS MESSIAH; and they completely and dramatically lose** the war against the Creator of the universe and are thrown into the Lake of Fire!

- The climax of the story comes when in Chapters 19–20, the King of Kings and Lord of Lords returns with millions *(perhaps billions)* of His Saints, who in spite of all of satan's efforts to stop them, have been redeemed from their sins and have received their eternal reward. On the other hand, satan, the antichrist, and those who have refused Jesus' salvation are eternally destroyed with a single sentence from Jesus' mouth!

That is what is supposed to stand out to us when we study the book that is called the *"Revelation of Jesus Christ" because:*

Jesus is the conquering hero of the book!

- Our modern formula for storytelling is based on this ultimate good versus evil. We see it in books and movies where the villain seems to have the upper hand in the middle of the movie, but by the end, the hero completely defeats the villain and brings him to justice.
- *But this is not just storytelling.* A cosmic battle IS raging that is far bigger than we humans who are living in this world. We are *supposed* to read our Bible and be able to see beyond the characters and events of any given Bible story to the much larger battle that is going on: **the eternal salvation of humanity (good) versus the eternal destruction of humanity (evil).**
- When we read the book of Revelation, we are supposed to see the final, all-out, once-and-for-all, conflict that ends with God finally winning and wiping out sin and satan! When the Early Church received the book of Revelation, it ignited them to spread the Gospel all over the civilized world in the next 200 years. It was like a shot of adrenaline straight into their spiritual hearts because for the first time, they had a clear-cut, inspired, Biblical assurance that satan was finally going to be defeated and eternally destroyed. Sin would be conquered, and righteousness would prevail. **<u>God wins and satan loses</u>!**

The Early Church was catapulted forward! "With truth like this at our fingertips, we will chance anything. We will walk right into the teeth of personal danger to get this truth out to the rest of the world." And they did! *(Ironically, it's odd that now, some 2,000 years later, many Christians aren't particularly inspired by Jesus' Revelation at all!)*

- We tend to often see this book as if it were about the antichrist versus Christians, when in fact it really isn't! *It's about Jesus versus satan! It's not about the destruction of Believers, it's about the eternal salvation of Believers (billions of them)!*

- Imagine the utter desperation of satan and the antichrist when they realize that even as they are making their last stand to defeat the Creator of the universe *(whom they have fought against for so long)*, that billions of additional people are being swept into Christ's eternal kingdom. *(I have a picture in my head of a huge number—perhaps even a majority—of the people on Earth when the End Times unfold coming to believe in the true God of Heaven and embracing Jesus Christ as the true Messiah, mankind's Redeemer.)*

The vicious cosmic battle between God and satan!

In order to fully understand what is happening at the "End of Time" we really need to be able to link it back to the "beginning of time." What we see ending with a vicious battle between God and satan is the final chapter of what starts at the beginning of the Bible more than 6000 years earlier.

Isaiah says this of satan's original fall:

Isaiah 14:12–17: "How you are fallen from heaven, O shining star, son of the morning! You have been thrown down to the earth, you who destroyed the nations of the world. For you said to yourself, 'I will ascend to heaven and set my throne above God's stars. I will preside on the mountain of the gods far away in the north. I will climb to the highest heavens and be like the Most High.' Instead, you will be brought down to the place of the dead, down to its lowest depths. Everyone there will stare at you and ask, 'Can this be the one

who shook the earth and made the kingdoms of the world tremble? Is this the one who destroyed the world and made it into a wasteland?'"

Over the years, it has become my strong belief that Lucifer (*former archangel, perhaps the original worship leader of Heaven*) rebelled against the God of Heaven. He led a coup involving one-third of the angels *because he was seriously ticked off about one thing*—that Almighty God had the gall to create human beings and elevate them above angels, both in God's personal love for them, and in their planned and promised future. *God gave them "dominion" over all that He had made (Genesis 1:28).*

- Satan became God's sworn enemy. The focus of his wrath, from day one, was to destroy the cherished human race that he felt had stolen his deserved position before God.
- The story of the Fall is not really the story of a snake, a man, a woman, and an apple. It was the massive opening shot in the "ultimate battle of all that Is Good vs. all that is evil."

Genesis 3:15: "And I will put enmity between you and the woman, and between your seed and hers; he will crush your head, and you will strike his heel."

This is not some inconsequential verse of Scripture that we can afford to pass over so we can get to more important matters. It is the **first prophecy in the Bible**, and it is God laying out the rules of engagement *(to satan)* for a war He is going to win!

As the first part of Genesis unfolds, we find two hugely important events—the Flood and the Tower of Babel. Why did God destroy every living person on earth except those in the Ark and start over? The Bible tells us why:

Genesis 6:5: "The LORD observed the extent of human wickedness on the earth, and he saw that everything they thought or imagined was consistently and totally evil."

How in the world did every single person on the earth, except a small handful, become so evil?

- This is no nice children's Bible story about a shipbuilder and a bunch of cute animals. It is a description of where the world was in "the universe-sized conflict between God and satan." Satan, for the second time in 1,500 years, felt that he had beaten God, but "Noah found grace in the eyes of the Lord!"

Was the Tower of Babel the story of some brash guys who had some time on their hands and set out to see how tall a building they could build?

- No! It, also, was a battle in the universe-sized war between God and satan. Noah's great grandson, Nimrod, married a woman named Semiramis. Both of their names are all over ancient literature as the founders of an ancient pagan satanic religion. God did not scatter people all over the world and scramble their languages because they got too carried away with brick and mortar. This was the first attempt by satan to set up a single person as political and spiritual ruler of the world. And *God said, "you are not going to get away with it, because at the extreme other bookend of this thing, we will battle this out, and I am going to destroy you and your false religious systems once and for all!"*

"In the meantime, I am determined to build a People of God, a Bride of Christ, and for that I need people who will fall in love with me with all of their hearts!"

I will send my incarnate Son to fulfill the first prophecy in the Bible *(Genesis 3:15)* and redeem all of humanity from their sins. Then I will raise up a Church of "overcomers" who will spread that Gospel of my salvation to the ends of the earth.

- We can follow satan's ancient pagan religion as it spread across the world. Every place it went it took on a different name based on the local language, but the basic humanity-destroying features were always there. It was part of the Canaanite religion in the Old Testament. It was the "temple of satan" that we find in Revelation Chapters 2 and 3. Roman Emperor Caesar Augustus became the chief priest of this ancient pagan religion, and every Emperor who followed him assumed that role right up to the destruction of the Roman Empire. When Constantine "converted" to Christianity, history says, he maintained his role as high priest of this pagan religion. And some of the early practices that were brought into the Christian Church probably led to a time in history we often call the Dark Ages when Christianity was all but snuffed out!

- It doesn't take a huge amount of spiritual discernment to figure out that what brought the world to the brink of spiritual darkness in those Dark Ages was more than just the fumbling of faulted humans.

- And the Almighty, who already has gone to unimaginable lengths to save humanity, will not tolerate systems of belief that pull people away from what He, in His infinite wisdom, has already established as the Truth.

- *There are not multiple pathways to God in this world* as some truth-deniers like to pretend. There never have been! And throughout all of Scripture, beginning with Adam and Eve, and Noah, and Nimrod at Babel, *every single time somebody said, "I have another pathway," God said, "Oh, no, you don't!"*

- Whenever somebody comes to you and suggests that they have "discovered" an alternate path to God or they've discovered the fact that there is no God or that there really is no absolute truth in this world, know this:

- *That "alternate truth" has an author, and it is always the same author!* Going back all the way to Nimrod, when anything appears on your horizon that pulls you in the opposite direction from the God of Heaven, every single time, you are a small bit player in a universe-sized cosmic battle! **Satan does not care about you. His whole crazed focus is on beating your God!**

Let me show you the explosive conclusion to all this in the Book of Revelation. We'll jump ahead to Chapters 17–18—we'll come back!

> **Revelation 17:1–6: "One of the seven angels said to me, 'Come, I will show you the punishment of the great prostitute. With her the kings of the earth committed adultery, and the inhabitants of the earth were intoxicated with the wine of her adulteries.' I saw a woman sitting on a scarlet beast that was covered with blasphemous names and had seven heads and ten horns. The woman was dressed in purple and scarlet, and was glittering with gold, precious stones and pearls. She held a golden cup in her hand, filled with abominable things and the filth of her adulteries. The name written on her forehead was BABYLON THE GREAT...THE MOTHER OF PROSTITUTES...AND OF THE ABOMINATIONS OF THE EARTH. I saw that the woman was drunk with the blood of God's holy people, the blood of those who bore testimony to Jesus."**

The "Prostitute"—The mother of all false religions!

Does it not make logical sense that this "prostitute" is the *"mother of all false religion"? Her prostitution is not "sexual" but "spiritual."*

- That is a theme that runs heavily through Scripture. Her name, "Babylon the Great," traces back to Nimrod and the Tower of Babel and picks up every single godless religious and political system. The "seven heads and ten horns" are all about her connection with the political systems of this world.

Revelation 18 picks up the theme by bringing the whole corrupt system crashing to the ground.

> **Revelation 18:1–5: "After this I saw another angel coming down from heaven. He had great authority, and the earth was illuminated by his splendor. With a mighty voice he shouted: 'Fallen! Fallen is Babylon the Great!' She has become a dwelling for demons and a haunt for every impure spirit. For all the nations have drunk the**

maddening wine of her adulteries. The kings of the earth committed adultery with her, and the merchants of the earth grew rich from her excessive luxuries. Then I heard another voice from heaven say: 'Come out of her, my people,' so that you will not share in her sins, so that you will not receive any of her plagues; for her sins are piled up to heaven, and God has remembered her crimes."

As God strikes satan and the antichrist, He will fulfill His own prophesies: *"I'm going to bring the whole satan-inspired system of false religion intertwined with arrogant self-serving godless governments to an abrupt and final end!"*

- The last great corruption will be the final system of the antichrist. He will bring about what many have tried and failed. He will set up a one-world government, briefly. He will probably install a one-world currency, and he will accomplish what satan has set out to do since the beginning of time: *He will set up a one-world religion, declare himself to be god,* and demand the world worship him.

- The "anti-christ" will barely get all of these one-world systems in place before *the Almighty swinging arm of the Real Christ will lift the redeemed Believers off the earth into Heaven!* Then, with all of us safely out of the way, God will open the taps of His stored-up wrath against all that His arch-enemy satan has ever done, and He will begin to cleanse evil from every nook and cranny of the planet!

That's the view we are supposed to have when we read the book of Revelation!

That's what got the Early Church so excited—finally they knew the last chapter of the book!

Let's take one last hard look at Daniel's 2,600-year-old prophecy. Daniel paints a vivid picture of the antichrist 2600+ years before he arrives. But **DON'T MISS WHAT DANIEL PROPHESIES NEXT!**

Daniel 7:7–11, 13–14: "After that, in my vision at night I looked, and there before me was a fourth beast—terrifying and frightening and very powerful. It was different from all the former beasts, and it

had ten horns. While I was thinking about the horns, there before me was another horn, a little one, which came up among them; and three of the first horns were uprooted before it. This horn had eyes like the eyes of a human being and a mouth that spoke boastfully. *(That's the anti-christ.)*

"As I looked, thrones were set in place, and the Ancient of Days took His seat. His clothing was as white as snow; the hair of His head was white like wool. His throne was flaming with fire, and its wheels were all ablaze. A river of fire was flowing, coming out from before Him. Thousands upon thousands attended Him.

"Then I continued to watch because of the boastful words the horn was speaking. <u>I kept looking until the beast was slain and its body destroyed and thrown into the blazing fire.</u>

"In my vision at night I looked, and there before me was one like a <u>Son of Man,</u> *[It's the name Jesus constantly chose to call Himself]* coming with the clouds of heaven. *(It's the phrase Jesus often attached to his Second Coming.)*

"He approached the Ancient of Days and was led into His presence. <u>He was given authority, glory and sovereign power; all nations and peoples of every language worshiped Him. His dominion is an everlasting dominion that will not pass away, and His kingdom is one that will never be destroyed.</u>"

Can anybody say, "Hallelujah"?!!

How much do I know?

1) True or False: In the first prophesy in the Bible found in Genesis 3:15, God tells the serpent that Eve's offspring will "crush his head!" Revelation 6–19 is satan finally getting his scaly head crushed!

2) Why do you believe that Lucifer, once perhaps an archangel in heaven, rebelled against God and became his arch-enemy? What event would have been so mind boggling to the evil one that he would slip from the second most powerful position in all of heaven to the most evil being on our planet?

3) True or False: The obvious question arises, "If God made satan and satan is evil, did not God then create evil"? No!—Much like darkness is what is left when all light is sucked out of a room—evil is what is left when all the presence of God is removed!

4) True or False: Satan has known, at least since Daniel 7 (*written 600 years before Jesus was born*), that the "Son of Man" would one day be led before the Ancient of Days and be given authority, glory and sovereign power; all nations and peoples of every language would worship Him. His dominion would be an everlasting dominion!

You can check your answers beginning on page 243.

Number of correct answers on this page:

Eve's "offspring" has been "crushing satan's head" rather regularly since the beginning of time. We often notice satan's short-term wins, but the reality is that over the long term the evil one keeps losing to God over and over and over! Satan knows he is prophesied to completely lose in the end! All of God's prophesies have always been 100% fulfilled. So what motivates satan to keep on trying to beat God?

*There seems to be a major turning point when an angel shouts in **Revelation 10:7**: "__There will be no more delay__! **When the seventh angel blows his trumpet, God's mysterious plan will be fulfilled,**" and the 24 elders are saying to God in Revelation 11:17: "**Now you have assumed your great power and have begun to reign!**" What is the connection? What is happening?*

*True or False: The point of The Unveiling is not to glorify the efforts of satan and the antichrist, but to show us that d*espite how hard the antichrist tries, he still loses.

11

The Battle of the Ages II

Imagine what is going on in the antichrist's mind after the Rapture of the Saints. He and satan have poured every ounce of their combined evil energy into stopping the plan of God. They know what God's plan is because satan got his first read of this book we are studying over 1,900 years ago. He has had 31,124 verses of Scripture rubbed in his face for centuries.

- *8,352 are prophetic, speaking of events to come.*
- *6,312 verses have already been fulfilled, exactly as predicted. (Satan knows that. He has lived through every single claw-biting moment of it.)*
- *2,040 verses are yet to be fulfilled. (He knows that too!)*

Although satan is well aware of the final count, he is the ultimate narcissist. He believes he is right and still thinks he's going to win!

- Jesus walloped the evil one by incarnating in human form, living a sinless life in spite of satan's temptations, dying for the sins of humanity, and then rising victorious over death and hell and the grave, crushing the evil plans of satan. *Did you know that Jesus' life, death, and resurrection suddenly fulfilled as many as 353 more prophesies!*
- Think about this from satan's perspective. He not only lost the biggest battle to date in the "ultimate battle between good and evil," but he had to watch God tick 353 more prophesies off the list! He also has to know,

all too well, that toward the end of God's list of prophesies, he, satan, gets thrown for all of eternity into the Lake of Fire!

- Try to grasp the desperation in the evil one and eventually in his antichrist! Isaiah defines satan as insanely arrogant and narcissistic. He is still convinced that in spite of losing over, and over, and over, and over again, somehow, he is going to pull this thing out of the bag. But, even the most arrogant being, if they get thrown against the wall often enough, will eventually get an inkling that things may not end well!

God is Winning! lucifer is losing!

I illustrate again with Adolf Hitler. He was about as close to an antichrist as anyone we have seen in recent history. He, as satan's representative, set out to kill every Jew on the planet, and was halfway successful. I'm sure in satan's narcissistic mind he may have thought, *"Well I didn't quite stop God's plan, but I sure slowed it down for a few hundred years."*

- It is supposed to strike us as a stunning point of history and a much bigger point in the Ultimate Battle between Good and evil: ***From the day Hitler died until the Nation of Israel was reborn was just 3 years and 2 weeks—36½ months—1,110 days! GOD WINS—lucifer loses!***

Now—try to imagine what satan's mindset will be during the last seven years of human history!

- Back in ancient times, satan seemed to have free reign because most people were pagans. Except for a brief time right after Creation and again right after Noah's flood, the majority of this planet's inhabitants were not God-followers.

- The spread of Christianity after Jesus' resurrection, the pagan-transforming Early Church burning a wide swath of righteousness across the world, and Jesus' prediction that "the gates of hell would not prevail against it" seemed to be pushing back the powers of darkness. But again, in the Dark Ages, the early blinding light of Christianity was all but snuffed out.

- Then roaring into the pages of history the Protestant Reformation and the Catholic Counter-Reformation came, followed by the world-wide Missionary Movement spawned from England, Europe, and the United States, and then the great revivals of the 19th and 20th centuries. *Satan must have truly felt like he was losing his grip.* **He was!**

- Lately, the tide of the Ultimate Battle *(in the West)* seems to have shifted in satan's favor, starting in Europe and now in America. The Apostle Paul prophesied to the Thessalonians that before the Man of Sin appears there will be a "great falling away" *(2 Thessalonians. 2:3).* Clearly, a "falling away" wouldn't happen among unbelievers—that prophesied **falling away happens in the Church**! No doubt once again satan feels that he is on a roll to ultimate victory. He is not!

We are supposed to see the first part of "Daniel's 70th week" *(the first half of the last seven years)* as satan laying the ground-work for his last great battle to conquer humanity's soul, and in his sin-blinded mind, the final humiliation of Creator God. However, as satan is narcissistically going about his evil little plans, God is carefully setting the stage to carry out the greatest "spiritual harvest" of all time!

- Do you see the punch and bigger counter punch? As satan is unleashing his final strategy to wipe the earth clean of Jesus-followers, God is counter-punching with a world-wide revival that causes multiplied millions of people to turn from satan and embrace Jesus' gift!

"The Great Tribulation!"

- When the tide is clearly shifting against satan *(and his antichrist)*, he rips off the mask and declares all-out war. **That is the Great Tribulation!** It's not that satan is winning. He is like the boxer whose opponent is connecting virtually every blow, and he fights back like a maniac, knowing the knockout blow could be right around the corner.
- Then to cap it all off, as he is swinging wildly at everyone the Creator God passionately loves, God steps in and raptures billions of them off the planet and into His presence, leaving satan flailing wildly in the air with no one to connect with!
- Immediately after **multiplied millions/billions of Believers leave the planet**, comes this:

> **Revelation 10:1–3, 5–7: "Then [Kai Eidon] I saw another mighty angel [allon aggelon] coming down from heaven, surrounded by a cloud, with a rainbow over his head. His face shone like the sun, and his feet were like pillars of fire. He stood with his right foot on the sea and his left foot on the land. And he gave a great shout like the roar of a lion. And when he shouted, the seven thunders answered. Then the angel I saw standing on the sea and on the land raised his right hand toward heaven. He swore an oath [allegiance] in the name of the One who lives forever and ever, who created the heavens and every-thing in them, the earth and everything in it, and the sea and everything in it. He said, 'There will be no more delay. When the seventh angel blows his trumpet, God's mysterious plan will be fulfilled. It will happen just as he announced it to his servants the prophets.'"**

This is a very important moment! Everyone needs to follow closely the "kai eidon" storyline. The "angel" is relaying a *divine proclamation. There will be no more delay!*

> **1 Corinthians 15:23–24: "But there is an order to this resurrection: Christ was raised as the first of the harvest; then all who belong to Christ will be raised when He comes back [Rapture].**

__After that the end will come,__ **when He will turn the Kingdom over to God the Father, having destroyed every ruler and authority and power.**"

Now couple that with the phrase, "*There will be no more delay!*" And then add this from Revelation 11:

> **Revelation 11:16–17: "The twenty-four elders sitting on their thrones before God fell with their faces to the ground and worshiped him. And they said, 'We give thanks to you, Lord God, the Almighty, the one who is and who always was, *for now you have assumed your great power and have begun to reign.*'"**

"Time's up—no more delay!"

Once again, imagine this from the standpoint of satan and his antichrist. Billions of those whom the antichrist was trying to conquer have just been lifted off the planet. This "mighty messenger" appears with a new proclamation: **"Time's up—no more delay!"**

- There is a massive thundering chorus of voices from Heaven amid the final trumpet sound, saying: "The kingdoms of this world *(that is the antichrist)* have become the kingdoms of our Lord and of His Christ" *so get out of the way, Jesus is in charge now!*
- **Chapters 12 and 13 are a parenthesis**—( )—in the forward moving chronology as Jesus fills in some wider gaps in the storyline. Chapter 12, [IMO] is a **flashback** to the fall of satan and what led him to this End of Times. The "woman and her son" in Chapter 12 are Israel and Jesus. *(We'll look at that)* and then Chapter 13, as we have already studied, fills in more information about the antichrist.
- Again, the point of The Unveiling is not to glorify the efforts of satan and the antichrist, but to show us that despite how hard the antichrist tries, **he still loses!**

And that is where *(as we might expect if 12–13 are a parenthesis)* the next **"kai eidon"** in Chapter 14 begins. Here's how it starts:

> **Revelation 14:1–3: "Then I saw (kai eidon) the Lamb standing on Mount Zion, and with Him were 144,000 who had His name and His Father's name written on their foreheads. And I heard a sound from heaven like the roar of mighty ocean waves or the rolling of loud thunder. It was like the sound of many harpists playing together. This great choir sang a wonderful new song in front of the throne of God and before the four living beings and the twenty-four elders. No one could learn this song except the 144,000 who had been redeemed from the earth."**

Who is this Lamb? *There is only one Lamb,* the same Lamb we read about in Revelation 5 who was found worthy to break the seals and open the scroll. Now He is standing on Mount Zion. *There is only one place on Earth or in Heaven called Mount Zion* and that is, in Jerusalem.

- *Jesus Himself is on Earth,* in Jerusalem, *after* He has returned to rapture the Saints and *before* He comes back in His triumphal return! Trying to make it say anything else misses the storyline. This is another "kai eidon" *(and I watched or beheld)* moment, and if you take it quite literally, Jesus is standing on the Temple Mount, and He is not alone! He is surrounded by "the 144,000." So, who in the world are the 144,000?

- Back in Chapter 7, *(just before the rapture happens ☺)*, in the first part of that amazing chapter, we find "another angel" [*allon aggelon*] appearing with the seal of the living God, and he seals 12,000 Jews from each tribe, 144,000 in all. They had *"His name, and His Father's name, written on their foreheads" (Revelation 14:1).* This shows that these people are not only God-following Jews, but Jews who have completely embraced Jesus as their Messiah!

Revelation 14:4: "They have kept themselves as pure as virgins, following the Lamb wherever he goes. They have been purchased

from among the people on the earth as a 'first fruits' offering to God and to the Lamb."

These Jews have not only been purchased (redeemed) but are the **first-fruits of many more to come!** There is [IMO] going to be a vast secondary revival among the Jewish people, and notice where this is on the timeline—during the dreadful "Day of the Lord's Wrath." These 144,000 are "sealed" from the antichrist—he cannot kill them! They are alive at the end of the seven years, and God goes into overdrive protecting His newly converted chosen people—probably lots and lots of them!

- Amazing! *144,000 Christian Jewish evangelists* who are teaching fearlessly all over Israel. Add to that the constant preaching *of "two witnesses" (we'll meet them in the next chapter)* who preach Jesus' salvation right to the very end. **And the antichrist cannot do a thing about it!** God is pouring out His wrath on satan and the antichrist and on all who have willfully chosen to follow him. Yet, even as the "dreadful Day of the Lord" unfolds, *a new secondary vast spiritual reaping, the great End Times revival, marches on!*

- And there is yet another amazing thing recorded here:

- Revelation 14:6–7: "And I saw another angel flying through the sky, carrying the eternal Good News to proclaim to the people who belong to this world—to every nation, tribe, language, and people. 'Fear God,' he shouted. 'Give glory to Him. For the time has come when He will sit as judge. Worship Him who made the heavens, the earth, the sea, and all the springs of water.'"

- **God appoints an "evangelistic angel"** whose job it is to move across the earth pointing those remaining non-Jews who have not followed the antichrist or accepted his mark in the direction of Jesus and His salvation. Even as the antichrist, in this second half of Daniel's 70th week, is hunting down any who would embrace faith in Jesus as the true Christ, *God sends His special angelic evangelist to spread the Gospel around the world one more time.* It's yet another blow to satan in God's "Ultimate Victory"!

How much do I know?

1) Yes or No: Revelation 14 seems to suggest that there are 144,000 *redeemed Jews* who have "His name, and His Father's name, written on their foreheads," who "have been purchased from among the people on the earth as a 'first fruits' offering to God and to the Lamb." They seem to be spending their time evangelizing during the "Great Tribulation" and the term "first-fruits" would seem to suggest that they are evangelizing other Jews.

2) Yes or No: 1 Corinthians 15:23–24 says there is an order to this resurrection: 1) Christ was raised as the first of the harvest, 2) *all who belong to Christ will be raised when He comes [Rapture]*, 3) *after that the end will come. He will turn the Kingdom over to God the Father, having destroyed every ruler and authority and power. That doesn't tell us exactly when the "rapture" takes place, but it does put the rapture ahead of Revelation 11:17: "now you have assumed your great power and have begun to reign" statement.*

3) Even as the Great Tribulation rages, God has (*according to Revelation 14:6–7)* "another angel flying through the sky, carrying the eternal Good News to proclaim to the people who belong to this world—to every nation, tribe, language, and people." What do you think the response of the antichrist is to this guy?

You can check your answers beginning on page 243.

Number of correct answers on this page:

True or False: When God created Adam and Eve, he gave them "dominion" over all creation. But when they fell, they transferred that dominion to satan! Why else would Paul have called him "the god of this world," the "prince of the power of the air?" When Jesus died and rose victorious over sin and satan, he made a "public spectacle of satan" [and his cohorts] by his triumph over them through the cross (Colossians 2:15). The "wrestling back" of the "dominion of the earth" seems to be happening right here in Revelation.

Daniel 12:11–12 says: "From the time the daily sacrifice is stopped and the sacrilegious object that causes desecration is set up to be worshiped, there will be 1,290 days. (What? I thought the second half was 1260 days long?) And blessed are those who wait and remain until the end of the 1,335 days!" What do you think is taking place during this mysterious prophesied 30-day addition, and a second 45-day addition?

12

The Lamb Becomes King of Kings I

There is a distinct point in the storyline of Revelation *when "the Lamb becomes the King of Kings."* We refer to Jesus as the King of Kings often, and that is true in an overarching general way, because He was/is indeed the pre-incarnate God of the universe. It is also true in a personal way because He is the "King of Kings and Lord of Lords" in the heart of every Believer. It has been a bit more difficult to apply that truth literally to, say, present day Syria, or Egypt, or the Sudan where truly evil people have been hunting down Christians and executing them. What do you say to those persecuted brothers and sisters— "Take courage, people of God, Jesus is on the throne and reigns as King of Kings and Lord of Lords?"

- Technically, *that defining event is yet to come* according to Revelation. So far, Jesus has presented himself to this world as the Lamb of God come to take away the sins of the world, the suffering Savior, the ultimate sacrifice for the sins of us all. He even limited His control of the universe so satan and his followers could put Him to death.

Philippians 2:6–11: "Who, though he was in the form of God, did not count equality with a thing to be grasped, but emptied himself, by taking the form of a servant, being born in the likeness of men. And being found in human form, he humbled himself by becoming

obedient to the point of death, even death on a cross. Therefore God has highly exalted him and bestowed on him the name that is above every name, so that at the name of Jesus every knee should bow, in heaven and on earth and under the earth, and every tongue confess that Jesus Christ is Lord, to the glory of God the Father."

Then Jesus defeated death by rising triumphant from the grave, making a "public spectacle of satan" and his cohorts (*who really thought they had defeated the God of the universe*) by triumphing over them through the cross (*Colossians 2:15*). Jesus wrestles back the "dominion" that Adam and Eve had transferred to satan when they fell making the evil one what the Apostle Paul calls, "the god of this world," and the "prince of the power of the air." *Jesus broke the stranglehold satan held on the hearts of mankind!*

- That is not the same thing as saying that Jesus "took charge of the earth" reducing satan to utter impotence. **That has not happened yet, but it will!** When, when will it happen? When will Jesus take complete charge? *When will "the kingdoms of this world become the kingdoms of our Lord, and of His Christ"?*

   Revelation 11:15–17: "The *seventh angel sounded his trumpet,* and there were loud voices in heaven, which said: '*The kingdom of the world has become the kingdom of our Lord and of his Messiah, and He will reign for ever and ever.*' And the twenty-four elders, who were seated on their thrones before God, fell on their faces and worshiped God, saying: 'We give thanks to you, Lord God Almighty, the One who is and who was, *because you have taken your great power and have begun to reign.*'"

(*See if you can put your finger on the chart where this takes place.*)

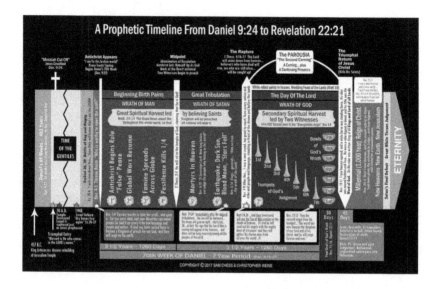

In fact, the timing makes sense of a prophecy that Daniel wrote 2,600 years earlier:

> Daniel 12:11–12: "From the time the daily sacrifice is stopped and the sacrilegious object that causes desecration is set up to be worshiped, there will be 1,290 days. [30 extra days for the bowl judgments to be poured out] And blessed are those who wait and remain until the end of the 1,335 days!" [45 more days for the Battle of Armageddon to take place—for Jesus to return, destroy satan, and throw the antichrist and false prophet into the Lake of Fire, and satan into the pit!] *Note the big white descending arrow on your chart.*

When we get deep into these last 1290 days, the pent-up wrath of God begins to rain down on this earth (The Seven Trumpet Judgments). Then, during the **last 30 days**, the "Bowl Judgments" are the absolute and utter destruction of this sin-soaked planet.

- *I have no intention of focusing heavily on that last 1335 days of "time" as we know it. For the vast majority of those final days we believers will be in heaven with Jesus! There will still be plenty of "brand new Jesus-followers" on earth during the chaos—the fruit of the evangelism of the 144,000, the two*

*witnesses, the evangelistic angel—but you and I won't be here on day 1200!
We'll be at the Marriage Supper of the Lamb! (Hang on, we're getting there.)*

It is so important to remember this perspective: **Revelation is not about punishing Believers; it is about punishing sin and satan!** *Revelation is the story of the eternal salvation of Believers and the eternal destruction of satan, the antichrist, sin itself, and all the effects of the curse of sin on this earth.* Revelation is the story of eternal triumph for God and for all who chose to follow Him!

• Now, with the raptured Saints securely in Heaven, *God does begin to pour out His wrath* against satan, and the antichrist, and all who have stubbornly resisted Him. We are, for a few pages, going to slip back to Chapter 8 to briefly unfold the scene of the blowing trumpets.

"The Seven Trumpets!"

Only those who have openly rebelled against their *Creator (along with those who accept Jesus Christ during the final Day of God's Wrath)* will endure the following horrors *(This comes after the Believers have been "raptured" in Chapter 7!)*:

> **Revelation 8:7–10: "The *first angel blew his trumpet*, and hail and fire mixed with blood were thrown down on the earth. One-third of the earth was set on fire, one-third of the trees were burned, and all the green grass was burned. Then the *second angel blew his trumpet*, and a great mountain of fire was thrown into the sea. One-third of the water in the sea became blood, one-third of all things living in the sea died. Then the *third angel blew his trumpet*, and a great star fell from the sky, burning like a torch. It fell on one-third of the rivers and on the springs of water."**

We don't know how long it takes these events to unfold, but the language indicates that it is not immediate—perhaps months. The antichrist is no longer strutting around demanding this and demanding that. Any pretense that he is in charge of world circumstances is clearly just bluster, because the circumstances of the world are completely out of his control. **They are now firmly in God's control!**

- Nobody is looking at the latest commodity prices or endorsing a political candidate. This is no longer something a "think tank" can get together and solve because nobody on Earth has any control over the source.
- This is clearly no longer "wrath from human to human," or "wrath from the antichrist toward believing humanity." This wrath is all coming from above. *Something "up there" is causing it!*
- There are still people, perhaps a lot of them, who have not followed the antichrist. *People are still very much redeemable!* Just because God is raining down judgment on a sinful Earth does not mean He has given up on saving people. In fact as we read Chapters 8–18, much of which deals with this dark section called "the Day of God's Wrath," **we continually see God all over the place trying to rescue every last person before it is too late!**
- Even as we read through the trumpet judgments, we get a sense of God saying: "Wake up! See where all this is coming from!" *There is a God in Heaven!* And that God is reaching out to you trying to save you from a doomed world!
- Some might shrug and say, "Where do you come up with the notion of a compassionate God during a time in the Bible when He is clearly all wrath and judgment?"

"The Two Witnesses"

We find the answer, amid the bellowing of Trumpets in Chapter 11. It's part of the message of the "strong angel with the little scroll." *(Revelation 10)* We can get so caught up with the angel and his "there will be no more delay" message, and John "eating the mini-scroll," that we forget to look at what was actually written in the scroll. Read Chapter 11—it's the prediction of "two witnesses."

Revelation 11:3, 5: "'I will give power to my two witnesses, and they will be clothed in burlap and will prophesy for those 1,260

**days.' If anyone tries to harm them, fire flashes from their mouths
and consumes their enemies."**

The question we constantly hear asked about these two witnesses is: *Who
are they?* The far more important questions should be: *What in the world are
they doing?* What is the divine purpose of these two witnesses? Who are they
witnessing to? What are they witnessing about?

Can there be any question? According to the 1260-day figure, they start at
the midpoint of the seven-year period and continue witnessing (*and breathing
fire*) right up to the end (*up until, and including, the 30-day and 45-day extension
periods*).

- So, all during this "Day of the Lord's Wrath" these two guys are pointing
  everyone who will listen in God's direction—it's not that they need a
  lot of help proving God's existence. (*All this is happening right as the
  "trumpets" are blowing.*)

**Revelation 8:12: "Then the *fourth angel blew his trumpet*, and
one-third of the sun was struck, and one-third of the moon, and
one-third of the stars, and they became dark."**

**Revelation 9:1–6: "Then the *fifth angel blew his trumpet*, and I
saw a star that had fallen to earth from the sky, smoke poured out
as though from a huge furnace. Then locusts came from the smoke
and descended on the earth, and they were given power to sting like
scorpions, but only the people who did not have the seal of God on
their foreheads. They were told not to kill them but to torture them
for five months with pain like the pain of a scorpion sting. In those
days people will seek death but will not find it. They will long to die,
but death will flee from them!"**

**Revelation 9:13–15: "Then the *sixth angel blew his trumpet*, and
I heard a voice speaking from the four horns of the gold altar that
stands in the presence of God. And the voice said to the sixth angel**

who held the trumpet, 'Release the four angels who are bound at the great Euphrates River.' Then the four angels who had been prepared for this hour and day and month and year were turned loose to kill one-third of all the people on earth."

Let me say again that I believe many people, even at this late date, will not have embraced the antichrist and taken his "mark." The antichrist at this point is probably not focused on running around the world tracking down people to brand. He will be busy with a world that is crumbling all around him.

- There is a little phrase here in Revelation 9:4 that is probably a lot more important than we give it credit for:
- The locusts of the fifth trumpet could only touch *"those who did not have the seal of God on their foreheads."*
- What if the "protected ones" are a larger number than we tend to imagine? *(What if it's all who embrace Jesus?)*

What is the "sheep and goat judgment"?

- By the time we get to the "sheep and goat judgment" described by Jesus in Matthew 25, there are, of course, a lot of "goats," but there are also *a lot of "sheep"! (These people had to have become "sheep" after the rapture!)*

Matthew 25:31–34: "When the Son of Man comes in His glory, and all the angels with Him, He will sit on His glorious throne. All the nations will be gathered before Him, and He will separate the people one from another as a shepherd separates the sheep from the goats. He will put the sheep on His right and the goats on His left. Then the King will say to those on His right, 'Come, you who are blessed by My Father; take your inheritance, the kingdom prepared for you since the creation of the world.'"

These seem to be the people who make their way through the last part of the seven years and have rejected the anti-christ, completely embracing Jesus the true

Christ. These are the people who move right on into the 1,000-year millennial reign of Christ. **They, in fact, must be the ones whom all the returning Saints (all of us Believers) will "reign over"!** (*We're coming to that.*)

In the same breath, understand that *the wretched sin-filled beast-followers are not going to populate the Millennium* in any way, shape, or form. So, what happens to them?

> **Matthew 25:41, 46: "Then he will say to those on His left, 'Depart from me, you who are cursed, into the eternal fire prepared for the devil and his angels.' Then they will go away to eternal punishment, but the righteous to eternal life."**

God continues to bring in a great final harvest!

The important point here is there is **going to be a bunch of late Tribulation sheep!** God is going to bring a great final harvest in, even as He is raining down judgment on satan, sin, and the antichrist!

And let's not forget this "evangelist angel" in Chapter 14. He's one of the "Day of Wrath" harvesters.

> **Revelation 14:6–7: "And I saw another angel flying through the sky, *carrying the eternal Good News to proclaim to the people who belong to this world—to every nation, tribe, language, and people.* 'Fear God,' he shouted. 'Give glory to Him. For the time has come when He will sit as judge. Worship Him who made the heavens, the earth, the sea, and all the springs of water.'"**

• This "evangelistic angel" who is flying around through the sky—is preaching to who? Not the raptured Saints—they're in Heaven. The flame-breathing witnesses have their hands full *(around Jerusalem),* so as we already noticed, God adds an angel who speaks from the sky *to every nation, tribe, language, and people!*

The antichrist by this time will have his plate very full of locusts and such, and his preoccupation seems to focus on the Jews. As an extension of satan, his final obsession is on God's chosen people. Meanwhile, Mr. Evangelistic Angel is travelling the world, at warp speed, proclaiming that the Good News is still available. And, what do you know, he even has two angelic partners. Watch this:

Revelation 14:8: "*A second angel followed* and said, 'Fallen! Fallen is Babylon the Great,' which made all the nations drink the maddening wine of her adulteries." (*This refers to the toppling of fake religious systems described in Chapters 17–18.*)

Revelation 14:9–12: "*A third angel followed them* and said in a loud voice: 'If anyone worships the beast and its image and receives its mark on their forehead or on their hand, they, too, will drink the wine of God's fury, which has been poured full strength into the cup of His wrath. "They will be tormented with burning sulfur in the presence of the holy angels and of the Lamb. And the smoke of their torment will rise for ever and ever. There will be no rest day or night for those who worship the beast and its image, or for anyone who receives the mark of its name.' *This calls for patient endurance on the part of the people of God who keep His commands and remain faithful to Jesus.*" (*Did you see that—these people were saved after the Rapture!*)

One more huge thing is occurring during this same time. We've discussed the 144,000 Jews who were sealed with God's protective seal at the exact same time that Jesus raptures His Saints in Revelation 7. Their task is not to leave Earth in the Rapture, but to stay here during the final days of Daniel's 70th week.

Revelation 14:1: "Then I looked, and there before me was the Lamb, standing on Mount Zion, and with Him 144,000 who *had His name and His Father's name written on their foreheads.*"

- *Remember we noticed that, at some point, the Lamb (Jesus) is going to be back here on Earth, on Mount Zion, during the Day of Wrath having a heart-to-heart (instruction giving time) with the sealed 144,000 (Jews).*

Revelation 14:4: "They have kept themselves as pure as virgins, following the Lamb wherever He goes. They have *been purchased from among the people on the earth as a 'firstfruits' offering to God and to the Lamb.*"

What does "first-fruits" mean?

The fact that the Bible says they are the "first-fruits" suggests *(from the biblical principle that giving first fruits brings in a large harvest)* that **there are more to come**—many, many more to come. In fact, the Bible seems to say that the antichrist becomes pathologically fascinated with finding these wretched Messiah-following Jews–and devotes all his energy on tracking them down and wiping them out.

Now, "move forward" in the story by "returning to" the *"woman and the dragon"* in Chapter 12:

- **Wait a minute Chess!** You keep telling us that the "kai eidons" unfold as a chronological storyline, but you move us from the antichrist in 13, to the collapse of the corrupt religious system in 17–18, then "on" to the blowing trumpets in 8–9. Then we reverse "back" to the 144,000 in Chapter 14, and now you top it off with the woman and the dragon in Chapter 12. Are you still trying to say this is one unfolding story? Yes, yes I am.

- It doesn't unfold like a novel, but the "kai eidons" *(listed on page 64)* cannot be interpreted as random events. The Bible, even in the Gospels and Epistles uses parenthesis ( ), passages to give more information about what is unfolding. Just because God sets aside chapter 13 to discuss the antichrist in detail—doesn't mean the "counterfeit Jesus" isn't there during the trumpets blowing in 8 and 9—he is! Chapter 12 gives the story of the woman *(Israel)* and the dragon *(satan)*. It is a ( ).

- The Chapter 12 ( ) goes back to satan's rebellion, and Adam's fall—up to the birth of Jesus, and on through his ascension back to heaven. It doesn't conclude until the end of Daniel's 70th week. *When a modern novel or movie does a parenthesis, it doesn't mean the story line has stopped!*

Revelation 12:5–6: "She [Israel] gave birth to a son (Jesus) who was to rule all nations with an iron rod. And her child was snatched away from the dragon and was caught up to God and to his throne. *(Add 2000+ years)* **And** *(then)* **the woman fled into the wilderness, where God had prepared a place to care for her for 1,260 days."**

Picture this: The antichrist is right there in Jerusalem where he is going to be until Jesus victoriously returns and plants His feet on the Mount of Olives. The planet by this time has been largely reduced to rubble, and the *30 days of seven bowl judgments have not even started yet.*

The antichrist is probably stuck in Jerusalem with 144,000 people sharing Jesus all day, every day, and the two "witnesses" who are also proclaiming Jesus in Jerusalem in between fire blasts; and there is nothing the antichrist can do to slow down any of them. Finally, he manages to kill the "witnesses" *(Revelation 11:7–11)* only to see them rise back to life three-and-a-half days later! Because he can't eliminate the 144,000, he goes after their Jewish converts.

Revelation 12:13–14: "When the dragon realized that he had been thrown down to the earth, he pursued the woman who had given birth to the male child. But *she was given two wings like those of a great eagle so she could fly to the place prepared for her in the wilderness. There she would be cared for and protected from the dragon for a time, times, and half a time"* (3½ years—1260 days).

- God does some kind of miraculous thing to preserve all the millions (?) of Jewish converts right through the end of the "bowl judgments." These become part of that great group of "sheep" that are separated from the "goats" into the Great Millennial reign of Jesus here on this earth!

Revelation 12:15–17: "*Then the dragon tried to drown the woman with a flood of water* **that flowed from his mouth. But the earth helped her by opening its mouth and swallowing the river that gushed out from the mouth of the dragon. And the dragon was angry**

at the woman and declared war against the rest of her children—all who keep God's commandments and maintain their testimony for Jesus."

The "anti-Jesus" is running out of steam!

- The problem is, the antichrist and satan himself, are running out of gas. They have nothing left. **God, on the other hand, has infinite energy for the battle!** We are arriving at the end of the 1260-day "Wrath of God" on the earth.

> **Revelation 11:15–17:** *"The seventh angel sounded his trumpet, and there were loud voices in heaven, which said: 'The kingdom of the world has become the kingdom of our Lord and of His Messiah [Christ], and He will reign for ever and ever.'* And the twenty-four elders, who were seated on their thrones before God, fell on their faces and worshiped God saying: 'We give thanks to You, Lord God Almighty, the One who is and who was, *because You have taken Your great power and have begun to reign.'"*

And with that, "the final seven bowls of judgment" come crashing down on sin and satan in the span of 30 days! *(The last 30 days of human time.)* All the armies of the world begin gathering around Jerusalem for the **final Battle of Armageddon**. The battle rages, "blood flows to the height of a horse's bridle."

- Do not miss what we've been stressing, that at this time there are still people all over the world—perhaps millions of them—who have embraced Jesus as their Savior and millions of Jews are tucked away in the "wilderness" awaiting the day of God's final redemption.
- **Jesus victoriously wins—satan miserably loses!!!**

How much do I know?

1) True or False: If a Jesus-follower refuses to take the "mark of the beast" and the antichrist has said no one can buy food without it; that means that everyone on the planet without the "mark of the beast" will starve to death? If not, why not?

2) Did you notice after the flying evangelistic angel, there is a second and third angel? The third is warning in Revelation 14:9–12: "'If anyone worships the beast and its image and receives its mark on their forehead or on their hand, they, too, will drink the wine of God's fury, which has been poured full strength into the cup of His wrath. They will be tormented with burning sulfur in the presence of the holy angels and of the Lamb. And the smoke of their torment will rise for ever and ever. There will be no rest day or night for those who worship the beast and its image, or for anyone who receives the mark of its name.' *This calls for patient endurance on the part of the people of God who keep His commands and remain faithful to Jesus.*" *Is this not saying his message is for the "people of God" who have rejected the "mark" and are "keeping God's commands" and "remaining faithful to Jesus?" How can this be? Aren't all the Christians supposed to be already "raptured" or martyred?*

You can check your answers beginning on page 243.

Number of correct answers on this page:

True or False: The following is a description of the "rapture." 1 Thessalonians 4:16–17: "For the Lord Himself will come down from heaven with a commanding shout, with the voice of the archangel, and with the trumpet call of God. First, the believers who have died will rise from their graves. Then, together with them, we who are still alive and remain on the earth will be caught up in the clouds to meet the Lord in the air. Then we will be with the Lord forever."

Jesus himself describes this exact same event in Matthew 4:30–31: "They will see the Son of Man coming on the clouds of heaven with power and great glory. And He will send out His angels with the mighty blast of a trumpet, and they will gather His chosen ones from all over the world—from the farthest ends of the earth and heaven." But notice that Jesus says this event follows verses 29–30: "Immediately after the anguish [tribulation] of those days, the sun will be darkened, the moon will give no light, the stars will fall from the sky, and the powers in the heavens will be shaken. [That's the same as Seal Six in Revelation 6:12–14] And then at last, the sign that the Son of Man is coming will appear in the heavens, and there will be deep mourning among all the peoples of the earth. And they will see the Son of Man coming on the clouds of heaven." When does Jesus himself say His "rapture" of the saints is going to have taken place?

13

The Lamb Becomes King of Kings II

We have been unfolding the End Times story from the opening of the seven seals, beginning in Revelation 6, right up through the pouring out of the Trumpet Judgments and then comes the final flurry of earth-shattering Bowl Judgments ending in Revelation 18.

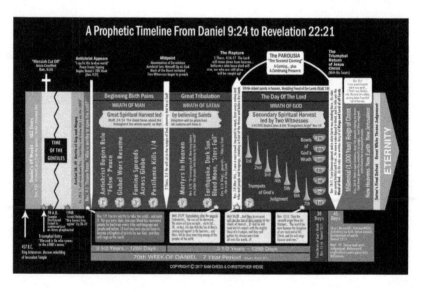

I hope our minds are not locked on "the sea becoming blood," but rather on the many wonderful positive high notes surrounding this final seven-year period:

(1) The amazing glimpse into the Throne Room of Heaven (Revelation 4) is awesome!

(2) The Lamb who is found worthy to open the seven seals (Revelation 5) is gripping!

(3) The Great Spiritual Harvest during the first five-plus years is beyond exciting!

(4) The vast throng—too great to count, from every nation, tribe, people, and language—that suddenly shows up in Heaven *(Revelation 7:9)* is supposed to lift us up (literally) into the presence of God *(Rapture)*!

1 Thessalonians 4:16–17: "For the Lord Himself will come down from heaven with a commanding shout [not down to the earth itself, see below!], **with the voice of the archangel, and with the trumpet call of God. First, the believers who have died will rise from their graves. Then, together with them, we who are still alive and remain on the earth will be *caught up in the clouds to meet the Lord in the air*. Then we will be with the Lord forever."**

Let's add to that one more passage on this point that we have not emphasized before. I think *its meaning is startlingly clear:*

Matthew 24:29–31: "Immediately after the anguish *[tribulation]* **of those days, the sun will be darkened, the moon will give no light, the stars will fall from the sky, and the powers in the heavens will be shaken.** *[That's the same as Seal Six in Revelation 6:12–14]* **And then at last, the sign that the Son of Man is coming will appear in the heavens, and there will be deep mourning among all the peoples of the earth.** *[Revelation 6:15–17]* **And they will see the Son of Man coming on the clouds of heaven with power and great glory. And He will send out His angels** *[Note: He does not come down to the Earth surface.]* **with the mighty blast of a trumpet, and they will gather His**

chosen ones from all over the world—from the farthest ends of the earth and heaven."

There are indeed wonderful positive high notes throughout the final seven years of human history. We're supposed to focus on them!

- The book of Revelation is not supposed to make us want to hide in the closet! Say it with me: It is the prophetic story of the final defeat of the antichrist, and satan! It "screams out" the ultimate triumph of Jesus and of all those who have been forgiven, redeemed, and cleansed by accepting Jesus' sin payment on their behalf!

The trumpet and bowl judgments of God's wrath are poured out on the antichrist, and those who have *willingly chosen him as their messiah,* and even on the sin curse itself. All of that submits to the cleansing fire of God's judgment. (It's *not fun reading, and not the stuff of which inspirational bumper stickers are made.*)

- But, once we finish those difficult verses, God immediately follows them with a "heavenly cleansing."
- I remember when I was a kid in Findlay, Ohio, our septic tank backed up, and apparently there weren't a fleet of cute little trucks with catchy sayings on the side that would pull up, clean everything out and haul it to wherever they haul such stuff. So, my grandfather opened the top of the tank, and we shoveled out five-gallon buckets and dumped them in a big hole on the back of our property. I was the young agile one, so I got the privilege of climbing down into the tank. After that event, there came a time of "great personal cleansing"!

The Mother of all Cleansings!

Revelation 19:1: "*After these things,* I heard what sounded like a vast crowd in heaven shouting." After these things—(*meta tauta eidon*)—is the same Greek phrase that introduced the "Rapture" passage (*Revelation 7:9*). **After *what* things?**

After the "mother of all septic tanks" has been cleansed!

After the seventh trumpet sounds and Scripture tells us that the 24 Elders fall down in worship shouting to God and His Christ, **"Now you have begun to reign on the earth."**

After satan's final claw-full of power over the earth has been sentenced to its final doom and Jesus has His "King of Kings and Lord of Lords" hands firmly on the steering wheel of the earth! *After those things!*

Revelation 19:1–3: "After this I heard what sounded like the roar of a great multitude *in heaven* shouting: '*Hallelujah!* Salvation and glory and power belong to our God, for true and just are His judgments. He has condemned the great prostitute who corrupted the earth by her adulteries. He has avenged on her the blood of His servants.' And again they shouted: 'Hallelujah! The smoke from her goes up for ever and ever.'"

Who is the multitude? John is not seeing them at this point. He is hearing them. He gets to look inside of Heaven *(again)* when we get to verse 11. But for now, he hears a "vast, too great to count" multitude shouting in a roar with "one voice": *"Hallelujah!* Salvation and glory and power belong to our God!"

- Since John cannot see them, let's help him figure out who the vast throng is.

- We've seen *(or heard)* three vast throngs in this book. In Chapter 5 we saw/heard a vast throng of angels singing, **"Worthy is the Lamb that was slain. You have purchased men, for God, from every tribe, language, people, nation."**

- In Chapter 7 we saw/heard a **"vast crowd, too great to count, from every nation and tribe and people and language, standing in front of the throne and before the Lamb. They were clothed in white robes and held palm branches in their hands. And they were shouting with a great roar, 'Salvation comes from our God who sits on the throne and from the Lamb!'"** *(I believe that throng is us—the raptured living and dead!)*

- In Chapter 14, we were startled to find the Lamb, Jesus, standing on the Temple Mount conferring with the 144,000 sealed Jewish witnesses. We didn't mention that something was going on in the background:

- Revelation 14:2–3: "And I heard a sound from heaven like the roar of mighty ocean waves or the rolling of loud thunder. It was like the sound of many harpists playing together. This great choir sang a wonderful new song in front of the throne of God and before the four living beings and the twenty-four elders. No one could learn this song except the 144,000 who had been redeemed from the earth."

- **WHO would be qualified** to teach the redeemed 144,000 a song that would empower them to take on the antichrist "and his beast-ers," and bring millions of Jewish people to faith in Jesus as the true Messiah during that last two years of the final seven?

- **I believe it is going to be US**—"the redeemed, raptured, glorified Saints," who are in Heaven awaiting the next event on the prophetic calendar!

That brings us to *this fourth look into Heaven* where a "too great to count" multitude are shouting with one voice ***"Hallelujah!"*** The word hallelujah occurs only four times in the New Testament. It is a Hebrew word that means "Praise you LORD/Yahweh!"

Hebrew – הַלְלוּ־יָהּ
Greek – αλληλουια
Latin – Alleluia
English – Hallelujah/Alleluia

In the New Testament, Jesus and the New Testament writers talk often about praising God, but they do not use an old Hebrew word to do it.

- *So, why does this vast crowd in Heaven use this old Hebrew word to express their adoration and praise to God?* I will tell you why: Because this vast crowd of raptured people in Heaven was using this very same word to express their adoration to God here on Earth before they arrived in Heaven! **This "vast crowd" was here before they got there!**

The Greek New Testament, literally, has to coin a new word to describe what the vast multitude is shouting to God in Heaven.

Revelation 19:1–3: "After this I heard what sounded like the roar of a great multitude *in heaven* shouting: '*Hallelujah!*'"

[1] "*Salvation* and *glory* and *power* belong to our God."

[2] "For true and just are His judgments." *(Jesus did exactly the right thing.)*

[3] "He has condemned the great prostitute who corrupted the earth by her adulteries."

[4] "He has avenged on her the blood of His servants." *[Remember Seal 5?]*

[5] "Again, they shouted: 'Hallelujah! The smoke from her goes up forever and ever.'"

Why is everybody shouting "Hallelujah"?

All this makes what comes next even more fascinating!

Revelation 19:4: "Then the twenty-four elders and the four living beings fell down and worshiped God, who was sitting on the throne. *They cried out, 'Amen! Hallelujah!'*"

So, these heavenly creatures are picking up the wording of the earthlings, those recent arrivals in Heaven! Not only do they start shouting "Hallelujah," but they shout the word "Amen" which is another Hebrew word that means "faithful, always consistent." Those are the two Biblical words that even now cross over into multiple languages all across the world. *(and apparently heaven!)*

Revelation 19:5–7: "And from the throne came a voice that said, 'Praise our God, all His servants, all who fear Him, from the least to the greatest.' Then I heard again what sounded like the shout of a vast crowd or the roar of mighty ocean waves or the crash of loud thunder: 'Praise the LORD! For the Lord our God, the Almighty, reigns! "Let us be glad and rejoice, and let us give honor to Him. For the time has come for _the Wedding Feast of the Lamb, and His bride has prepared herself._"

What in the world is the "Wedding Feast"?

Revelation 19:7–9: "'For the time has come for the _Wedding Feast of the Lamb, and His bride has prepared herself._ She has been given the finest of pure white linen to wear.' For the fine linen represents the good deeds of God's holy people. And the angel said to me, 'Write this: _Blessed are those who are invited to the Wedding Feast of the Lamb._' And he added, 'These are true words that come from God.'"

Before we dismiss this as just some symbolic way of saying "the Saints have come marching in," we need to note that the phrase "the time has come" in

Greek means that this event is ***"a new, never done before event" that is about to start.***

- Jesus used the same phrase in the Garden of Gethsemane when He said, "*My hour is come.*" And we know what happened there!

This is the long-awaited "wedding ceremony" for Jesus and His redeemed Bride! This idea of "being married to God" goes back to the beginning of time when God made a covenant with Israel. He committed Himself to them forever in an "eternal covenant" by which they would/could/should return the favor.

> **Isaiah 54:5: "For your Creator will be your husband; the Lord of Heaven's Armies is His name! He is your Redeemer, the Holy One of Israel, the God of all the earth."**

It sounds a bit weird to 21st Century Westerners—far less weird to the First Century Church. They understood that God had established His faithfulness to His chosen children—and He expected them to be faithful in return. When they ignored God, and embraced the wood and stone idols of their pagan neighbors, God said they were being "unfaithful," committing "spiritual adultery." In fact, it became so bad that God said He "would divorce them" and turn to the Gentiles with His offer of salvation. Gentiles were "grafted in." Those who accept Jesus' redeeming work are said, in the New Testament, to be:

"The Bride of Christ—Jesus' Bride"

In spite of their former "spiritual adultery"—the Jews can now, also, come into right relationship with God as part of the Bride of Christ. In fact, as we saw in the last chapter, millions of them [IMO] will embrace Jesus as the true Messiah during that dark Day of the Lord's Wrath. The point is, *none need to wait to become the Bride of Christ.* When we accept His redeeming death in our place as the payment for our sins, when we come to Him in repentance for our sinful rebellion and turn over to Him the Lordship of our lives, *we become saved, redeemed, part of "Jesus' Bride."* This privilege is not some future event in Heaven.

Revelation 19:8: "'She *[the Bride]* **has been given the finest of pure white linen to wear.' For the fine linen represents the good deeds [righteous acts] of God's holy people."**

- There is no doubt whatsoever who these people in Heaven are. Don't get tripped up by the mention of their righteous acts. We don't get to Heaven because of our righteous deeds. Any deeds we ever do that are righteous are because, and only because, of His righteousness in us. The very best we can say is that we will be there because of Jesus' righteousness—*period*.

- The key here is: This multitude of white-robed, righteousness-absorbing, Hallelujah-shouting people are, I firmly believe, the redeemed, raptured Saints! Now, here they/we are robed in white, members of the new worship choir of Heaven.

"The King of Kings, and the Lord of Lords!"

We see a massive throng "robed in white" mounting up with the King of Kings and Lord of Lords at the end of Chapter 19, ready to return to once-and-for-all destroy the antichrist and redeem the whole earth from satan's clutches. *If you are a Believer, you can count yourself among that number!* What a scene! The only way to accurately describe it is: There is going to be one massive heavenly celebration!

Revelation 19:7, 9: "For the time has come for the Wedding Feast of the Lamb, and His bride has prepared herself. And the angel said to me, 'Write this: Blessed are those who are invited to the Wedding Feast of the Lamb.' And He added, 'These are true words that come from God.'"

1) Before Jesus mounts up to descend in His triumphal Second Coming,

2) Before He takes on the antichrist and the armies of the world in the famous Battle of Armageddon,

3) Before He finally, completely, destroys the effects of in this world and throws the antichrist and the false prophet into the Lake of Fire and satan into the pit,

4) Before the sheep and goat judgment at the end of Armageddon where He sends the wicked to join the antichrist in the Lake of Fire, and separates those who have embraced Him as Messiah and ushers them into His "millennial" 1,000-year reign on this earth,

Before any of that takes place, Jesus gathers all the saints from all the ages—Abraham and Sarah, Moses, David, Mary his mother, and Mary Magdalene, and invites them/us to the Marriage Supper of the Lamb. Think of it, the "thief on the cross" may be sitting across the table from you! *(We'll expand this in Chapter 15.)*

- Remember when Jesus said to the Church in Revelation 3 that "to those who overcome He would write on them the name of His God," and then added "and I will write *on them my new name" (Revelation 3:12)?*
- I suspect that somewhere on a banquet table the size of the United States is a place setting with a card emblazoned with not only your name but a "special name" God has only for you—because you are His special invitee.

But, there is one condition: You must embrace Jesus' redeeming gift of salvation!!

How much do I know?

1) Notice the distinctions between the Rapture of the Saints and the Second Coming of Jesus. In the Rapture the trumpet blows, the dead rise first and then all Believers rise to meet Jesus in the air. In the Second Coming the white-robed Redeemed are already with Jesus and are coming back to earth with him. At the Rapture all the people of the earth are hiding in caves screaming "save us from the wrath of God." In the Second Coming all the armies of the world are surrounding Jerusalem when Jesus arrives, and they turn to attack Jesus himself! Can you name other distinctions between the Rapture and the Second Coming?

2) Right after the ultimate "Hallelujah Chorus" in heaven comes the "Wedding Feast of the Lamb" or "the Marriage Supper of the Lamb." What do you think that Feast is all about, how long does it last, and who of us will be in attendance?

3) True or False: The book of Revelation was never designed to be weird and symbolic. It is the step-by-step description of the final triumph of Jesus and of all those who have been forgiven, redeemed, and cleansed by embracing His sin payment on their behalf!

You can check your answers beginning on page 243.

Number of correct answers on this page:

The Greek word "parousia" is used to describe the Rapture. It is also used to describe Jesus' Second Coming. Why would the same word be used for both events? Does that mean the two events actually happen at the same time?

Perhaps Jesus' Rapture and his Second Coming are all part of one larger event. Was there more than one major event in Jesus' First Coming? Can you name some of them? How long did Jesus' First Coming last?

If Jesus' Second Coming is one event with many parts, what are some more of the individual pieces that might make up His "Second Triumphant Return"? How long do you think this whole event will last?

14

The Second Coming of Jesus Christ

As Ethan's eyes poured over the Revelation letter, they were drawn like a magnet to one paragraph. *(Ours are too!)*

> **Revelation 19:11–14, 16: "Then I saw heaven opened, and a white horse was standing there. Its rider was named Faithful and True. His eyes were like flames of fire, and on His head were many crowns. He wore a robe dipped in blood, and His title was the Word of God. The armies of heaven, dressed in the finest of pure white linen, followed Him on white horses. On His robe at His thigh was written this title: King of all kings and Lord of all lords."**

Ethan knew exactly whose robe was "dipped in blood." He knew exactly who bore the title, "the Word of God." His buddy John had made that very clear in the introduction to his "Gospel."

- He could picture, to the square foot, where this "DESCENT" of Jesus and the "armies of heaven" were going to land because he had been standing there when the ASCENT happened—and he and John had heard the angels' specific instructions.

- That "army of heaven dressed in white linen" sure wasn't talking about the angels. The "white linen" phrase was always reserved for those "Redeemed" through Jesus' blood. And there has to be a direct connection between those who "return with Jesus" in his Second Coming—and those who went up to meet him in the "rapture"!

1 Thessalonians 4:15–17: "We who are still living when the Lord returns will not meet Him ahead of those who have died. For <u>the Lord Himself will come down from heaven with a commanding shout</u>, with the voice of the archangel, and with the trumpet call of God. First, <u>the believers who have died will rise from their graves. Then, together with them, we who are still alive and remain on the earth will be caught up in the clouds to meet the Lord in the air.</u> Then we will be with the Lord forever."

The Greek word *"parousia"* was/is critical to understanding the Second Coming. It is used 24 times in the New Testament, four times in the Gospels, three directly from the mouth of Jesus. Ethan and the info-nerds had spent hours studying that one key word—most importantly the three critical times it was used in Jesus' final Matthew 24 sermon, the passage in which Jesus Himself described how the End Times will unfold.

"Parousia" is a compound word formed from "para" meaning "a visitation/an arrival" and "ousia" meaning "being with/ an ongoing presence."

"Par-ousia" means "an arrival," followed by "an on-going presence."

A huge key to anyone understanding the Second Coming of Jesus—was/is to figure out when Jesus will again make *"an arrival" (parousia) to be with His Redeemed, who then enjoy His* **"continual, ongoing presence"** from that moment forward.

That was the chief thing the Early Church most wanted to know from the day Jesus ascended back to heaven. They knew from the "dazzling angels" announcement and from the Zechariah 14 prophesies—that Jesus was, indeed, going to one day arrive back on this earth! But how could they square that with "the Believers rising to meet Jesus in the air" and then "forever being with him"?

- Surprisingly, some verses that use the word *"parousia"* seem to be speaking of our being *raptured up* to meet Jesus in the air—while other passages seem to be referring to *our returning with Him* in His triumphal landing back on this earth to defeat satan, and the antichrist, fight the Battle of Armageddon, and establish His earthly reign.

- How could that be? Why would the same word be used for both events? Does that mean that the two events happen at the same time? Do Believers rise up to meet Jesus in the air, and then come right back with him to this earth? What does that do to the "Hallelujah-ing Redeemed Saints" pictured in heaven? What about the "Marriage Supper of the Lamb" that clearly seems to take place "in heaven."

- There is an answer to this mystery! Ethan knew instantly what it was. He spoke Greek and had an Eastern mindset. But even to 21st Century Western minds, the answer, once seen, is just pure logic (theo-logic).

1) Jesus' First Coming was one event that lasted 33 years spanning the period between the angel's announcement of His birth, through His death and resurrection, and ending with His ascension back to Heaven. It started with Gabriel's first word to Mary, and ended with the last view of Jesus disappearing in the clouds—Yes?

2) Jesus' Second Coming is, also, one long event! It starts with the: **a)** rising of the dead saints, **b)** rapture of the living saints, the **c)** Day of the Lord's Wrath on Earth, and **d)** Marriage Feast of the Lamb with the saints in Heaven. Jesus' Second Coming <u>includes</u> the: **e)** Triumphant Return of Jesus with His saints, **f)** fighting of the Battle of Armageddon, **g)** destruction of the antichrist, **h)** condemning of satan to the abyss, **i)** sheep and goat judgment, and **j)** 1,000-year reign of Christ.

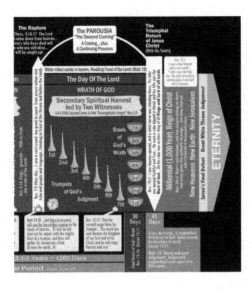

This is from Jesus' mouth in the famous Mathew 24 passage: **"His disciples came to Him privately. What sign will signal your return (parousia) and the end of the age (aionos)?"** *What follows is very important:*

> **Matthew 24:29–31:** *"**Immediately after the anguish** [tribulation] **of those days, the sun will be darkened, the moon will give no light, the stars will fall from the sky, and the powers in the heavens will be shaken** [Seal 6]. **And then at last, the sign that the Son of Man is coming will appear in the heavens** [the sign is visual—Jesus and his angels] **and there will be deep mourning among all the peoples of the earth. And they** [everyone] **will see the Son of Man coming on the clouds of heaven with power and great glory. And He will send out His angels with the mighty blast of a trumpet, and they will gather His chosen ones from all over the world."* (See Mark 13:24–27; and Luke 21:25–28)

- Jesus' account in Matthew 24 perfectly matches that of the Apostle Paul in 1 Thessalonians 4:

> **1 Thessalonians 4:15–17:** **"We who are still living when the Lord returns will not meet Him ahead of those who have died. For**

the Lord Himself will come down from heaven with a commanding shout, with the voice of the archangel, and with the trumpet call of God. First, the believers who have died will rise from their graves. Then, together with them, we who are still alive and remain on the earth will be caught up in the clouds to meet the Lord in the air. Then we will be with the Lord forever."

"An arrival," followed by a "continual, ongoing presence"

That is the "Parousia," or at least the beginning of the "Parousia," the Second Coming of Jesus Christ! It is without doubt the time when the Believer experiences the **personal arrival** of Jesus Himself—and then enjoys His "**continual, ongoing presence**."

But *both of those passages are describing the Rapture of the Saints, not the Triumphal Second Coming of Christ because according to Revelation 19, when Jesus returns, the redeemed Saints are already with Him*—we mount up with Jesus *(Revelation 19:14)* and accompany Him on the final trip back to this earth.

- Plus, there are two very different visuals in these passages **describing two distinct parts of Jesus' "Parousia."**

- Jesus' first coming was a "silent night advent," under the radar. He was born in a stable with a few sheep and his crib was a livestock trough. The huge angelic choir performed, only for the benefit of a few Bedouin shepherds. No one five miles away in Jerusalem even bothered to walk over to find out if the "moving star" was the fulfillment of a long-awaited Messianic prophecy.

- But, whatever the First Coming was in secluded quietness, the two main parts of the Second Coming will be with universe-shattering visuals and ear-piercing noise! I do not believe for a moment that the Rapture will unfold as many popular books and movies depict—where nobody on Earth is aware that Jesus has returned for His Saints, except that Uncle Fred's truck seems to have veered driverless off the road, and Grandpa's coveralls are left empty in the barn. **That is *not* the picture that the**

end of Revelation 6 paints and, it's *not* the picture that Jesus Himself paints in Matthew 24, *nor* is it the picture the Apostle Paul paints in 1 Thessalonians 4.

The unmistakable changes in the sun, moon, and stars *(Matthew 24)* get the attention of everyone on Earth *(electrifying to Believers, terrifying to unbelievers)*.

- This is not something we have to search for and adjust to fit the storyline! *(Please look at your 2nd chart.)* **This is the exact order presented by Jesus himself in Matthew 24** in response to his disciples "What will be the signs of your coming" question. *(See Mark 13:24–27; Luke 21:25–28)*
- It was Jesus, in his final sermon, who gave us the order of: 1) vs. 15—"the sacrilegious object that causes desecration being set up in the Holy Place" as Daniel prophesied (antichrist); 2) vs. 29—"immediately after the anguish of those days the sun will be darkened, the moon will give no light, and the stars will fall from the sky;" 3) vs. 30—"Then at last the sign that the Son of Man is returning will appear—they will see the Son of Man coming on the clouds of heaven"—vs. 31 "He will send out his angels with the mighty blast of the trumpet and gather his chosen ones from all over the world!"
- **THAT'S <u>JESUS' ORDER OF EVENTS</u>!**—read the chapter!

The image of perhaps millions of resurrected bodies rising out of their graves, and millions or billions more living people being lifted off the earth to meet this glorified Savior who comes down from Heaven with a commanding shout and the trumpet call of God—is *very* different from the silent-night First Coming with a cooing baby in an out-of-the-way bed of straw. *It is not logically possible to open millions of graves and lift millions more people off the earth without anyone else noticing!*

Look again at the words of Jesus Himself!

Matthew 24:30: "And *then* at last, the sign that the Son of Man is coming *will* appear in the heavens, and there will be deep mourning

among _ALL_ the *peoples of the earth*. **And** *they [all—everyone]* **will see the Son of Man coming** on the clouds of heaven with power and great glory."

- This event must take at least long enough for the earth to make one complete rotation so that everyone on the earth will see it. (*This is not a watch-it-on-your-iPhone thing*!)
- Whatever these people see and hear during the Rapture, the first part of the "Parousia," leads to deep mourning among all the *(unbelieving)* people of the earth. *The Believers are not mourning; they are rising to meet Jesus!*
- *Remember, the parallel passage* in Revelation 6 sheds even more light:

  Revelation 6:15–16: "Then *everyone*—the kings of the earth, the rulers, the generals, the wealthy, the powerful, and every slave and free person—all hid themselves in the caves and among the rocks of the mountains. And they cried to the mountains and the rocks, 'Fall on us and hide us from the face of the one who sits on the throne and from the wrath of the Lamb.'"

- The beginning of the "Parousia," the Rapture, starting with the cosmic signs in the sky has to be a big enough and visible enough event and has to take a long enough period of time that it *brings panic to every unbeliever on the earth.* And it has to allow enough time for *everyone* to go hide out and *scream, "Hide us from the face of the One who sits on the throne."*

Notice, again, this cannot be referring to Jesus' final Second Coming with His Saints from Heaven. In that "coming," the saints are coming back with Him, not rising to meet Him in the air!

- By the time of Jesus' Triumphal Second Return with His Saints, the kings of the earth are not hiding in caves from the Lamb on the throne. What's left of them are all gathering their armies and heading for the valley of Meggido *(Har Meggido: Armageddon)* for the final battle against the King of Kings and Lord of Lords!

- By the time of Jesus' Triumphal Return with His Saints, there are only two types of people left on the earth—those who have come to faith in Christ after the Rapture, and those who are viciously sold out to sin, satan, and the antichrist and hate God with every fiber of their being.

When we get to the 2nd half "Day of the Lord's Wrath" on sin, satan, and the antichrist, there is not one storyline, but three storylines all occurring at the same time *(See chart)*.

- The **first storyline** in Revelation 19 gives us a stark look into Heaven where the raptured, redeemed Saints are praising *(the "Hallelujah" scene)* for the final cleaning up of the sin problem on earth, attending the Wedding Feast of the Lamb, and mounting up to return with Jesus.

- At the same time, on Earth, a **second storyline** is the final push for people to come to salvation with *the two witnesses constantly* preaching, the 144,000 reaching the Jews with what seems to be a massive turning to Jesus as the true Messiah—and even the evangelistic angels of Revelation 14 moving above the earth, preaching to every nation, tribe language, and people. Those who embrace God's salvation at this late hour are then protected by God to the end. *These are the people who will populate the earth during Jesus' 1,000-year reign! They are who we (the raptured, redeemed Saints) will "reign" over!*

- At the same time a **third storyline** on Earth is the part of Revelation that people tend to focus on most—the pouring out of God's judgments on a furiously rebellious remnant. This is part of a crescendo of events leading to Jesus' final Triumphant Return.

After the horrible trumpet judgments, come the rapid-fire final bowl judgments (we're in the final 30 days). Here's the first five:

    Bowl #1: Horrible, malignant sores break out on everyone who has the mark of the beast and who worships his statue *(Revelation 16:2)*.

    Bowl #2: The sea becomes like the blood of a corpse, and everything in the sea dies *(Revelation 16:3)*.

Bowl #3: The rivers and springs become blood *(Revelation 16:4).*

Bowl #4: The sun scorches everyone with its fire and "Everyone was burned by this blast of heat, and they cursed the name of God, who had control over all these plagues. They did not repent of their sins and turn to God and give Him glory" *(Revelation 16:8–9).*

Bowl #5: The fifth angel poured out his bowl on the throne of the beast, and his kingdom is plunged into darkness. His subjects grind their teeth in anguish, "and *they cursed the God of heaven for their pains and sores. But they did not repent of their evil deeds and turn to God*" *(Revelation 16:10–11).*

By this time, the antichrist, as the world leader, must have terribly low favorability ratings. After he was assassinated and resurrected *(Revelation 13:14),* the world believed in him. He led "the whole world" to worship himself and satan; all who followed him and took his "mark" on their hand or forehead.

- But, in the seven years since he came to power promising to right all the wrongs of the world, the earth has gone from a seemingly peaceful place to a seething ball of complete destruction.
- Well over half the world's population has died! Instead of economic recovery, the antichrist has ruled over a complete worldwide economic collapse. There is no money to buy the supplies that aren't available in stores anyway—no lights to turn on to cut through the pitch darkness outside day and night. Complete anarchy reigns everywhere. Temperatures are intensely hot at all times, and there is no clean water to take a bath in or drinkable water to satisfy one's thirst.

Revelation 16:12–14, 16: "Then the sixth angel poured out his bowl on the great Euphrates River, and it dried up so that the kings from the east could march their armies toward the west without hindrance. And I saw three evil spirits that looked like frogs leap from the mouths of the dragon, the beast, and the false prophet.

They are demonic spirits who work miracles and go out to all the rulers of the world to gather them *for battle against the Lord on that great judgment day of God the Almighty. And the demonic spirits gathered all the rulers and their armies to a place with the Hebrew name Armageddon.*"

Satan's demons are gathering the armies of the world to fight against the returning Jesus. But those armies are not purposely coming to fight Jesus. I don't believe they know or care anything about a returning Jesus. *The armies are coming to take on the antichrist!* They've had enough of his awful leadership! What's left of the world's armies come from every direction to dethrone him.

- These are not unified armies. They are going to fight each other too, until the last group standing becomes the new world leader. So they come, by the millions, from every direction toward Jerusalem.

- Note: While these armies may *think* they are coming to fight the antichrist, that is not why s*atan is assembling them.* Satan is bringing the remaining might of the world to take on the returning Jesus! How does satan know that Jesus is going to return at that point? *Because he's read the same Book we're reading, and he believes it!*

- Satan knows exactly what God says He is going to do at the End. Yet he still foolishly believes that he can thwart God's plan! Like a moth drawn to a flame, he will walk right into the trap of setting the stage for God's final judgment on himself, the antichrist, and the willfully rebellious.

Picture the scene that is now unfolding:

From all over the globe, like salmon instinctively called upstream, angry, hate-filled people migrate toward Jerusalem, stumbling in the darkness, burning from the heat, with the stench of diseased, sweat-pouring, filth-ridden bodies—a glut of pure evil and hatred filling the air, the monumental clash of evil people killing any and all who do not think just like them.

And then, in the middle of that pounding chaos, out of the corner of their eye *people start to see a light way up in the heavens.* Although the sky is pitch black and they haven't seen a star in weeks, there is one there now! At dusk the next day the same light appears but this time it's larger.

- *Each night it gets bigger and brighter until it seems to fill the sky.* The brightness seems to come from the center, extending outward for thousands of miles in every direction. The sun-like brilliance is bouncing off what looks like layers of clouds, *but it cannot be clouds because there are none out there. ("He's coming on the clouds!")*

- Imagine if what is coming toward earth is brighter by far than any comet (*because it is lit from within*) and has a combined mass larger than the largest continent. **Every time the earth turns, every eye is fixed toward the east as this insanely bright spectacle, that IS Jesus' Triumphant Return to Earth, draws ever closer.**

- As this brilliant new threat fills the sky, obviously hurtling directly toward the earth, *what is left of the hate-filled throngs lose interest in fighting each other and position themselves and their weapons to take on this new enemy. Every remaining missile on earth is pointed in the direction of the center of the light.*

What is it?

Revelation 19:11–14, 16: "Then I saw heaven opened, and a white horse was standing there. Its rider was named Faithful and True. His eyes were like flames of fire, and on His head were many crowns. He wore a robe dipped in blood, and His title was the Word of God. The *armies of heaven, dressed in the finest of pure white linen, followed Him on white horses.* On His robe at His thigh was written this title: King of all kings and Lord of all lords!"

How much do I know?

1) Revelation 19 seems to be running three storylines all at the same time. Can you fill in what all is unfolding at the same time:

   a) 1ˢᵗ Storyline:

   b) 2ⁿᵈ Storyline:

   c) 3ʳᵈ Storyline:

2) Lots and lots of people seem to be coming to faith in Jesus during the Great Tribulation (the last 3½ years). If they are too late to be carried up in the rapture, too late to attend the Marriage Supper of the Lamb—if the first time they get to see Jesus is at his Triumphal Second Coming—what is going to ultimately happen to these people?

3) As the final bowls of God's Wrath against sin and satan are poured out, all the remaining armies of the world are gathered at Jerusalem for the famous Battle of Armageddon. We know that they try to fight the returning Messiah and are instantly defeated. But that can't be the reason they gathered there. They wouldn't have known anything about a returning Messiah. So what does bring them all at the same time to the valley of Meggido?

You can check your answers beginning on page 243.

Number of correct answers on this page:

The Revelation of Jesus Christ

PART IV

REVELATION 19–22:

Unveiling Eternity

Revelation, in fact all of biblical prophecy, *was written as a single storyline.* (*That's so important!*) 1) In Daniel 9:25, the prophet Daniel prophesied (*600 years before Jesus was born*) that there would be 69 weeks (*of years*)—483 years—from the time King Artaxerxes decreed the rebuilding of Jerusalem until the Anointed One would come. 2) Sure enough, it was exactly 483 years later when Jesus, the Messiah, rode into Jerusalem on the back of the donkey, on Palm Sunday, and was mobbed by people shouting, *"Blessed is He who comes in the name of the Lord."*

- 3) Daniel then prophesied (*Daniel 9:26*) that the Messiah *would be "cut off appearing to have accomplished nothing."* And sure enough, a handful of days after Palm Sunday, Jesus was led to Golgotha and crucified (*leap forward 2000 years*).

- 4) Daniel prophesies to the day the events of "the 70ᵗʰ week:" **Daniel 12:11–12: "From the time the daily sacrifice is stopped and the sacrilegious object that causes desecration is set up to be worshiped, there will be 1,290 days. And blessed are those who wait and remain until the end of the 1,335 days!"**

- How it must have excited the Early Church info-nerds to be able to take the detailed information in Jesus Unveiling and fill in with so many newly revealed details!

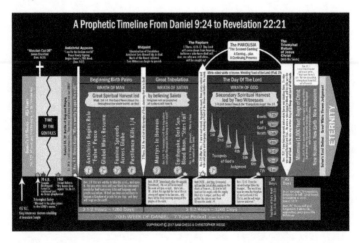

But all that detailed to-the-day prophetic information seems to come to a screeching halt at Jesus' Triumphal Return!

- **All of Revelation 19:11–22:6 fills only 59 verses in Revelation.** We can read it all in about 15 minutes, but it covers all the rest of eternity!

We do have 3 ½ chapters of inspired Scripture and we will explore every part of it—but it does open the door wide for some holy imagination. Perhaps Jesus is going to close out the Marriage Feast of the Lamb and start off the next billion years by saying something like this:

- "OK—It's time for all of you 'Redeemed in the Blood of the Lamb' Saints to join me as I make my final journey back to Earth to finish the destruction of satan, the antichrist, and their minions.
- "Out of all the humans who are still left on the earth, there now remain only two types:
  - Those who have rejected satan and the antichrist and received my salvation and my protection. They will be kept safe until we arrive.
  - All the rest of humanity who are filled with blind hatred and rage toward me—their Creator. They have completely embraced satan and the antichrist, and our **task now is to eliminate sin from the earth**.
- "So, before my Millennial Reign can begin *(where you all will reign with me, as kings and priests)*, **all sin must be purged from the planet!**"

If the Rapture does indeed happen in Revelation 7, just before the Wrath of God is poured out, and if the Wedding Feast of the Lamb begins soon after the Saints arrive in Heaven and doesn't end until we all mount up to return with Jesus (Revelation 19), about how long might the Wedding Feast of the Lamb last?

If the Marriage Supper of the Lamb does last for months—What would you imagine will be going on all that time? One imagines that we will all, finally, be in the very presence of Jesus. What might he be saying?

15

The Marriage Feast— and Jesus' Return

So—the Saints, both living and dead, have been raptured! Revelation 7:9 pictures a vast crowd too great to count from every nation, tribe, people, and language standing in front of the throne and before the Lamb. That's when the "four Hallelujah" events unfold. The Saints in Heaven are really beginning to catch on to the magnitude of what they are now a part of.

Then comes this:

> **Revelation 19:7–8: "'Let us be glad and rejoice, and let us give honor to Him. For the time *has come* for the Wedding Feast of the Lamb, and *His bride* has prepared herself. She has been given the *finest of pure white linen to wear.' For the fine linen represents the righteous deeds* of God's holy people."**

- Here again, the phrase *"has come"* in Greek, (ἔρχω) is a very potent phrase. *(It is the phrase Jesus used in the Garden of Gethsemane when He said, "my hour has come.")* It means that a very real, and very important, event is about to take place.

- And it does—**a divine marriage feast!** We should think of the "Marriage Supper" in this way: *If I am a Believer—I will, someday, be right there, with Jesus, in Heaven, at this long-awaited Marriage Feast of the Lamb!*
- The Day of the Lord's Wrath back on Earth lasts for 18–24 months, and this Feast of the Lamb going on in Heaven is no "one-evening-only" occasion either. It will last as long as God thinks necessary, and I suspect that it includes far more than a steak and baked potato.

Picture yourself sitting there around the heavenly banquet table as Jesus begins to explain all the things in this life that just didn't make any sense, all the things that brought you, and me, and millions of other people, such pain and confusion. *Imagine hearing Him answer once and for all every anguished "Why?" question ever posed.* Imagine Jesus patiently unveiling every tormented "If there is a loving God, then why?"

- And you will hear one after another after another of the redeemed Saints begin to say, *"Oh, now I get it! Now it all makes sense! It was so worth it all!"*

Picture us coming back day after day *(maybe 24 hours a day)* for maybe a year and a half *(Earth time)*, the "Bride of Christ" resting in the love of her "Bridegroom." And the grace that has been working in our lives here on this earth, that so often seems to be trying to travel over broken wires inside of us, begins to connect in all its fullness. *The truth of God's complete salvation begins to explode into every fiber of our being! (Think what that will be like for you!)*

As God's "poured out wrath" on earth begins to wind down, Jesus then says, "Now let me explain—what I *(and you)* are going to do next."

You will be part of the final Triumphant Return of Jesus!

- If it is starting to sound like we are in storybook mode here, know this: *According to Revelation 19, you will indeed be part of this final Triumphant Return of Jesus to purge sin from the earth and set up an earthly millennial reign!*

Revelation 19:11–14, 16: "Then I saw *heaven opened,* and a white horse was standing there. Its rider was named Faithful and True. His eyes were like flames of fire, and on His head were many crowns. He wore a robe dipped in blood, and His title was the Word of God. The *armies of heaven, dressed in the finest of pure white linen, followed Him on white horses.* On His robe at His thigh was written this title: King of all kings and Lord of all lords."

- There is no doubt who is wearing the white robes. Verse 8 already told us it is the threads worn by the Bride of Christ! **The key here is that *this is your future reality*!**

As we approach the Earth, we have been given enough prophesied information to tell us what we can expect. We are now in the last few hours of the last 30 days—the *6th bowl.*

Revelation 16:12–14, 16: "Then the sixth angel poured out his bowl on the great Euphrates River, and it dried up so that the kings from the east could march their armies toward the west without hindrance. And I saw three evil spirits—leap from the mouths of the dragon, the beast, and the false prophet. They—go out to all the rulers of the world to gather them for battle against the Lord on that great judgment day of God the Almighty—And the demonic spirits gathered all the rulers and their armies to a place with the Hebrew name *Armageddon.*"

Revelation 19:19: "Then I saw the beast and the kings of the world and their armies gathered together to fight against the one sitting on the horse and His army."

All the hate-filled, satan-worshiping armies of the world cram into Megiddo, a 180-mile long valley in Israel that covers Nazareth and Cana and surrounds the Sea of Galilee. They are fighting each other in the utter darkness that has become their world until, *finally, their attention is consumed by the brilliant arrival of the*

King of Kings and Lord of Lords, all His angels, and all the redeemed Saints who have hitched up their white robes and galloped to Earth from outer space!

- The prophet Zechariah prophesies that Jesus will land on the Mount of Olives where He prayed to the Father, "not my will but your will be done," and where He rode from on the donkey amid palm branches and shouts of Hosanna. Zechariah tells us that as Jesus lands on the Mount of Olives, it splits from the east to the west.

> **Zechariah 14:2–4: "I will gather all the nations to fight against Jerusalem. Then the LORD will go out to fight against those nations, as he has fought in times past. On that day his feet will stand on the Mount of Olives, east of Jerusalem. And the Mount of Olives will split apart, making a wide valley running from east to west."**

Bowl seven → the final bowl of God's judgment → brings "time" to an end!

> **Revelation 16:17–21: "Then the seventh angel poured out his bowl into the air. And a mighty shout came from the throne in the Temple, saying, 'It is finished!' Then the thunder crashed and rolled, and lightning flashed. And a great earthquake struck—*the worst since people were placed on the earth.* The great city of Babylon split into three sections, and the cities of many nations fell into heaps of rubble. And *every* island disappeared, and *all* the mountains were leveled. There was a terrible hailstorm, and hailstones weighing as much as seventy-five pounds fell from the sky onto the people below. They cursed God because of the terrible plague of the hailstorm."**

It is interesting to note that Africa, the Arabian Peninsula, and Israel sit on top of the deepest rift in the world.

- There will be a shaking in the earth's crust so severe that it "stretches every mountain into flatlands and sinks every island under the sea" (where everything has died because of the 2nd bowl).
- This is certainly no mere natural disaster because 75-pound hailstones fall from the sky.
- All of this takes place in the pitch darkness left by the 5th bowl and the scorching heat left by the 4th bowl.

The end of the antichrist!

Finally, *two verses* are all we get to end the long story of the antichrist, the false prophet, and the willfully rebellious—who have committed their lives to satan's leadership:

> **Revelation 19:20–21: "And the beast was captured, and with him the false prophet who did mighty miracles on behalf of the beast— miracles that deceived all who had accepted the mark of the beast and who worshiped his statue. Both the beast and his false prophet were thrown alive into the fiery lake of burning sulfur. Their entire army was killed by the sharp sword that came from the mouth of the one riding the white horse."**

And so satan's messiah, who has terrorized the world for years, and all the remaining military might of the world is gone—*poof!*—with a word from the mouth of the King of Kings and Lord of Lords. *We Believers will be there to witness that universe-shaking event!*

- *If you are not spiritually prepared when Jesus returns* to Rapture His Saints, if you have not placed your faith in Jesus' sin payment on a cross to redeem you and wash your sins away, if you have not embraced Jesus' resurrection over death, and sin, and satan, and hell to bring to you eternal life—then *none of the "with Jesus" material above applies to you!*
- This is not just something a preacher says as he approaches the end of his sermon to pressure you into making a decision for Christ. ***This is***

the truth! I want to share with you something I had never seen prior to working on this study of Revelation.

We need to refer again to the chart. Notice the section near the bottom—the bright-yellow boxes. Jesus' own words in His final sermon before His crucifixion came so alive to me that I realized I had never understood a fraction of this before.

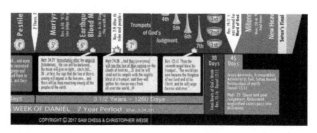

This we've already seen:

Matthew 24:29–31: *"Immediately after* the *anguish (tribulation)* of those days, the sun will be darkened, the moon will give no light, the stars will fall from the sky, and the powers in the heavens will be shaken. And *then* at last, the sign that the Son of Man is coming will appear in the heavens, and there will be deep mourning among all the peoples of the earth. And *they* [everyone] *will see the Son of Man coming* on the clouds of heaven with power and great glory. *And He will send out His angels with the mighty blast of a trumpet, and they will gather His chosen ones from all over the world."* (That's the Rapture!)

Now add this: Jesus' sermon is not over—but goes on to/through Chapter 25 of Matthew. Jesus has something so pressing on His mind that He put it in the last words of His last sermon before He was crucified.

Matthew 24:32–34: "Now learn a lesson from the fig tree. When its branches bud and its leaves begin to sprout, you know that summer is near. *In the same way, when you see all these things,* [24:1–29] **you can know His return is very near, right at the door. I**

tell you the truth, *this generation will not pass from the scene until all these things take place.*"

1) "All these things" are the carefully laid out words of Scripture that we have studied detailing the Ezekiel battle, the rise of the antichrist, the mark of the beast, and so on.

2) "This generation" is the generation of people who see the rise of the antichrist and all the events leading up to the Rapture *(Matthew 24:1–29)*.

Then Jesus repeats a familiar theme in **Matthew 24:42: "*So you must keep watch!* For you don't know what day your Lord is coming!"**

- Jesus is not saying He is going to sneak up behind Christ-followers and catch them unaware. He has already spelled out, to them/us, in great detail what we are to be looking for to understand when He will arrive.
- Rather, He is saying to a different group of people, **"Don't let down the guard of your life.** Don't live in such a way that you know what you should do but have chosen to do something else. Don't find yourself at my coming saying, 'I knew what I was supposed to do, and I should have done it, I meant to do it. Life just slipped by and caught me on the outside looking in.'"

Jesus then added this very familiar story—and it's certainly not by accident:

Matthew 25:1–13: "Then the Kingdom of Heaven will be like ten bridesmaids who took their lamps and went to meet the bridegroom. Five of them were foolish, and five were wise. The five who were foolish didn't take enough olive oil for their lamps, but the other five were wise enough to take along extra oil. When the bridegroom was delayed, they all became drowsy and fell asleep. At midnight they were roused by the shout, 'Look, the bridegroom is coming! Come out and meet Him!' All the bridesmaids got up and prepared their lamps. Then the five foolish ones asked the others,

'Please give us some of your oil because our lamps are going out.' But the others replied, 'We don't have enough for all of us. Go to a shop and buy some for yourselves.' But while they were gone to buy oil, the bridegroom came. Then those who were ready went in with Him to the marriage feast, and the door was locked. Later, when the other five bridesmaids returned, they stood outside, calling, 'Lord! Lord! Open the door for us!' But He called back, 'Believe me, I don't know you!' _So you, too, must keep watch! For you do not know the day or hour of my return._ "

- It's not the Jesus-followers who are unprepared for the Rapture. They are fully ready to meet Jesus. It is the *"almost-Jesus followers" who are left open-mouthed repeating over and over to themselves, "If only—!"*
- Missing the Rapture doesn't mean one will slip into hell without the chance to repent. It does mean that those people will enter the Day of God's Wrath and may very well give his or her *(newly redeemed)* life as a martyr!
- However—those who are still rejecting Jesus' loving invitation at the time of his final victorious Second Coming will be forever separated from God!

How much do I know?

1) Zechariah 14:2–4 prophesies the 2nd return of Jesus It was probably confusing to the Israelites because they hadn't quite grasped Jesus "First Coming" yet. Daniel, one generation before Zechariah, had prophesied that "the Anointed One will be killed, appearing to have accomplished nothing, and a ruler will arise whose armies will destroy the city and the Temple." Zechariah knew those prophesies yet saw far enough ahead to see a restored Jerusalem and a living Messiah returning to the Holy City! Where does he say Jesus will land when he arrives a second time?

2) In Matthew 24:32–34: "Now learn a lesson from the fig tree. When its branches bud and its leaves begin to sprout, you know that summer is near. *In the same way, when you see all these things,* you can know His return is very near, right at the door. I tell you the truth, *this generation will not pass from the scene until all these things take place.*" Which generation will not pass away? Is he talking about the generation he is living in? Or is he talking about the generation that will experience the events he has just described in 24:1–29?

3) True or False: Clearly there are some "signs" described by Jesus that will tell us that "His return is very near, right at the door?"

You can check your answers beginning on page 243.

Number of correct answers on this page:

Daniel 9:25 prophesies that from the time the Persian King Artaxerxes decreed the rebuilding of Jerusalem's walls until the time the "Messiah Prince" came would be a period of exactly 483 years. It was exactly 483 years later when Jesus rode over the hill from Bethany on what we now call Palm Sunday. If God was so specific and literal in his prophetic timing in the Old Testament, would he not be just as specific and literal when he speaks of a 1,000-year reign of Jesus in Revelation 20?

True or False: When we think of living forever in heaven with Jesus, few of us ever include in those plans—living and reigning with Jesus, for 1,000 years, right here on this earth.

If Jesus is reigning on this earth for a thousand years, and we are reigning with him, who in the world are we going to be reigning over?

16

The Millennial Reign of Christh

The Marriage Supper of the Lamb is over! The redeemed Saints have mounted up and returned to earth with Jesus landing in Jerusalem just as the dazzling angels told James, and John, and Ethan he would all those years before. When Jesus and his massive entourage land, the Mount of Olives splits to the east and west as Zechariah prophesied it would! "Next on the prophetic calendar," Elder Ethan ponders, "seems to be a rather mysterious, yet clearly prophesied, 1,000-year period with Jesus and his Saints 'reigning on earth.'"—the Millennial Reign of Jesus Christ.

- This "mysterious event" is not just something that is mentioned in Revelation 20. Several of the major and minor prophets in the Old Testament wrote about it—some in great detail, and they were prophesying about this "Millennial Reign" 400–700 years before Jesus' first coming!
- They did not all necessarily grasp the fact that the Messiah would have to FIRST come to this world to die for the sins of all humanity. Yet, somehow, they did all believe that their Anointed One would one day *reign over this whole Earth.*

I am struck by the back story of Zechariah's famous prophecy about the Messiah's mountain-splitting return:

Zechariah 14:4, 6, 9: "On that day his [the Messiah's] feet will stand on the Mount of Olives, east of Jerusalem. And the Mount of Olives will split apart. On that day the sources of light will no longer shine, yet there will be continuous day! And the *LORD will be King over all the earth.* On that day there will be one LORD—"

Zechariah would have been a young prophet in Persia while Daniel was still alive. He would have been completely aware that Daniel had prophesied the arrival of the Messiah in Daniel 9:25, and that in 9:26, he had prophesied that soon after the Messiah arrived, he would be killed! **Yet Zechariah still saw a day when the Messiah would return ALIVE to reign from Jerusalem!**

This is your future reality—prophesied in Jesus' Unveiling: If you are a Believer, you will spend 1,000 years of your "eternity" back on Earth reigning with Jesus! Why? Some have said this must be some kind of figurative number—it is surely not to be taken as a literal 1,000 years. Really?—Why not?

1) If everything in Revelation seems to be lining up as a literal part of the End Times storyline, and

2) If Daniel's 483 prophesied years from the time of King Artaxerxes' decree until the coming of the Messiah turned out to be exactly 483 (lunar) years, and

3) If the 70th week of Daniel turned out to be exactly seven years divided into two exact three-and-a-half year parts *(each exactly 1,260 days)*, and

4) If the final bowl judgments last exactly 30 days, and Jesus' taking over the reins of the earth as King of Kings and Lord of Lords lasts 45 prophesied days,

5) **Why in the world would anybody get to the prophecy of the 1,000-year reign of Jesus the Messiah and suspect it was anything other than exactly what it says it is?**

6) So many people have adjusted their theology over the last 70 years because the final elusive pieces of the puzzle are clearly starting to slip into place.

All the pieces are falling into place!

The storyline marches with perfect precision on *toward eternity*! John reports that right after Jesus annihilates the Armageddon armies:

> **Revelation 19:20–21: "But the beast was captured, and with it the false prophet. The two of them were thrown alive into the fiery lake of burning sulfur. The rest were killed with the sword coming out of the mouth of the rider on the horse."**

Jesus then deals with satan himself:

> **Revelation 20:1–3: "And I saw an angel coming down out of heaven, having the key to the Abyss and holding in His hand a great chain. He seized the dragon, that ancient serpent, who is the devil, or satan, and bound him for a thousand years. He threw him into the Abyss, and locked and sealed it over him, to keep him from deceiving the nations anymore until the thousand years were ended."**

Notice this: The fact that Jesus ascended to Heaven from the Mount of Olives and will land on the Mount of Olives when He returns—is a "prophetic completion." Whenever we see something start on one side of Biblical prophecy, we should always look for where it closes on the back side—it's God's perfectly logical mind!

- When Jesus ascended from the Mount of Olives, He was all alone. The angels assured the onlookers, **"in the same way you have seen Him go. He will come again"** *(Acts 1:11)*.
- What the angels didn't mention was *when Jesus returns in His triumphal landing on the Mount, He will have several billion angels filling the sky, along with millions, perhaps billions of believing, raptured Saints landing* in wave after wave onto the Earth.

A brand-new sequence of events begins to unfold, and every one of them will be God's way of "completing a prophesy"—and we Believers are going to help Him do it. In God's complete, infinite, perfect mind, if a door was opened in history, from the Garden of Eden on, and God's plan was interrupted so that the door was left open, God will systematically tie off every historical loose end.

Let's not make the mistake of thinking that God started His plan, but then satan got in the way of God's plan, forcing Him to alter His original divine design. That's nonsense! **God's plan will end exactly the way He intended it to end. God's plan, from before the foundations of the earth, will land in the center of the bull's eye. There is not one thing that satan, or the antichrist, or any of rebellious humanity has ever done that will deviate God's ultimate objective by even a fraction!**

Once we return with Jesus and dismount, God will start His earthly reign by mopping up the effects of more than 6,000 years of sin and the curse on the Earth. The 2–3 years of judgments during the Day of the Lord's Wrath were about hammering a sin-cursed creation into submission, but now, finally, God goes after the source.

With a "completing the prophetic" theology in mind, watch God's binding of satan:

> **Revelation 20:1: "And I saw an angel coming down out of heaven, having the key to the Abyss and holding in his hand a great chain."**

Satan was the very first thing that came into God's perfectly created masterpiece to bring sin's destruction, and now he is the very last thing God deals with as Jesus wrenches complete control of the earth out of his hands.

> **Revelation 20:1 (NLT): "An angel comes down out of heaven, having the key to the Abyss"** (bottomless pit).

We have seen this *Abyss* several times throughout the book of Revelation. It's always under the control of satan and the antichrist. Out of the abyss have come demons to do this and the hordes of satan to do that. And now, from the "master key safe in Heaven" comes perhaps the archangel Michael with the "master key of the universe" and corrals the evil one and his hordes.

Revelation 20:2: "He seized the dragon, that ancient serpent, who is the devil."

One of the characteristics of ancient languages was "emphasis by understatement." This is a monumental event. It isn't just satan who has to leave the Earth so that the next phase of God's plan can get underway. It is all his demons and every "willfully rebellious" person left on Earth. Every idol, every sinful image, every sinful tool to commit evil must be purged from the Earth.

The Abyss *(whatever and wherever it is)* seems to have been the source from which all that is evil came. Now picture God reversing the swirl inward so that all that demonic, all that leads humanity away from God goes screaming back into the pit—the last of which is the evil one himself, God's one-time archangel.

Revelation 20:2–3: "He seized the dragon, that ancient serpent, who is the devil, or Satan, and bound him for a thousand years. He threw him into the Abyss, and locked and sealed it over."

- It is important to our understanding of the Millennium that the 1,000-year reign of Jesus on this earth starts with all that is evil—all that is sinful, eradicated from the earth. That means that one more thing has to happen.

Jesus closed His final Matthew sermon with this final warning:

Matthew 25:31–34, 41: *"But when the Son of Man comes in His glory,* and all the angels with Him, then He will sit upon His glorious throne. *All the nations will be gathered in His presence, and He will separate the people* as a shepherd separates the sheep from the goats. He will place the sheep at His right hand and the goats at His left. Then the King will say to those on His right, 'Come, you who are blessed by My Father, inherit the Kingdom prepared for you from the creation of the world. Then the King will turn to those on the left and say, 'Away with you, you cursed ones, into the eternal fire prepared for the devil and his demons.'"

Only **two groups of people** are going to be left on the earth at this point in time, and both of them are "redeemed"!

(1) The **RAPTURED, GLORIFIED, RETURNED SAINTS** who will rule with Jesus during the Millennium, and

(2) The **redeemed, unraptured, unglorified Believers** who they/we will reign over.

Remember Zechariah 14 which tells us that Jesus gets off His white horse and plants His feet on the Mount of Olives? That same book *(along with many others)* begins to describe what the Earth will be like now that the Day of the Lord's Judgment is over, now that satan has been banished, now that everyone on Earth has embraced Jesus as Lord.

Zechariah 14:6–9: "On that day the sources of light will no longer shine, yet there will be continuous day! Only the LORD knows how this could happen. There will be no normal day and night, for at evening time it will still be light. *On that day life-giving waters will flow out from Jerusalem, half toward the Dead Sea and half toward the Mediterranean, flowing continuously in both summer and winter.* [Note that this is not normal water from a normal spring and also how it flows in two directions.] **And the LORD will be King over all the earth. On that day there will be one LORD—His name alone will be worshiped."**

- Are you looking forward to reigning with Jesus during the *(1,000-year)* Millennium? It's not something most Christians ever think about. In the Lord's Prayer, Jesus begins with the words:

"Our Father which art in heaven, Hallowed be Your name, Your kingdom come, Your will be done on earth, as it is in heaven" *(Matthew 6:9–10).*

- At most levels, we spiritualize this in our daily lives and say, "His coming kingdom has already started in us on this Earth." That's true! But the real foundational meat of the second sentence in the Lord's Prayer is, at least in part, in our *asking Jesus to hurry back to Earth to set up His eternal reign*.

I've preached whole series of sermons on how God wants to unfold His kingdom in and through us in the here and now. That truth, however, doesn't replace the reality that **someday soon we will be part of reigning with Jesus on this Earth in His eternal kingdom**!

- This is something we are all supposed to be excited about, but somehow many Christians have missed all the excitement. We've replaced all this biblical theology we are studying with the phrase, "I'm going to Heaven to be with Jesus when I die." (*What exactly does that mean?*)

Notice another "prophetic completion:"

> **Zechariah 14:10–11: "All the land from Geba, north of Judah, to Rimmon, south of Jerusalem, will become one vast plain. But Jerusalem will be raised up in its original place and will be inhabited all the way.** [Jerusalem becomes Mt. Jerusalem; a six-mile-wide mountaintop with the suburbs reaching east to the Euphrates River, in Iraq.] **And Jerusalem will be filled, safe at last, *never again* to be cursed and destroyed."**

Let me summarize what several of the Old Testament prophets say about this coming Millennial period:

The Millennial Earth!

(1) The atmosphere will be completely renewed; the new Divine "light" will make plant growth outrageous. The Earth will again be like the Garden of Eden was. Harmful radiation will be gone.

(2) This will affect the non-glorified humans who are still reproducing. Revelation 20 tells us that the entire Earth will be re-populated in the

1,000 years. There will be no disease or deformity. People will, perhaps, once again live for hundreds of years.

(3) There will be no political election season *(How about another Hallelujah!)* because Jesus Himself will be the perfect ruler, and He will be surrounded by other rulers, redeemed rulers (us Believers) who will help Him administrate the New Earth.

Revelation 20:4: "Then I saw *thrones*, and the *people sitting on them* had been given the *authority to judge*."

Those followers of Jesus who died as martyrs after the Rapture and before the Second Coming—those who had "proclaimed the Word of God," and had "not worshiped the beast or accepted his mark"—THEY ALL CAME BACK TO LIFE AGAIN and they reigned with Christ for a thousand years *(Revelation 20:4)*!

Revelation 5:9–10: "And they sang a new song, saying: 'You are worthy to take the scroll and to open its seals, because You were slain, and with Your blood You purchased for God persons from every tribe and language and people and nation. *You have made them to be a kingdom and priests [believers] to serve our God, and they will reign on the earth.*'"

(4) The animal kingdom will apparently be completely at peace with humans and with each other—*"the wolf and the lamb will feed together and the lion will eat straw like the ox"* (Isaiah 65:25). *And so much more!*

- This New Earth under the Millennial Reign of Jesus *completes the circle begun with the Garden of Eden*. Now, instead of a handful of people in the Garden, millions are filling the Earth. Instead of God "ruling" over two people in Eden, more than 6,000 years of human history has produced *millions of redeemed Saints who join with God in "ruling" over all the rest of God's "renewed" creation.*

How much do I know?

1) What is this Abyss that the antichrist is confined to? The angel in Revelation 1 seems to have a key to it. Satan is going to be thrown into the Abyss, and it will be locked and sealed it over. Where is the bottomless pit and where did it come from?

2) If after Jesus' Triumphant Second Coming there are only two groups of people on the earth: The raptured, glorified, returned Saints and the redeemed, unraptured, unglorified Believers who came through the last of the Tribulation—what will be our relationship to each other?

3) During the 1,000-year reign of Christ, the earth is once again repopulated. Where do all the kids come from? Are they all automatically followers of Jesus?

4) Might this be some part of what our future "rulership" will involve? Does that make Heaven seem less inviting to you?

You can check your answers beginning on page 243.

Number of correct answers on this page:

We are quick to quote the phrase: "Every knee will bow, and every tongue will confess that Jesus is Lord" found in Philippians 2:10, but do we have any idea when that truth actually becomes a reality?

Revelation 21:1 says: "Then I saw 'a new heaven and a new earth,' for the first heaven and the first earth had passed away." Does that mean we will be living back on this same planet, one day, but it will somehow be "new"? What does that mean?

Zechariah 14:9 says: "And the LORD will be King over all the earth. On that day there will be one LORD—His name alone will be worshiped." Does that mean that Jesus will be right here on this planet "ruling" over all its inhabitants?

Revelation 20:4 says: "Then I saw thrones, and the people sitting on them and they reigned with Christ for a thousand years." Does that mean we will be right here on this planet "ruling" with Jesus?

17

The New Heaven and New Earth

Many long-time Christians have a mindset about their future *(their after-this-life future)* that we can summarize this way:

(1) I am going to die and I'm going to go to Heaven or

(2) If Jesus returns before I die, I am going to be raptured and carried up to be with Him in Heaven.

(3) Either way, "I am on that great glory train bound for Heaven."

A hymn by Eliza Hewitt (1898), "When We All Get to Heaven" reads, *"Sing the wondrous love of Jesus; sing His mercy and His grace, In the mansions bright and blessed, He'll prepare for us a place. When we all get to heaven, what a day of rejoicing that will be! When we all see Jesus, we'll sing and shout the victory."*

- I am not in any way mocking this old hymn. I have sung it scores of times and been deeply blessed, but *(pardon me Eliza)*, it's a little light on specifics. Is Heaven about more than "singing and shouting the victory"?

- Actually, if we want to know what our eternal, heavenly future as Christians will be *(at least 1,000 years of it),* the Bible spells it out.

- If Jesus' return is less than 100 years away *(and of course we do not know if it is or not)*, we can know with absolute certainty where we Believers will be and what we will be doing 100 years from now and 500 years from now. This is no obscure mumbo-jumbo; it is our prophesied future *(and remember that 6,512 verses of prophecy in the Bible have all happened exactly as predicted).*

- With all due respect to the song, aren't we going to be doing far more than *sitting "in our mansion bright and blessed"*?

Let's go back to unfolding the storyline of Revelation and pick up after Jesus' Second Coming and Triumphal Return with his Saints.

Since, the Rapture of the Saints is detailed in Revelation 7 and reinforced in Matthew 24 as indicated on the chart by the first big white "up" arrow.

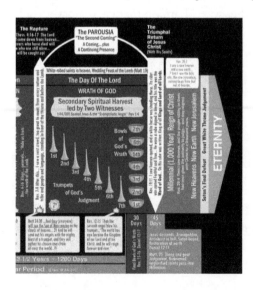

Since the *"Parousia," the Second Coming*, encompasses the whole time between the Rapture of the Saints and the Triumphal Return of Jesus with His Saints. *(Big white arrow down on chart.)*

Since the last 11 verses of Chapter 19 have Jesus coming back with His white-robed Saints, and as He lands on the Mount of Olives, He takes on all the gathered armies of the world in the famed Battle of Armageddon.

- If you are still wondering what you are going to be doing let me help: *You are going to be there with Jesus at the Battle of Armageddon mounted on a white horse.*
- You will be there with millions or billions of other redeemed, glorified *(no longer in an earthly body)* Saints surrounded by billions of angels.

Refer to the green box labeled 45 Days on the chart that lists all the things that will unfold in your Millennial future. You will watch the following events tick off *(and perhaps even play some role in them):*

(1) The Armageddon finale.

(2) The destruction of the antichrist *(Revelation 19)*.

(3) The exile of satan to the Abyss *(Revelation 20)*.

(4) The sheep and goat judgment *(Matthew 25)*.

(5) The redeemed, unglorified entering the Millennium, still in human bodies with a sin nature and reproducing.

(6) The restoration of the Earth.

Imagine what you will be seeing when you are standing there with Jesus as the 45-day period unfolds. The last verse in Revelation 19 speaks of all the world's birds being gathered for a "feast" at the end of the Battle of Armageddon. Frankly, that sounds a bit gross—the whole planet has just come through the pouring out of the Trumpet Judgments and then the horrendous destruction of the last 30 days of the final Bowls of God's Wrath. The last bowl levels every mountain and sinks every island. Scripture seems to indicate that God's judgments, particularly those in the last 30 days, are God's way of "cremating" the effects of sin's curse on the Earth.

2 Peter 3:7, 10, 12–13: "The present heavens and earth are reserved for fire, being kept for the day *of judgment* and destruction of the ungodly. But the *day of the Lord* will come like a thief. *The heavens will disappear with a roar; the elements will be destroyed by fire, and the earth and everything done in it will be laid bare. That day will bring about the destruction of the heavens by fire, and the elements will melt in the heat.* But in keeping with His promise we are *looking forward to a new heaven and a new earth, where righteousness dwells.* "

- The Apostle Peter makes it clear: God is going to get rid of this old sinful Earth and replace it with "a New Heaven and a New Earth." Peter tells us exactly when "the heavens will disappear with a roar, and the elements will be destroyed by fire." It will be at the end of the "Day of the Lord's Wrath"—after which we look forward to a New Heaven and a New Earth! That's the same wording John uses in Revelation:

Revelation 21:1: "Then I saw *'a new heaven and a new earth,'* for the first heaven and the *first earth had passed away.* "

- The Greek word translated "new" in this verse is *kainos*, which means *new in substance and quality, not new in time (neos)*. It is the word used of the "new birth" and of us becoming "a new creation in Christ Jesus."
- When we arrive with Jesus, will we be viewing a planet that looks like a world-wide atomic bomb just went off, or will we be watching as the restoration of the planet unfolds? Will we then finally step down onto a newly-minted Earth with a brand-new Heaven spreading out above the earth?

Isaiah 65:17–20, 25: *"See, I will create new heavens and a new earth. The former things will not be remembered, nor will they come to mind.* **But be glad and rejoice forever in what I will create, for I will create Jerusalem to be a delight and its people a joy. I will rejoice over Jerusalem and take delight in My people; the sound of weeping and of crying will be heard in it no more. Never again will there be in it an infant who lives but a few days, or an old man who does not live out his years; the** *one who dies at a hundred will be thought a mere child. The wolf and the lamb will feed together,* **and the lion will eat straw like the ox."**

Let's expand even further what we started at the end of the last chapter—a Scriptural condensing of Jesus' 1,000-year earthly reign.

1) The atmosphere changes: The new "light of God" replaces sun and accelerates plant growth. Isaiah suggests that agricultural production will be outrageous. The earth will again be like the Eden greenhouse—No drought, no strong storms, no natural catastrophes. True "prosperity" will finally reach every corner of the earth; poverty and hunger will not exist.

2) The non-glorified humans will be reproducing—a lot. The entire Earth will again be filled with people without any of the effects of the curse to make everyone's life a living hell.

3) It will no longer be "us vs. them" with the bears and the mosquitoes. **"The wolf and the lamb will live together,** the leopard will lie down with the baby goat," A child will lead around a lion *(Isaiah 11:6)*. Poisonous will become non-poisonous; carnivores will "eat their veggies." Spiders and snakes will become beautiful?

4) Jerusalem will be the undisputed spiritual center of the Earth. People will come from all over the world to worship Jesus in Jerusalem. **Zechariah 14:9: "And the LORD** *will be King over all the earth.* **On that**

day there will be one LORD—His name alone will be worshiped."
(Every knee will bow, and every tongue will confess that Jesus is Lord!)

Jesus is reigning with a "rod of iron," why?

The Unveiling does tell us, however, that Jesus will be reigning over this growing population with *a rod of iron (Revelation 2:27). Why the heavy-handed approach?* If all the rebellious sinners are dropped into the Lake of Fire at the beginning of the 1,000-year Reign of Christ—why would there be problems, of any kind, in the new Millennial Kingdom where "the Lord is King over all the earth"?

- If the antichrist, and then satan himself, are banished from the Earth, why would anybody 200 years into the Millennium say, "I don't like following Jesus. I don't want to go up to Jerusalem and worship Him"?

- If true prosperity has surged through the entire world and everyone has more than enough to eat, and disease and deformity are no longer afflicting anyone, and nobody is bouncing a check at the local bank, what could possibly require the Lord's heavy hand?

- This exposes the modern myth that politicians and social scientists sometimes screech—"people act unrighteously because of the perceived 'lack' in their lives; if everybody lacked nothing—the world would become a perfect place."

The Redeemed people during the Millennium, who came STRAIGHT OUT OF DANIEL'S 70TH WEEK, still have the sin nature lurking in their *(non-glorified)* human hearts. **Rebellious actions come from an un-submitted heart!** In a final solution where God has completed the prophetic circle of re-creating a Garden of Eden on the Earth and gives humanity everything their hearts desire—some of humanity will still turn their backs away from the righteous leadership of the King of Kings and Lords of Lords. *(Amazing!)*

Revelation tells us exactly who it is who helps the One sitting on the eternal throne of David to govern this earth for 1,000 years:

Revelation 20:4: "Then I saw *[kai eidon]* **thrones, and the people sitting on them had been given the authority to judge."** *That has to be a direct fulfillment of:*

Revelation 5:9–10: "And they sang a new song, saying: 'You are worthy to take the scroll and to open its seals, because You were slain, and with Your blood You purchased for God persons from every tribe and language and people and nation. You have made them to be a kingdom and priests to serve our God, and they will reign on the earth.'"

Have you ever seriously thought of being raptured and going to Heaven only to spend the next thousand years back on Earth ruling with Jesus over a world-full of non-glorified humans, some of whom openly reject His righteous rule, and become participants in a final rebellion when Satan is temporarily released? We Believers are destined to be part of that! *(Who knew?)*

* For many who long for Heaven, the prospect of reigning with Christ on Earth might sound a little less than inviting. But what if the presence of God, the very Throne Room of God came down to Earth where you, and Jesus, and the rest of the Believers already were—and your overwhelming focus was inside the very place Jesus went to prepare for you? The place where Believers of all ages really are "singing and shouting the victory"?

Seriously? Reigning with Jesus = One final Harvest?

Actually, our additional extracurricular activities of "reigning with Jesus" on this earth are not going to be so much about "corralling the bad guys" as about **drawing in one final harvest of those who will join the glorified redeemed at the end of the 1,000 years.** *(Remember, the non-glorified are still reproducing new people.)*

For any of that to be true, however, one additional major Divine piece has to be "unveiled," and this is where the Millennial picture really begins to swivel. It is not difficult to picture a New Heaven and a New Earth coming at the beginning of the 1,000 years. In fact, from a logical standpoint it is hard to see it any other way. The Millennial Earth is clearly not the devastated, destroyed Earth left after the Day of the Lord's Wrath.

Jesus' Revelation **ties two amazing things together** like two sides of a single coin.

> **Revelation 21:1–3:** "Then I saw *a new heaven and a new earth,* **for the old heaven and the old earth had disappeared. And I saw the Holy City, the *New Jerusalem, coming down from God out of heaven like a bride beautifully dressed for her husband.* I heard a loud shout from the throne, saying, '*Look, God's home is now among His people! He will live with them,* and they will be His people.'"

> **Revelation 21:16–17:** "When he [the angel] measured it, he found it was a square, as wide as it was long. In fact, its length and width and height were each 1,400 miles. Then he measured the walls and found them to be 216 feet thick."

- It sounds like something out of a Star Trek movie. This 1,400-mile cubed, descending Holy City is going to be massive! If one corner of it lands near Jerusalem the rest could cover most of the Middle East. If each level was one-mile high (*imagine if the ceiling in your mansion were one mile up), the total surface area would be 2,628,072,000 square miles, which is more than 13 times the surface area of the Earth!*

This is the place Jesus went back to Heaven to prepare for us!

> **John 14:1–4:** "Don't let your hearts be troubled. Trust in God, and trust also in me. There is more than enough room in my Father's home. If this were not so, would I have told you that I am going to prepare a place for you? When everything is ready, I will come and get you, so that you will always be with me where I am."

"God's home"–the Throne Room of God!

Revelation 21:22–27: *"I saw no temple in the city, for the Lord God Almighty and the Lamb are its temple. And the city has no need of sun or moon, for the glory of God illuminates the city, and the Lamb is its light.* The nations will walk in its light, and the kings of the world will enter the city in all their glory. Its gates will never be closed at the end of day because there is no night there. And all the nations will bring their glory and honor into the city. Nothing evil will be allowed to enter, nor anyone who practices shameful idolatry and dishonesty—but only those whose names are written in the Lamb's Book of Life."

The image of being "with Christ" for 1,000 years takes on a whole new perspective when we consider *HEAVEN IS GOING TO COME DOWN TO EARTH*. We will spend a lot of our time in the presence of the Lamb and the Lord God Almighty, being illuminated by the Light of God Himself and dwelling in a place that the Bible calls the "home" of God. This is the stunning setting where all the worship around God's Throne in the "Throne Room of Heaven" takes place.

- **If all of that is here on Earth during the Millennium, who would want to be anywhere else?**
- But, doesn't the Bible say that the 1,000-year Millennium happens in Revelation Chapter 20 and that the New Heaven, New Earth, and New Jerusalem do not occur until Chapter 21? Does this not disrupt the notion that the storyline in Revelation unfolds in chronological order?

Even though I have been harping on the importance of drawing a chronological timeline through the Unveiling—in this instance, the New Jerusalem *is, [IMO],* going to be here during the entire Millennium. It would not be improper to interpret that **the events of Chapter 20 and 21 are unfolding at exactly the same time.**

- Revelation 20:1–3: Satan is bound and locked into the Abyss.
- Revelation 20:4: "Then I saw thrones, and the people sitting on them— and they reigned with Christ for a thousand years."

- Revelation 20:7–8: "When the *thousand years come to an end*, Satan will be let out of his prison. He will go out to deceive the nations."
- Revelation 20:10: "Then the devil, who had deceived them, was thrown into the fiery lake of burning sulfur, joining the beast and the false prophet."
- Revelation 20:11: "And I saw a great white throne and the one sitting on it."
- Revelation 21:1–2: "Then I saw a New Heaven and a New Earth, for the old heaven and the old earth had disappeared. And the sea was also gone. And I saw the Holy City, the New Jerusalem, coming down from God out of heaven like a bride beautifully dressed for her husband."

The thrones and "reigning people" sitting on them in Revelation 20:4 and the great white throne in Revelation 20:11 ARE IN THE NEW JERUSALEM! (One has to assume it has already come down to Earth and that the mention of the end of 1,000 years when "satan will be let out of prison" *(20:7–8)*, and Satan's final incarceration *(20:10)* are a flash forward in time.)

Revelation 21:23–27: "And the city has no need of sun or moon, for the glory of God illuminates the city, and the Lamb is its light. The *nations will walk in its light, and the kings of the world will enter the city in all their glory*. Its gates will never be closed at the end of day because there is no night there. *And all the nations will bring their glory and honor into the city*. Nothing evil will be allowed to enter, nor anyone who practices shameful idolatry and dishonesty— but only those whose names are written in the Lamb's Book of Life."

- The discussion of the nations and the kings of the world only makes sense if people other than the Redeemed glorified Saints, who are ruling over it, are populating the Earth. The statement that "nothing evil will enter the city" implies that there are still unrighteous people on the Earth who will need to be kept out.
- The statement that "only those whose names are written in the Lamb's Book of Life" *implies that there are those whose names are not written in it!*

Revelation 22:1–2: "Then the angel showed me *a river with the Water of Life*, clear as crystal, flowing from the throne of God and of the Lamb. It flowed down the center of the main street. On each side of the river grew a Tree of Life, bearing twelve crops of fruit, with a fresh crop each month. *The leaves were used for medicine to heal the nations.*"

Revelation 22:14–15: "Blessed are those who wash their robes. They will be permitted to enter through the gates of the city and eat the fruit from the tree of life. Outside the city are the sorcerers, the sexually immoral, the murderers, the idol worshipers, and all who—<u>live a lie</u>."

It seems clear that this "City of God's home," the New Jerusalem, descends while we are ruling the Earth with Jesus. Perhaps *(I am speculating)* it is only the first few levels where the "Redeemed of the nations of the earth" are permitted to enter and where our judgment over them takes place. At other levels, perhaps *(remember the City is 1,400 miles high)*, only the Redeemed are permitted to enter.

"I'm going to prepare a place for you!"

- This New Jerusalem is most certainly the place that "JESUS WENT BACK TO HEAVEN TO PREPARE" for you.
- Some*where (occupying perhaps 100 miles worth of floors, now I'm really speculating)* is the unimaginable Throne Room of God. **There we will fall down and worship our wonderful Creator and Savior!**

How much do I know?

1) Who started that phrase "The Lion and the Lamb will lie down together" anyway? What does Isaiah 11:6 actually prophesy about the relationship of animals to each other in the Millennium?

2) True or False: This passage in Revelation 5:9–10: "And they sang a new song, saying: 'You are worthy to take the scroll and to open its seals, because you were slain, and with your blood you purchased for God persons from every tribe and language and people and nation. You have made them to be a kingdom and priests to serve our God, and they will reign on the earth.'" This is fulfilled in Revelation 20:4: "Then I saw [kai eidon] thrones, and the people sitting on them had been given the authority to judge," and the "fulfillers," the "throne-sitters," are us—the redeemed Believers!

3) True or False: The New Jerusalem is the place Jesus went to prepare for us (John 14:1–3). The New Jerusalem, heaven—at least that part of it, is going to come down to earth? "Heaven is going to come to earth?"

You can check your answers beginning on page 243.

Number of correct answers on this page:

True or False: The New Jerusalem originates back at Abraham, who some 4,200 years ago "was confidently looking forward to a city with eternal foundations, a city designed and built by God" (Hebrews 11:10).

True or False: Even though Revelation 19:11–22:6 uses up only 59 verses in the book and we can read the whole thing in about 15 minutes—we must not rush past it because it is detailing all the rest of our eternity.

True or False: Two of the things that are going to mean the most to us in heaven throughout all eternity, are going to be: "walking through those pearly gates" onto those "streets of gold"!

18

Heaven—Our Eternal Home

The truth about Heaven affects the eternal future of every single Believer! If we are going to experience the "direct and continual presence" of Jesus during the Rapture, Marriage Feast, Triumphant Return, 1,000-year reign on this Earth—and then **spend all of eternity enjoying Heaven with Him**, it should be normal that we would be interested in, and even fascinated by, any nugget of information we can find on the subject!

Most of us are familiar with the key Bible passages on Heaven. Jesus made it a point to leave us with the truth that one of His primary activities after His ascension and before His return to Rapture His church—was going to be preparing "a place" for us.

> **John 14:1–3: "Let not your heart be troubled; you believe in God, believe also in me.** *In My Father's house are many mansions;* if *it were* **not** *so,* **I would have told you.** *I go to prepare a place for you.* **And if I go and prepare a place for you,** *I will come again and receive you to myself; that where I am, there you may be also.***"

Jesus is preparing your "mansion" in Heaven, and when it is ready, He is going to come back for you—and take you to your new heavenly digs!

- Where is this mansion some might ask? In Heaven, is the response - Where is Heaven? Up there!—somewhere?

- What are we going to be doing "up there"? We don't really know for sure, but we can't wait to get there! *(Huh?)*

Let's pick up this final part of the storyline and follow it through Chapters 21 and 22 for some more definite answers to those questions. After the final Triumphal Return of Jesus with His already raptured, glorified Saints *(Revelation 19)*, the final Battle of Armageddon, the defeat of the antichrist, and the consignment of satan to the abyss, the sheep and goat judgment of Matthew 25 takes place in which the goats *(the Christ-rejecters and antichrist followers)* are consigned to the Lake of Fire, and the sheep *(those who have embraced Jesus as Messiah)* move into the Millennium as those believers whom we will reign over.

- So many people read through the exciting and dramatic End Time events and then coast over the final few chapters of Revelation to get to the finale: *"Surely I am coming soon, Amen."* We don't allow ourselves to fill in the last few pieces of the puzzle.
- Imagine working a complex and beautiful jigsaw puzzle, and just before you fit the final pieces that complete the picture on the box lid, you break it all up and toss the pieces back into the box!

For us Believers, the last three chapters of the book of Revelation are our future! They are the final culmination of living out this present life as Jesus' followers. This is our ultimate goal. We are running the race of life, sprinting toward the spiritual finish line, pouring every drop of our spiritual energy into "completing the race" for which we were put on this Earth.

It will dawn on us that we have won the race during the Rapture *(Revelation 7)*, when we are among all the Saints in Heaven at the Marriage Supper of the Lamb, when we accompany Jesus in His Triumphant Second Coming *(Revelation 19)*, and when we start reigning with Christ as residents of "God's home" the New Jerusalem *(Revelation 21–22)*.

Revelation 21:1–5: "Then I saw a new heaven and a new earth, for the old heaven and the old earth had disappeared. And the sea was also gone. *[This rather strange phrase may not quite mean there is no ocean. The Israelites viewed lakes and streams as things of life, and the sea* *was considered a place from which bad things came, such as, the antichrist who "came out of the sea." So, this may just be an idiomatic way of saying, that people have nothing to be afraid of anymore.]* **And I saw the Holy City, the New Jerusalem, coming down from God out of heaven like a bride beautifully dressed for her husband. I heard a loud shout from the throne, saying, 'Look, God's home is now among His people! He will live with them, and they will be His people. God Himself will be with them. He will wipe every tear from their eyes, and there will be no more death or sorrow or crying or pain. All these things are gone forever.' And the one sitting on the throne said, 'Look, I am making everything new!'"**

The New Jerusalem originates back with Abraham, who some 4,200 years ago *"was confidently looking forward to a city with eternal foundations, a city designed and built by God" (Hebrews 11:10).*

- How long has the New Jerusalem been in existence? When Jesus went back to Heaven to prepare a "room" for us, was He building the whole city or just custom tailoring a room/mansion for each person who embraces Him as Lord and Savior? The Bible doesn't say, but I tend to think it was the latter. This city is said to be God's home *("my Father's house")*. When it comes here to Earth, God Himself will live with His people and be with them.

Revelation 21:16–17: "When he *[the angel]* measured it, he found it was a square, as wide as it was long. In fact, its length and width and height were each 1,400 miles [12,000 stadia]. Then he measured the walls and found them to be 216 feet thick."

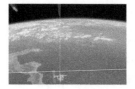

Think about this: The City is 1,400 miles high! The International Space Station is orbiting 205 miles up, so this city will extend seven times higher than the space station in orbit.

In verse 10, John lays it out even more clearly suggesting that this is something God really wants us to get, or perhaps we are supposed to grasp that it is ungraspable by our modern frame of reference. When we finally see this New City descending from Heaven, slowing down as it approaches Earth, and finally settling into what appears to be its final resting place, we will be beyond stunned—just from what we see on the outside. God does try to give our weak human minds a mental picture:

Revelation 21:10–12, 14: "And he showed me the Holy City, Jerusalem, coming down out of heaven from God. It shone with the glory of God, and its brilliance was like that of a very precious jewel, like a jasper, clear as crystal. It had a great, high wall with twelve gates, and with twelve angels at the gates. On the gates were written the names of the twelve tribes of Israel. The wall of the city had twelve foundations, and on them were the names of the twelve apostles of the Lamb."

- Clearly we are supposed to draw the conclusion that Saints from both Old and New Testament times will live in the city. *Jews will be as important as redeemed Gentiles.* So, it's possible that you will have a room right next to one of the Children of Israel who trudged across the wilderness. He can tell you what it was like when his shoes never wore out, and you can explain how many sets of tires you burned up on your car in 40 years.

Revelation 21: 18–19, 21: "The wall was made of jasper, and the city was pure gold, as clear as glass. The wall of the city was built on foundation stones inlaid with twelve precious stones. The twelve gates were made of pearls—each gate from a single pearl! And the main street was pure gold, as clear as glass."

"I'm gonna walk on those streets of gold!"

- This is where the often-quoted expressions of "walking on streets of gold," and St. Peter meeting us at the "pearly gates" come from. We reduce it to images we can relate to because there is no way our brains can grasp the reality. The gold is so pure that it is crystal clear, and the idea of a whole gate being made out of a single pearl is simply to say to us, *"You're not going to believe this when you see it!"*

- I seriously doubt that many of us will spend our days gawking at the beauty of a "pearly gate," because it will be *what's inside that makes Heaven—Heaven!* Heaven is not Heaven because of the gold! Things that are so valuable here will not impress us there. *(God is stoking the fire in our minds.)*

Revelation 21:22–27: "I saw no temple in the city, *for the Lord God Almighty and the Lamb are its temple. And the city has no need of sun or moon, for the glory of God illuminates the city, and the Lamb is its light.* The nations will walk in its light, and the kings of the world will enter the city in all their glory. Its gates will never be closed at the end of day because there is no night there. And all the nations will bring their glory and honor into the city. Nothing evil will be allowed to enter, nor anyone who practices shameful idolatry and dishonesty—but only those whose names are written in the Lamb's Book of Life."

- I really do firmly believe that the New Heaven and the New Earth happen at the beginning of the 1,000-year reign of Christ. That's the only explanation for the totally destroyed Earth after the "Day of the Lord" turning into the global Garden of Eden that Isaiah and Zechariah describe.

- I just as firmly have come to believe that the New Jerusalem comes down from Heaven at the beginning of the 1,000- year "Millennium" as well—It's the only possible explanation for what we just read:

Revelation 21:24–27: "The nations will walk in its light, and the kings of the world will enter the city in all their glory. Its gates will never be closed at the end of day because there is no night there. And all the nations will bring their glory and honor into the city. Nothing evil will be allowed to enter, nor anyone who practices shameful idolatry and dishonesty—but only those whose names are written in the Lamb's Book of Life."

Those Believers who trusted Christ during the last days of the "Lord's Wrath" are thriving in the New Earth, the renewed Garden of Eden. There is no want, no disease—the wolf and the lamb have become best buds.

- People will be trekking from all over the world to worship Jesus in Jerusalem as He sits on the renewed eternal throne of David.

Zechariah 14:9: "And the *LORD will be King over all the earth. On that day there will be one LORD. His name alone will be worshiped.*" *(Every knee will bow, and every tongue confess!)*

Even though every person entering the Millennium will be a Believer, and even though the Savior of the world will be personally available to pour out His grace on every person, and even though the glorified, raptured, returned Saints are there ruling with Jesus—In spite of the fact that all of "Maslow's hierarchy of felt needs" are being fulfilled in spades, some unregenerate sinful human hearts will still say, "I am not following the King of Kings and Lord of Lords. Just because the majority of people on the earth worship Him as God Almighty does not mean I am going to accept Him."

- At the end of the 1,000 years, Jesus releases satan from the Abyss for a brief time. Satan runs to every corner of the planet gathering up every rebellious person *(a great number, we read) who will not follow this King of Kings*. And in one final cleansing of the Earth, *Jesus sends down fire from Heaven and consumes them all and finally consigns satan to the Lake of Fire forever.*

"The Great White Throne Judgment!"

- All those who have rejected Almighty God and His Christ are eternally consigned to the Lake of Fire.
- During Jesus' 1,000-year reign on Earth—we will reign with Him. I believe our role is to nurture, teach, and disciple *(much as we do right now)* all who accept Jesus' Lordship during the Millennium. Every time a child is born into the world, we are there, for who is better to explain what truly following Jesus is all about than those raptured Redeemed who had to learn to overcome through the toughest of life circumstances.
- We Believers right now have to "overcome" in a sin-cursed world with a devil who just seems to be everywhere all at once. We have to overcome in a world full of pain and death and vast need. Surely we can teach the Millennium Believers to overcome in a world where every need is met and Satan is chained in the Abyss. *(We should probably assume that those who make it through the Millennium and are committed to following Christ are then glorified right along with the rest of us.)*

Remember those letters to the seven churches in Revelation 2–3? We learned that Jesus' function during the Church Age *(the present time in which we are living)* is to carve out of a sinful world those who "overcome" sin and satan. Remember the focus of those great promises at the end? All who are victorious, all who overcome:

(1) Will be clothed in white *(Revelation 19)*.

(2) Will not be harmed by the second death *(Revelation 20)*.

(3) Will sit with me on My throne *(Revelation 20)*.

(4) I will give them authority over all the nations to rule the nations with an iron rod *(Revelation 20)*.

(5) They will be citizens in the City of my God—the New Jerusalem that comes down from Heaven *(Revelation 21–22)*.

(6) I will give them the right to eat from the Tree of Life, which is in the paradise of God *(Revelation 22)*.

- **Everything we are doing now is preparing us to live in the world of Revelation 19–22!** That truth should lead each of us to examine ourselves and ask, "How am I overcoming sin and satan now"?

It's hard to even imagine Early Elder Ethan and the 1st–2nd Century Church leaders, living in their small stone houses, trying to get their heads around this last part of the Unveiling. After the final 45 days of time as we know it—the New Heaven and New Earth will rise out of the destroyed Earth. Then, we will all live and reign with Jesus right from "the Home of God," the place Jesus has prepared just for them, you, me, and every other Believer.

Revelation 22:1–2: "Then the angel showed me a river with the Water of Life, clear as crystal, flowing from the throne of God and of the Lamb. It flowed down the center of the main street. On each side of the river grew a Tree of Life, bearing twelve crops of fruit, with a fresh crop each month. The leaves were used for medicine to heal the nations."

For the next 1,000 years, and on into eternity, you will be living in God's Home, *which has come down to Earth*. Turns out, Heaven is not going to be "up there" at all—at least not for long!

We will be worshiping God in the very Throne Room mentioned in Revelation 4 and 5!

Your heart begins to sing–then out of your glorified lungs in perfect pitch comes the song: "Holy, Holy, Holy, Is the Lord God Almighty! You are worthy, O Lord our God, to receive glory and honor and power!"

Revelation 22:3–5: "No longer will there be a curse upon anything! For the throne of God and of the Lamb will be there, and His servants will worship Him. And they will see His face, and His name will be written on their foreheads. And there will be no night there—no need for lamps or sun—for the Lord God will shine on them. And they will reign forever and ever."

Revelation 22, the last chapter of Jesus' unveiling, the final chapter of Divine Revelation for all time—has a line-up of final powerful statements topped off with a loving, open-armed invitation:

Revelation 22:7, 12–13, 17: "Look, I am coming soon! Blessed are those who obey the words of prophecy written in this book. Look, I am coming soon, bringing My reward with Me to repay all people according to their deeds. I am the Alpha and the Omega, the First and the Last, the Beginning and the End. The Spirit and the Bride say, 'Come.' Let anyone who hears this say, 'Come.' Let anyone who is thirsty come. Let anyone who desires drink freely from the Water of Life."

And then comes this warning to anyone who would dare to minimize a single word of "this Revelation from Jesus Christ":

Revelation 22:18–19: "And I solemnly declare to everyone who hears the words of prophecy written in this book: If anyone adds anything to what is written here, God will add to that person the plagues described in this book. And if anyone removes any of the words from this book of prophecy, God will remove that person's share in the Tree of Life and in the Holy City that are described in this book."

We who have been carefully digging through these pages are not in any danger of "losing our share in the Tree of Life or the Holy City"! In fact, when we cap off our time spent in deep study with this verse, again, from Chapter 1, we find just how pleased God has been with the time we have invested:

Revelation 1:3: "God blesses the one who reads the words of this prophecy to the church, and He blesses all who listen to its message and obey what it says, for the time is near."

If you have dug your way through the reading of the Unveiling of Jesus' Revelation and the study of this Unmasking book—that promised "blessing" is yours! You will find, in yourself, a new level of understanding for this present life—because you have increased your level of understanding of "the life to come"!

Revelation 22:20: "He who is the faithful witness to all these things says, 'YES, I AM COMING SOON!' AMEN! COME, LORD JESUS!"

How much do I know?

1) Do you think it is at all possible that those redeemed Believers who trusted Christ during the last days of the "Lord's Wrath" on earth and are thriving in the New Earth, may not get to enjoy quite as many blessings offered in the New Jerusalem as the Saints who met with Jesus up at the Marriage Supper of the Lamb?

2) Do you believe that people will still be coming to faith in Christ during the Millennium?

3) Will it be possible for a person to turn away from Jesus, the ruler of all the earth, and choose not to follow him? How do you know?

4) What will be happening in the Throne Room of God during the Millennium?

5) Which floor of the 1,400-mile high New Jerusalem do you think your "mansion" will be on?

You can check your answers beginning on page 243.

Number of correct answers on this page:

EPILOGUE

Ethan is now very old. His earthly eyes are shot, but his spiritual eyes are as strong as ever. He had committed his whole adult life to one consuming focus—the Second Coming, the Second Advent, the Victorious Return—of his beloved Messiah—Jesus the Christ!

He had lived through the cruel executions of James, and Peter, and Paul, all of the Apostles except John—and many of his family members and friends. Jesus' prophesies about his future followers being "arrested, persecuted and killed" was his everyday news—news that some days was more painful than it seemed possible to bear. Ethan himself had lost virtually all he once possessed in his single-minded focus on proclaiming Jesus as the soon-coming sin-Savior of the world.

Sin <u>was</u> rampant everywhere! False prophets had risen up! While spiritual passion burned hot in many—others ran far and fast away from the Messiah, rather than face the wrath of the "evil one." Everything around him seemed to be a preview of what Jesus had prophesied the End Times would be.

Ethan had watched with sorrow, yet fascination, as Jerusalem was leveled to the ground, exactly as Jesus has predicted! Sadly, there was no indication that anybody had any thoughts of rebuilding the Holy City anytime soon. The Jews that hadn't been massacred remained scattered to the "four winds" of the earth. Zechariah's prophecy remained unfulfilled—that Jerusalem would be the place where Jesus returned and set up an everlasting rule. For that to happen, some huge unknowable developments were going to need to occur!

Ethan was still receiving weekly reports of how Jesus' Church was spreading throughout the Empire—but it was far, far from reaching "the whole world." Some Greek named Galileo had come up with a new theory 300 years before that the earth was round! That would have to mean that there was another whole side to the planet—and a top and a bottom! How in the world could they ever get to all those places with the message of the Gospel? There didn't just need to be people "saved" on the other side of the globe—Jesus' Church had to be formed, people in every village and town had to be discipled. They had to all be taught "everything Jesus had taught them" and **then, and only then, would "the end" come!**

Maybe this "Good News about Jesus Kingdom being preached throughout the whole world, so that all nations will hear it," was going to take longer than any of them ever imagined. What if it took 50 more years? What if Jesus didn't plan to return for 100 years—or even *(gasp)* 200?

As Ethan's dying body began to succumb to his final sickness, his eyes turned toward heaven. "I may be sick now," he prayed, "but THERE IS COMING A DAY! This body may go into the ground, but one day my left-over-dust will hear the sound of the Trumpet through six feet of solid dirt… and my body will gather back together and come crashing through the surface and rise straight up to meet my Jesus in the air!"

"The precious Son of Man, the Son of God—now with all authority, glory and sovereign power will *(amidst darkened sun, lightless moon and stars falling from the sky)* be coming on the clouds of heaven with his power and great glory. And you will send out your angels with that mighty blast of a trumpet, and they will gather your chosen ones *(me, and James, and John and millions more both living and dead)* from all over the world—from the farthest ends of the earth!"

"And I, insignificant unworthy former Jerusalem Commissioner Ethan— will be invited into your everlasting dominion that will not pass away. I will join with you in ruling over an eternal kingdom that will never, never come to an end! Oh, thank you my blessed Savior, my Messiah!"

- **"I can hear your voice calling out to me Jesus, 'YES, I AM COMING SOON!'"**
- **"I respond to you with all of my heart and all of my soul, and all of my mind, 'AMEN! EVEN SO, <u>COME, QUICKLY LORD JESUS!</u>'"**

SPECIAL ACKNOWLEDGEMENT

In the course of researching, and preaching, a four-and-a-half-month series of sermons, one consults many, many different sources, which contribute a thought here—a new direction there. Some sources have been, decidedly, most helpful—not least of which were the writings of some of those men I was privileged to learn from in seminary: Dr. Gary Cohen, Dr. Paul Feinburg, Dr. Douglas Moo, and Dr. Gleason Archer. Dr. Cohen, in fact, was the translator of Revelation for the *New King James Version* of the Bible, and taught me the Book of Revelation, in Seminary.

However, *there is one person who has most influenced my thinking:*

When wrestling with the entire chronology of the Book of Revelation, trying to understand the book, not as a hodgepodge of symbolism but as a literal prophetic storyline in time, the writings of one man kept rising to the surface. **Marvin J. Rosenthal, President of *"Zion's Hope Ministries,"* in Winter Park, Florida.** So many authors would make positional statements without proving, logically, (theo-logically) how they arrived at their conclusions. Time after time I would come back to Rosenthal who would explore every passage, wrestle with every possibility, until the pieces of the puzzle finally clicked into a clear picture. I am forever indebted to Marvin Rosenthal for his powerful insights.

There are no intended direct quotes from Mr. Rosenthal's writings. However, his influence will be felt throughout the book. In a few places I have used phrases which came from his pen like "Battle of the Ages" and

"The Antichrist is coming." However after multiple edits and revisions I do believe the flow of words is my own. However, for those who are familiar with his thinking and writings, his fingerprints will be seen.

ACKNOWLEDGEMENTS

I am thankful to so many who have helped birth this book. My dear wife, of 41 years, Sue Chess who worked patiently around my ADD mind as I pecked at my laptop day after day, then read the manuscript offering valuable input.

Cass Everett poured untold long, long hours into repeatedly editing and reviewing the manuscripts. She tirelessly worked over and over through the use of every Scripture, culminating in two indexes at the end of the book. (Her "mansion" in the New Jerusalem should be very close to the Throne Room.)

My ministry colleagues Christopher Weise, Bill Howe, Kevin Pierce, Geof Hoge, Ian Crawshaw, Bill Mirti, and Jim McKeegan who wrestled through this material with me around a conference table as we consumed five months of church ministry life. Penny Worley was faithful to print several hundred manuals from original CD's that predate this book, and then continued responding to so many "help me" requests, including modifying the original cover.

Pastor Christopher Weise poured in countless hours designing the End Times chart that is such an important part of this book. He designed, and redesigned, the original cover for this book.

Debi Boerckel did a letter by letter proofread catching all the punctuation and grammar errors the rest of our eyes missed.

Pastor Kevin Pierce worked through the Greek vocabulary and grammar making sure of accurate interpretation.

My dear daughter, Heather Brogan, worked with me designing and photographing the scroll on the book cover, and drew the Four Horsemen drawing used in the book.

And for Dr. Scott Philip Stewart (and Lena, his wife) at Christian Author Services whose initial expert editing moved this material from 23 sermons into the first manuscript working copy.

Thank you all so, so much for the sacrifice of your time!

ANSWERS TO END-OF-CHAPTER QUESTIONS

Chapter 1:
1. Long dark hair
2. Getting his church ready for heaven (perhaps c and b).
3. "Whoever has ears let him hear what the Spirit says to the churches."
4. Churches that do not preach truth exactly as stated in Scripture or who do not call people to a transformed Biblical lifestyle.

Chapter 2:
1. Matthew 18:15–17—Jesus must have been "forming local churches" earlier than we tend to think.
2. The Church is supposed to "hold the keys of the Kingdom, bind and loose on earth what has already been bound and loosed in heaven," and "the gates of hell will not prevail against it"!
3. Apparently not—there must be Believers at the end of the Tribulation who were not previously raptured. They must be who the raptured, redeemed reign over.

Chapter 3:
1. True
2. True
3. True

Chapter 4:
1. That started it! It won't come completely to an end until the Tribulation is over.
2. No!—No!

3. Satan, the antichrist, the willfully unrepentant unbelievers.

Chapter 5:
1. The antichrist
2. All of the above
3. No!—"The nations will know that I am Lord!"
4. If the vast crowd are "all those who came out" of the Tribulation, then they aren't all martyrs—this is the Rapture of the Saints!

Chapter 6:
1. Palm Sunday, with the crowd shouting "Hosanna" declaring Jesus the Messiah!
2. They were supporting pre-conceived ideas. [IMO ☺]
3. True
4. Ezekiel Battle—God answers with fire—worldwide revival—Rapture—another worldwide revival.

Chapter 7:
1. True! World rule—brings peace—dies then resuscitated.
2. Murder of babies in Bethlehem—attempted massacre in Esther's day, tremendous opposition as Nehemiah builds walls, Hitler killing 6 million Jews.
3. Yes! Yes, he does!

Chapter 8:
1. True!—The "man of sin" (antichrist) must be revealed.
2. Yes, it is!
3. If it is not that—we are left with a big fat nothing-burger! [IMO ☺]

Chapter 9:
1. They have to be seriously desperate because of some catastrophe that has befallen them.
2. In the last 50 years we have seen a dramatic shift where what used to be called evil is now called good, and what used to be called good is now called evil!
3. We must relentlessly walk precisely in the light of God's Word!

4. It seems to be a "branding" of some sort (either physical or electronic) that defines who each person is, for autocratic control purposes. The followers of the antichrist think they will die without it.

Chapter 10:
1. True
2. God creating human beings and elevating them in his affections above the angels.
3. True
4. True

Chapter 11:
1. Yes!
2. Yes!
3. He probably tries to shoot him out of the sky!

Chapter 12:
1. False—There are many new Believers still alive when Jesus returns!
2. No—many more people are turning to Christ even after the original Believers are raptured.

Chapter 13:
1. R—Believers taken off earth.
   SC—Believers stay on earth.
   R—Jesus rescues before the hour of trial.
   SC—Jesus returns after the hour of trial.
   R—Believers given glorified bodies.
   SC—Believers left on earth keep unglorified bodies.
2. All redeemed, raptured Believers will share a time of soul communion with Jesus that could last 18–24 months. [IMO]
3. True

Chapter 14:
1. Storyline #1: Wedding Feast of the Lamb.
   Storyline #2: Final great harvest of souls.
   Storyline #3: The pouring out of God's judgments.
2. They will enter the Millennium; they are who Jesus and the redeemed will "rule over."

3. They are completely fed up with the antichrist who has let the world spiral out of control.

Chapter 15:

1. On the Mount of Olives.
2. No—He is talking about those who live through the events of Matthew 24:1–29.
3. True

Chapter 16:

1. Some say the center of the earth. Some say in the sun. Who knows?
2. The raptured Saints will be "ruling over" the unraptured, unglorified Believers.
3. They come from the unraptured, unglorified Believers, and not all of them will follow Jesus or "obey our rule."
4. Yes. I hope not!

Chapter 17:

1. Who knows?—The wolf will live with the lamb—leopard + goat—calf + lion—a child will lead them!
2. True
3. True, true, true!

Chapter 18:

1. Probably not, at least not until the Millennium is over.
2. Yes
3. Yes, satan has one final reaping.
4. Revelation 4
5. Floor 948 ☺

TOTAL NUMBER OF CORRECT ANSWERS

SCRIPTURE BY CHAPTER INDEX

Unless otherwise indicated, all Scripture quotations are taken from the Holy Bible, **New Living Translation,** copyright © 1996, 2004, 2007, 2013 by Tyndale House Foundation. Used by permission of Tyndale House Publishers, Inc., Carol Stream, Illinois 60188. All rights reserved.

Scripture Indexes compiled by Cass Everett

Prologue

Matt. 16:18-19   vii

Matt. 16:21   vii

Matt. 16:22-23   viii

Luke 24:5-7   viii

Matt. 28:11-15   viii

1 Cor. 15:3-6   viii

Matt. 16:21   ix

Matt. 20:19   ix

Matt. 24:30   ix

John 14:1-3   ix

Acts 1:9   x

Acts 1:10-11   x

John 14:2-3   x

Zech. 14:4   xi

Zech. 14:9   xi

Mark 14:61-64   xi

Dan. 7:9 NIV   xii

Dan. 7:13-14 NIV   xii

Matt. 24:30-31   xii

Matt. 24:3   xiii

Matt. 24:2   xiii

Jer. 23:3   xiii

Ezek. 34:13   xiii

John 16:7   xiii

John 16:13-14   xiii

Acts 3:18-21   xiii

Zech. 14:4   xiv

Zech. 14:6-9   xiv

Zech. 14:11   xiv

Matt. 24:2   xv

Matt. 24:5-15   xv

Matt. 24:30-31   xvi

Matt. 24:2   xvi

Zech. 14:4   xvi
Zech. 14:9   xvi
Matt. 28:19   xvi
Matt. 24:14   xvi
Acts 8:1   xvii
Acts 8:3-4   xvii
Acts 9:1-2   xvii
Acts 10:22   xvii
Acts 12:1-3   xvii
Acts 13:50   xvii
Acts 14:4-5   xvii
Acts 14:22   xvii
1 Thess. 4:13-18   xviii
Matt. 24:30   xix
Matt. 24:28   xx
Matt. 24:32-34   xx
1 Cor. 15:51-57   xxi

Introduction
Acts 1:11 NIV   xxiii
Rev. 1:1   xxv
Rev. 1:3   xxv
Rev. 1:19   xxvi
Rev. 1:7-8   xxvi
Rev. 22:3   xxvii
1 John 5:19   xxviii
Rev. 22:12-14   xxviii
Rev. 22:17   xxviii
Rev. 22:20   xxviii

Part I
Rev. 1:3   2

1.
Rom. 8:34   5
1 Pet. 1:18-20   5
Rev. 1:12-17   5
Dan. 7:13   5
Rev. 1:17-18   6
Rev. 1:19-20   7
John 14:3   7
Matt. 16:18   8

2.
John 16:13   13
Matt. 16:18   14
Matt. 16:19   14
Eph. 5:23   14
Eph. 5:25   14
Eph. 5:27   14
Eph. 1:22-23   15
Eph. 3:10   15
Rev. 2:7 NIV   16
Rev. 2:1-7 NIV   16
Rev. 2:6   17
Rev. 2:7 NIV   17, 18
Rev. 2:11   18
Rev. 2:17 NIV   18
Rev. 2:26-29   18
Rev. 3:5   18
Rev. 3:12   19
Rev. 2:5   20
Rev. 3:20-21   20
Rev. 3:21-22 NKJV   21
James 1:12   21

Part II

Rev. 5:5-7   25

3.

Rev. 3:21   27

Rev. 4:1-2   27

James 1:12   28

Rev. 2:10   28

Rev. 6:11   28

Rev. 3:21   28

Ps. 47:8   28

Ps. 99:1   28

Matt. 23:22   28

Rev. 4:1   29

Rev. 4:2-8   29

Dan. 7:9-10 ESV   31

Ezek. 1:1   31

Ezek. 1:4-6   31

Ezek. 1:26-27 NKJV   32

Rev. 1:17   32

Rev. 4:9-11   32

Matt. 24:1-2   33

Gen. 1:3   34

Rev. 4:1-2   34

Heb. 13:14-15   34

1 Thess. 4:17   35

Rev. 20:6   35

2 Cor. 4:8-9   36

2 Cor. 4:10   36

2 Cor. 4:16-18   36

Rev. 4:2-6 NKJV   37

Rev. 4:9-11   38

Rev. 5:1-14   38, 39

4.

Rev. 4:8-11   44

Luke 21:24   45

Jer. 31:8-12   46

Ezek. 38:3   48

Ezek. 38:5-9   48

Rev. 5:1   49

Rev. 5:1-2   50

Rev. 5:2-3   52

Rev. 5:4   52

Rev. 5:5-8   53

Rev. 5:9-10 NIV   54

Rev. 5:11-14   55

5.

Rev. 1:1   61

Rev. 1:13-16 TLB   62

Rev. 5:1   62

Rev. 5:5   63

Rev. 6:1-2   63

**("Kai   Eidon"   references   in
Revelation: 64**

6:1, 2, 5, 8, 12

7:2

8:2, 13

9:1

10:1

13:1, 11

14:1, 6, 14

15:1

16:13

17:3
19:11, 17, 19
20:1, 4, 11)

Rev. 6:2 65
Ezek. 39:1-4 67
Ezek. 39:6-8 67
Ezek. 39:7 67
Zeph. 2:2 70
Rev. 7:1-4 72
Rev. 7:9-10 72
Rev. 7:13-14 72
Rev. 7:15-17 73

Part III
1 Thess. 5:1-6 79

6.
Dan. 12:4 ESV 81
1 Thess. 5:4 82
Dan. 9:24-25 83
Dan. 9:26 84
Ezek. 36:17 84
Ezek. 36:19 84
Ezek. 36:22-24 84
Dan. 12:7-12 85
Ezek. 39:7 86
Matt. 24:14 ESV 86
Rev. 7:9-10 88
Rev. 7:13-15 88
Rev. 22:7 89
Rev. 22:17 89
Rev. 22:20 89

Rev. 8:1 89
Zeph. 1:7 90
1 Thess. 1:10 NIV 90
1 Thess. 5:9-10 NIV 90
Rev. 19:1-9 NIV 90
Rev. 19:11-16 NIV 91

7.
1 Thess. 1:10 NIV 96
1 Thess. 5:9-10 NIV 96
Rev. 3:10 96
Rev. 6:2 97
1 Pet. 5:8 NKJV 98
Rev. 13:3 98
Rev. 16:14 98
Rev. 16:16 98
Gen. 12:1-3 100
Zech. 14:4 101
Zech. 14:9 101
Gen. 12:1-3 101
Joel 2:1-2 102
Luke 21:24 102
Ezek. 39:1 102
Ezek. 39:3-4 102
Ezek. 39:6 102

8.
2 Thess. 2:1-4 107
Rev. 6:10 109
Rev. 6:12-14 109
Rev. 6:15-17 110
Rev. 6:12-14 111
Rev. 6:15-17 111

Rev. 7:1-4   111, 112

Rev. 7:9-10   112

Rev. 6:13   112

Rev. 7:14   113

1 Thess. 4:16-17   113

Ezek. 39:7   114

Matt. 24:14   114

Matt. 28:18-20   115

9.

1 Thess. 4:15-18   119

2 Thess. 2:1-5   120

1 Thess. 4:17   120

1 Thess. 1:10   120

2 Thess. 1:9-10   120

Dan. 9:25-26   121

Dan. 9:27   121

Dan. 12:7-8   122

Dan. 12:11-12   122

Rev. 13:1   123

Ezek. 38:18-20   124

Ezek. 38:21-23   124

Ezek. 39:12   124

Ezek. 39:21-22   124

2 Thess. 2:9   124

Rev. 7:9   125

1 John 4:3   126

2 Thess. 2:6-7   127

Rev. 13:5-8   127

Rev. 13:16-17   127

10.

Isa. 14:12-17   132

Gen. 1:28   133

Gen. 3:15   133

Gen. 6:5   133

Gen. 6:8   134

Gen. 3:15   134

Rev. 17:1-6 NIV   136

Rev. 18:1-5 NIV   136

Dan. 7:7-11 NIV   137

Dan. 7:13-14 NIV   137, 138

11.

Matt. 16:18   143

2 Thess. 2:3   143

Rev. 10:1-3   144

Rev. 10:5-7   144

1 Cor. 15:23-24   144

Rev. 11:16-17   145

Rev. 11:15   145

Rev. 14:1-3   146

Rev. 14:1   146

Rev. 14:4   146

Mal. 4:5   147

Rev. 14:6-7   147

12.

Rev. 17:14   150

Phil. 2:6-11 ESV   150

Col. 2:15   151

2 Cor. 4:4   151

Eph. 2:2 NKJV   151

Rev. 11:15-17 NIV   151

Dan. 12:11-12   152

Zeph. 1:15 NIV   152

Rev. 8:7-10   153

Rev. 11:3   154

Rev. 11:5   154

Zeph. 1:15 NIV   155

Rev. 8:12   155

Rev. 9:1-6   155

Rev. 9:13-15   155

Rev. 9:4   156

Matt. 25:31-34 NIV   156

Matt. 25:41 NIV   157

Matt. 25:46 NIV   157

Rev. 14:6-7   157

Rev. 14:8 NIV   158

Rev. 14:9-12 NIV   158

Rev. 14:1 NIV   158

Rev. 14:4   159

Rev. 12:5-6   160

Rev. 11:7-11   160

Rev. 12:13-14   160

Rev. 12:15-17   160

Rev. 11:15-17 NIV   161

13.

Rev. 8:8   164

Rev. 7:9   165

1 Thess. 4:16-17   165

Matt. 24:29-31   165

Rev. 6:12-14   165

Rev. 6:15-17   165

Rev. 19:1   166

Rev. 7:9   167

Rev. 11:17   167

Rev. 19:1-3 NIV   167

Rev. 5:9   168

Rev. 7:9-10   168

Rev. 14:2-3   168

Rev. 19:1-3 NIV   169

Rev. 19:4 NIV   170

Rev. 19:5-7   170

Rev. 19:7-9   170

Matt. 26:45   171

Isa. 54:5   171

Jer. 3:7-9   171

Rom. 11:17-18   171

Rev. 21:9   171

2 Cor. 11:2   171

Rev. 19:8   172

Rev. 19:7   172

Rev. 19:9   172

Rev. 3:12   173

14.

Rev. 19:11-14   176

Rev. 19:16   176

1 Thess. 4:15-17   177

Matt. 24:29-31   179

1 Thess. 4:15-17   179, 180

Rev. 19:14   180

Matt. 24:30   181

Rev. 6:15-16   182

Rev. 16:2   183

Rev. 16:3   183

Rev. 16:4   184

Rev. 16:8-9   184

Rev. 16:10-11   184

Rev. 13:14   184

Rev. 16:12-14 184

Rev. 16:16 185

Rev. 19:11-14 186

Rev. 19:16 186

Part IV

Dan. 9:25 190

Dan. 9:26 190

Dan. 12:11-12 190

15.

Rev. 7:9 193

Rev. 19:7-8 193

Matt. 26:45 193

Rev. 19:11-14 195

Rev. 19:16 195

Rev. 16:12-14 195

Rev. 16:16 195

Rev. 19:19 195

Zech. 14:2-4 196

Rev. 16:17-21 196

Rev. 19:20-21 197

Matt. 24:29-31 198

Matt. 24:32-34 198

Matt. 24:1-29 199

Matt. 24:42 199

Matt. 25:1-13 199

16.

Zech. 14:4 204

Zech. 14:6 204

Zech. 14:9 204

Dan. 9:25-26 204

Rev. 19:20-21 NIV 205

Rev. 20:1-3 NIV 205

Acts 1:11 NIV 205

Rev. 20:1 NIV 206

Rev. 20:2 NIV 207

Rev. 20:2-3 NIV 207

Matt. 25:31-34 207

Matt. 25:41 207

Zech. 14:6-9 208

Matt. 6:9-10 ESV 208

Zech. 14:10-11 209

Rev. 20:4 210

Rev. 5:9-10 NIV 210

Isa. 65:25 210

17.

Rev. 19:11-21 215

2 Pet. 3:7 NIV 216

2 Pet. 3:10 NIV 216

2 Pet. 3:12-13 NIV 216

Rev. 21:1 NIV 216

Isa. 65:17-20 217

Isa. 65:25 217

Isa. 11:6 217

Zech. 14:9 217

Rev. 2:27 218

Rev. 20:4 219

Rev. 5:9-10 NIV 219

Rev. 21:1-3 220

Rev. 21:16-17 220

John 14:1-4 220

Rev. 21:22-27 221

Rev. 20:1-3 221

Rev. 20:4   221

Rev. 20:7-8   222

Rev. 20:10   222

Rev. 20:11   222

Rev. 21:1-2   222

Rev. 20:4   222

Rev. 20:11   222

Rev. 20:7-8   222

Rev. 20:10   222

Rev. 21:23-27   222

Rev. 22:1-2   223

Rev. 22:14-15   223

Rev. 22:18-19   234

Rev. 1:3   235

Rev. 22:20   235

18.

John 14:1-3 NKJV   226

Rev. 21:1-5   227, 228

Heb. 11:10   228

John 14:2   228

Rev. 21:16-17   228

Rev. 21:10-12 NIV   229

Rev. 21:14 NIV   229

Rev. 21:18-19   229

Rev. 21:21   229

Rev. 21:22-27   230

Rev. 21:24-27   231

Zech. 14:9   231

Rev. 22:1-2   233

Rev. 4:8   233

Rev. 4:11   233

Rev. 22:3-5   234

Rev. 22:7   234

Rev. 22:12-13   234

Rev. 22:17   234

SCRIPTURE BY BOOK INDEX

"Kai Eidon" references in
Revelation: 64
  6:1, 2, 5, 8, 12
  7:2
  8:2, 13
  9:1
  10:1
  13:1, 11
  14:1, 6, 14
  15:1
  16:13
  17:3
  19:11, 17, 19
  20:1, 4, 11

Genesis
  1:3 34
  1:28 133
  3:15 133, 134
  6:5 133
  6:8 134
  12:1-3 100, 101

Psalm
  47:8 28
  99:1 28

Isaiah
  11:6 217
  14:12-17 132
  54:5 171
  65:17-20 NIV 217
  65:25 210, 217

Jeremiah
  3:7-9 171
  23:3 xiii
  31:8-12 46

Ezekiel
  1:1 31
  1:4-6 31
  1:26-27 NKJV 32
  34:13 xiii
  36:17 84
  36:19 84

36:22-24 84
38:3 48
38:5-9 48
38:18-20 124
38:21-23 124
39:1 102
39:1-4 67
39:3-4 102
39:6 102
39:6-8 67
39:7 67, 86, 114
39:12 124
39:21-22 124

Daniel
7:7-11 NIV 137
7:9 NIV xii
7:9-10 ESV 31
7:13 5
7:13-14 NIV xii, 137, 138
9:24-25 83
9:25 190
9:25-26 121, 204
9:26 84, 190
9:27 121
12:4 ESV 81
12:7-8 122
12:7-12 85
12:11-12 122, 152, 190

Joel
2:1-2 102

Zephaniah
1:7 90
1:15 NIV 152, 155
2:2 70

Zechariah
14:2-4 196
14:4 xi, xiv, xvi, 101, 204
14:6 204
14:6-9 xiv, 208
14:9 xi, xvi, 101, 204, 217, 231
14:10-11 209
14:11 xiv

Malachi
4:5 147

Matthew
6:9-10 ESV 208
16:18 vii, 8, 14, 143
16:19 vii, 14
16:21 vii, ix
16:22-23 viii
20:19 ix
23:22 28
24:1-2 33
24:1-29 199
24:2 xiii, xv, xvi
24:3 xiii
24:5-15 xv
24:14 ESV xvi, 86, 114
24:28 xx
24:29-31 165, 179, 198

24:30   iv, xix, 181
24:30-31   xii, xvi
24:32-34   xx, 198
24:42   199
25:1-13   199
25:31-34 NIV   156, 207
25:41 NIV   157, 207
25:46 NIV   157
26:45   171, 193
28:11-15   viii
28:18-20   115
28:19   xvi

Mark
14:61-64   xi

Luke
21:24   45, 102
24:5-7   viii

John
14:1-3   ix
14:1-3 NKJV   226
14:1-4   220
14:2   228
14:2-3   x
14:3   7
16:7   xiii
16:13   13
16:13-14   xiii

Acts
1:9   x
1:10-11   x
1:11 NIV   xxiii, 205
3:18-21   xiii
8:1   xvii
8:3-4   xvii
9:1-2   xvii
10:22   xvii
12:1-3   xvii
13:50   xvii
14:4-5   xvii
14:22   xvii

Romans
8:34   5
11:17-18   171

1 Corinthians
15:3-6   viii
15:23-24   144
15:51-57   xxi

2 Corinthians
4:4   151
4:8-9   36
4:10   36
4:16-18   36
11:2   171

Ephesians
1:22-23 15
2:2 NKJV 151
3:10 15
5:23 14
5:25 14
5:27 14

Philippians
2:6-11 ESV 150

Colossians
2:15 151

1 Thessalonians
1:10 NIV 90, 96, 120
4:13-18 xviii
4:15-17 177, 179, 180
4:15-18 119
4:16-17 113, 165
4:17 35, 120
5:1-6 79
5:4 82
5:9-10 NIV 90, 96

2 Thessalonians
1:9-10 120
2:1-4 107
2:1-5 120
2:3 143
2:6-7 127
2:9 124

Hebrews
11:10 228
13:14-15 34

James
1:12 21, 28

1 Peter
1:18-20 5
5:8 NKJV 98

2 Peter
3:7 NIV 216
3:10 NIV 216
3:12-13 NIV 216

1 John
4:3 126
5:19 xxviii

Revelation
1:1 xxv, 61
1:3 xxv, 2, 235
1:7-8 xxvi
1:12-17 5
1:13-16 TLB 62
1:17 32
1:17-18 6
1:19 xxvi
1:19-20 7
2:1-7 NIV 16
2:5 20
2:6 17

2:7 NIV   16, 17, 18
2:10   28
2:11   18
2:17 NIV   18
2:26-29   18
2:27   218
3:5   18
3:10   96
3:12   19, 173
3:20-21   20
3:21   27, 28
3:21-22 NKJV   21
4:1   29
4:1-2   27, 34
4:2-6 NKJV   37
4:2-8   29
4:8   233
4:8-11   44
4:9-11   32, 38
4:11   233
5:1   49, 62
5:1-2   50
5:1-14   38, 39
5:2-3   52
5:4   52
5:5   63
5:5-7   25
5:5-8   53
5:9   168
5:9-10 NIV   54, 210, 219
5:11-14   55
6:1-2   63
6:2   65, 97

6:10   109
6:11   28
6:12-14   109, 111, 165
6:13   112
6:15-16   182
6:15-17   110, 111, 165
7:1-4   72, 111, 112
7:9   125, 165, 167, 193
7:9-10   72, 88, 112, 168
7:13-14   72
7:13-15   88
7:14   113
7:15-17   73
8:1   89
8:7-10   153
8:8   164
8:12   155
9:1-6   155
9:4   156
9:13-15   155
10:1-3   144
10:5-7   144
11:3   154
11:5   154
11:7-11   160
11:15   145
11:15-17 NIV   151, 161
11:16-17   145
11:17   167
12:5-6   160
12:13-14   160
12:15-17   160
13:1   123

13:3 98
13:5-8 127
13:14 184
13:16-17 127
14:1 146
14:1 NIV 158
14:1-3 146
14:2-3 168
14:4 146, 159
14:6-7 147, 157
14:8 NIV 158
14:9-12 NIV 158
16:2 183
16:3 183
16:4 184
16:8-9 184
16:10-11 184
16:12-14 184, 195
16:14 98
16:16 98, 185, 195
16:17-21 196
17:1-6 NIV 136
17:14 150
18:1-5 NIV 136
19:1 166
19:1-3 NIV 167, 169
19:1-9 NIV 90
19:4 NIV 170
19:5-7 170
19:7 172
19:7-8 193
19:7-9 170
19:8 172

19:9 172
19:11-14 176, 186, 195
19:11-16 NIV 91
19:11-21 215
19:14 180
19:16 176, 186, 195
19:19 195
19:20-21 NIV 197, 205
20:1 NIV 206
20:1-3 NIV 205, 221
20:2 NIV 207
20:2-3 NIV 207
20:4 210, 219, 221, 222
20:6 35
20:7-8 222
20:10 222
20:11 222
21:1 NIV 216
21:1-2 222
21:1-3 220
21:1-5 227, 228
21:9 171
21:10-12 NIV 229
21:14 NIV 229
21:16-17 220, 228
21:18-19 229
21:21 229
21:22-27 221, 230
21:23-27 222
21:24-27 231
22:1-2 223, 233
22:3 xxvii
22:3-5 234

22:7 89, 234
22:12-13 234
22:12-14 xxviii
22:14-15 223
22:17 xxviii, 89, 234

22:18-19 234
22:20 xxviii, 89, 235

ABOUT THE AUTHOR

Sam Chess has served as a Pastor on the Treasure Coast, of Florida, for more than 40 years. He serves as the Senior Pastor of Grace Emmanuel Church (EFCA) in Port Saint Lucie. *(graceemmanuel.com)* He and his wife Sue founded the church in 1990.

Grace Emmanuel has two radio programs called "GRACE ALIVE" on the regional Christian radio station WCNO. *(WCNO.com)* The four times a week program reaches from Ft. Lauderdale to Melbourne, FL and across much of the state.

Sam serves on the board of the Treasure Coast Christian Alliance, which brings together local government officials, business leaders, and clergy in unity and purpose.

Sam and Sue have three grown children and eight wonderful grandchildren. Sue Chess serves as the Executive Director of Care Net Pregnancy Services of the Treasure Coast.

Sam holds a Bachelor's degree from Hobe Sound Bible College and a Master's degree from Trinity International University.

You can contact Sam on Facebook at Sam Chess – Author or at *unmaskingrevelation.com.*

Printed in the USA
CPSIA information can be obtained
at www.ICGtesting.com
JSHW022212140824
68134JS00018B/1015